God Is Love

Saint Teresa Margaret: Her Life

God Is Love

Saint Teresa Margaret: Her Life

Margaret Rowe

ICS Publications
Institute of Carmelite Studies
Washington, DC
2003

ICS Publications
Institute of Carmelite Studies
2131 Lincoln Road, NE
Washington, DC 20002-1199
800-832-8489
www.icspublications.org

Typeset and produced in the United States of America

Library of Congress Cataloging-in-Publication Data

Rowe, Margaret
God Is Love: the Life of Saint Teresa Margaret: her life / Margaret
Rowe. -- Rev. ed.
p. cm.
Includes bibliographical references
ISBN: 0-935216-33-2
1. Teresa Margaret of the Sacred Heart, Saint, 1747-1770. I. Title.
BX4700.T43R68 2003
282'.092-- dc21

2003013268

Contents

INTRODUCTION

There are countless "lives" of saints gathering dust on library shelves all over the world. Each year several new titles are added to them, and many would seem to be of dubious value, for readers continue to lay them aside with a sigh that such things are beyond their comprehension or abilities. Yet the chief value of spiritual biography lies in providing encouragement and a model or method upon which one might confidently base one's own interior life.

The earliest type of hagiography is very much out of favor today. The writer was concerned only with presenting a paragon of virtue, and usually contrived the portrayal of a totally inhuman figure, possessing no mortal frailties; when the supply of authenticated miracles dwindled, neither the narrator nor his amanuensis felt any scruple about concocting others to improve the recital or illustrate their point.

Today the reaction against these pious myths has resulted in a full swing in the opposite direction. We want our saints to be so much creatures of flesh and blood that they hardly qualify for canonization at all! In the feverish search for fully human traits and failings, many modern biographers have entirely overlooked the most important element in the formation of a saint—the action of divine grace. The techniques of psychoanalysis have been applied with (one feels) dubious success, for while such a process may and does reduce the saint to the level of our workaday lives, it is a seemingly impossible achievement to psychoanalyze a dead person. And so we are presented with a saint in whose life the supernatural is retired almost right out of the picture. New data is produced by equating the saint's experiences, incidents from daily life, conversations, etc., with known or imaginary historical events contemporaneous with her time, and with subsequent psychological discoveries; and from these are drawn conclusions which may or may not be correct, but which are unblushingly presented as attested and authenticated facts. Such experiments in hagiography mostly give a mere caricature of holiness, and readers turn from such unspiritual models with even more weariness.

The third (and seemingly increasingly popular) method is the so-called "historical novel," in which real and fictitious characters are introduced and manipulated at the will of the author. His own speculations can be applied indiscriminately, and very often the characters are no more than a convenient set of pegs upon which he hangs his own theories. This method has one great advantage of making the characters come to life, but its overriding drawback is that the reader tends to treat the whole work as a piece of devotional fiction; and in any case there is no way of knowing where truth ends and fantasy begins, or how far the saint herself is a creation of the author.

In these pages I have made a tentative assay at a fourth method. This is not a work of fiction; nor is it, strictly speaking, biography - that is, not in the critical sense that we use the term today. I have taken liberties here and there in interpreting certain incidents and in transposing some material. Matter given in retreat notes and letters is sometimes incorporated into conversations, and vice versa; for while the contents of spiritual diaries and letters of direction are of the greatest importance in assessing a saint's character and spirituality, they usually make extremely dull reading. But this has been done only when I knew who was speaking and what they were talking about. There is no fictitious character in these pages, and the subject and matter of all conversations are factual, although I have at times framed the actual words that have been put on the speakers' lips.

Margaret Rowe

Preface to the Second Edition

This book had been out of print since 1964. We are glad to make available a newly devised reprinted biography, so that the public can come to know or even reacquaint themselves with Saint Teresa Margaret (Redi) of the Sacred Heart. Considered a "little flower" of Florence, she deserves to be known and loved as her sister in Carmel Saint Thérèse, the Little Flower of Lisieux, is known and loved.

The elaboration of this edition did not bring extensive changes to the engaging narrative of Margaret Rowe. Typographical errors were corrected; and some spelling changes were introduced into the original text. Accompanying it now are a useful chronology of the saint's life and chapter headings that ensure easier reading of the whole.

ICS Publications hopes this fascinating account of one of Carmel's appealing women saints will provide inspiration for new reading audiences and deepen their spiritual lives.

September 1, 2002

Chronology

Who Is God?

> *"I know where I'm going,*
> *And I know who's going with me*
> *I know who I love... "*
> (Scottish Lyric)

Anna Sisti lay on the couch for a few minutes, eyes closed, listening to the tiny slivers of sound as the children's high-pitched voices floated up from the garden, shattering the stillness like little staccato showers of gravel thrown against a window-pane.

She sighed, and struggled to sit up, despite the oppressive headache. Now that they were at large there would be no chance of getting any sleep, although the blinds were drawn and the house was still and quiet in the siesta somnolence of a summer's afternoon.

"I may as well go out to the garden and see what the children are up to." She tiptoed lightly to the door, so as not to disturb the others, and stood on the loggia, blinking slightly in the blinding Italian sunshine.

Three children - two boys and a girl - were romping about, well away from the house, apparently in pursuit of a butterfly, to judge from their erratic course.

"Where's Anna Maria?" she was about to call, when suddenly she saw the child standing on the terrace, quite still, her bright hair glowing against the gray wall like the golden narcissi she so loved, her whole attitude strained with expectancy, her head slightly on one

The gravel crunched beside her, and she turned at her aunt's approach. "What are you doing, child?"

"I was thinking."

"Thinking? Big thoughts for a little head, I've no doubt."

Anna Maria turned her clear blue eyes on the older woman's face. "Aunt," she said, "tell me: Who is God?"

"God is the creator of heaven and earth, and the supreme Lord of all." She paused.

"Yes, go on," the little girl prompted. Once more Aunt Sisti had recourse to the catechism.

"God is infinite in all perfections, the supreme Spirit who alone exists of Himself."

"Yes, yes!" exclaimed Anna Maria almost impatiently. "But tell me, who is God?"

Gradually the house had begun to stir, and now the door opened again. Camilla Redi stood framed in the sunlight that splashed across the dark shadows of the hall behind her.

"Mama!" cried Anna Maria, running towards her mother, who caught her in her arms. "Will you tell me who is God?"

Camilla smoothed the hair away from the serene forehead of this serious-minded child of hers. "God is love," she said softly. "He loves you and wants you to love Him. He made you because He loves you and wishes to have you forever with Him in heaven - which you will be if you are good and love Him with all your heart."

Anna Maria seemed satisfied. She threw her arms around her mother's neck, gave her a quick hug, and then ran off to join her sister and brothers who had by now forgotten the butterfly, long escaped over the wall, and were engaged in paddling their sticky fingers in a shallow pool.

But the question was not forgotten, and suddenly she thought: "I'll ask Papa. Perhaps he will know why everyone tells me what God is, and I want to know *who* He is."

After her sister-in-law had returned to the house, Anna Sisti stood for a long time gazing thoughtfully across the cypress groves and terraced lace-work of grape-vines that trailed over the slopes below the

Redi summer villa outside Arezzo. What a precociously intelligent child this niece of hers was! She loved to watch the play of expression on the mobile little face, now serious, now gay, always interested and eager to find out about everything around her, especially the things of God whose nearness she seemed to feel almost consciously.

In later years, Anna Sisti would often recall the nine months spent as a guest of her brother in 1753 when her little namesake was six. "I discovered in her a way of thinking and acting above her age, which obviously required the guidance of a superior hand to regulate it. I never wearied of watching her, and I admit that I was much consoled by doing so. I used to notice how she would sometimes stand in the prayerful attitude of one making an offering to God; she seemed so composed, serene and joyful, that I was amazed."[1]

Anna Maria Redi was not a prodigy of infantile sanctity. She was a normal, healthy, happy child. But she was one in whom grace and nature perfected each other and developed side by side. "The child of a mother who speaks to her frequently of God," said Pope Pius XII, "learns early in life to practice the three theological virtues; she will believe in God, hope in Him, and love Him, long before she learns to recite her acts of faith, hope, and charity."

St. Thomas Aquinas, who at the age of five was placed as an oblate in the Benedictine Abbey of Monte Cassino, persistently sought from the monks an answer to the one question that obsessed him: WHAT IS GOD? The otherwise extraordinarily silent child had but one desire, to consecrate himself entirely to God. He had no need or wish to consider the problem of what he would do with his life. He knew where he was going, and he knew the way to get there.

Anna Maria Redi was as different from the burly Thomas in physical appearance as one could imagine. A Dresden-china figure with an oval face and delicate features, one could picture her as the gracious hostess of a comfortable country house, the belle of many a ball, carefully and daintily nurtured to a life of comfort, ease, and protection from the hardships and sufferings of life.

---

[1] Letter to Ignatius Redi, March 11, 1770.

But she also knew where she was going, and at the age of six, the little face was gravely expectant as she made the reiterated query: "WHO IS GOD?"

To this question she continued to seek an answer for the remainder of her brief life. The replies given by her mother, father, aunt, anyone who would speak to her on the subject that never failed to fascinate her, satisfied her only momentarily. As her understanding developed, so did her desire for knowledge grow. The capacity was always in advance of the supply. Her future confessor, the Discalced Carmelite Father Ildefonse of St. Aloysius, who knew her soul perhaps more intimately than any other, said of her later: "Scarcely was she able to understand that God is the supreme Lord and Creator than she felt drawn towards Him with a deep and sincere love ... which determined her to consecrate everything to Him and to have Him before her mind, in her heart, and on her lips. She desired not merely to avoid offending Him, but never to do anything even slightly displeasing to Him or not conformed to His glory and His will. All this she herself told me several times, adding: 'Jesus knows well that from my infancy I have never longed for anything but to please Him and to become a saint.'"

Many years later, Father Ildefonse questioned her about this statement, asking whether, as soon as she was old enough to distinguish spiritual realities, she had turned to God with the love of her heart. Astonished by the question, she replied, "Why, of course. Just like everyone else." This demonstrates an unbelievably precocious choice of the love of God. There was no sudden, dramatic decision to dedicate her life wholly to Him; it was merely the orientation of her whole being and aspirations. She had never desired anything else, never turned aside to follow after the pleasures of earth. As soon as she was capable of making a choice between good and bad - or, rather, between good and better - which in her life occurred at an earlier age than usual, she turned to God simply and naturally: a flower lifting her face to the rising sun and faithfully following it across the sky through the brief day of her life.

And - even more astonishingly - Anna Maria succeeded in this aspiration. Throughout the whole of her life she never lost sight of her goal and succeeded in reaching it very rapidly. It is no small thing to claim that a human being (even one who lived a sheltered life both at home and in a convent school before her early entry into a strictly enclosed religious order) passed through life without committing sin, or even any serious, deliberate fault.

The fact is inescapable; she was extraordinarily mature spiritually for her years, and her goodness was the fruit of piety - piety, that is, as a virtue, not a sentimental attachment to the devotional sweetness of prayers that attracted and made her feel "nice."

Often in biographies of Anna Maria one comes across the expression "angelic," and while this inaccurate term is commonly used to describe all well-behaved little girls who keep their pinafores clean and do as they are told, its application in this sense to so pious and obedient a child is not surprising. But there is more to it than that. Anna Maria was one of those children who seem almost too good to be true, certainly not one who was amenable and docile only because she had not enough spunk to be anything else. Her reason developed early, virtue attracted her, she saw that childish tantrums and naughtiness do offend God when deliberate and culpable, and she often had to check her high spirits and fiery temperament. Yet all who knew her were convinced of precocious but real holiness, and even at so early an age, many remembered the pretty, fair-haired child kneeling at her prayers, hands joined reverently, eyes down-cast, or gazing lovingly at the Tabernacle.

To say that Anna Maria committed no willful, culpable fault is not to say that she was already perfect, an angel incarnate as it were. She had defects and small faults and many imperfections throughout her childhood and youth, some of which she struggled with until the end of her life. As she grew in holiness, these assumed enormous proportions in her eyes, and caused her considerable anxiety lest by them she might be guilty of offending God.

An imperfection, however, is not sinful, because it does not constitute a formal offence against God, or the culpable transgression of a precept. As long as we are in the flesh, we will never be entirely free from faults and imperfections, particularly those that are involuntary and almost semi-instinctive. They are often a very necessary means to preserve humility, for through them we are brought face to face with our helplessness and complete reliance on God. And the knowledge is brought home to us that we are nothing but weakness and imperfection in ourselves, and that any good that is in us is solely the work of God.

In nothing may God be relegated to the second place, and even when there is no question of formal offence, we must learn not to act carelessly, inadvertently, unrecollectedly, or behave like some boorish person who always jostles and pushes himself into the first place, intent only that he be heard and served. And it is in this sense that Anna Maria Redi is called "sinless," for never from her earliest years was there any conscious and deliberate choice of self in preference to God; rather a genuine self-forgetfulness in the interests of His honor and glory.

It is to Father Ildefonse that we are indebted for much of our knowledge of Anna Maria's interior life and dispositions. He it was who related that "she had a continual, even impatient solicitude for occasions when she could ask others about our great God; she would listen intently to anyone who spoke to her of the divine perfections." And he adds: "That answer 'Just like everyone else' was given to me also in reply to questions about more spiritual matters - things which, however, she regarded as quite ordinary and in keeping with the normal behavior of Christians. Although from the age of five she had never given her affections to anything or anyone but God, she saw nothing unusual in this. She took it for granted that as soon as one learned to know about God, one automatically loved and gave oneself completely to Him. 'But everyone does that!' she would exclaim, astonished that such an attitude should appear singular or noteworthy."

However, Anna Maria was far from being a sanctimonious or introspective child. She possessed a lively disposition, and later her father described her as having "a fiery temperament." This was demonstrated occasionally in childish scuffles, for Anna Maria, being the eldest girl, often maintained her authority by force, and more than once resorted to physical shock treatment in persuading her sisters to conform, even though it was in the practice of virtue!

To Sir Ignatius Redi[2] the numerous children[3] who came tumbling rapidly into his domestic world were always something of a miracle, a source of perpetual wonder, and none more than his second child, the tall, well-built, blonde girl, before whose frank, steady gaze, her father often felt a sense of profound awe.

Not so Camilla. Children were no mystery to her, still less was there anything miraculous about them. They were creatures requiring love and care, but also demanding discipline and correction. Their needs were endless, and she was forced to forego most of the social contacts, the outings and gay parties that her lively, vivacious nature reveled in, as maternal obligations increasingly demanded her presence in the nursery. As babies followed one another rapidly into the world, they became ever less of a wonder; rather an increasing source of worry as infantile ailments multiplied, bringing trouble-filled days and sleepless nights; a cause for constant supervision and not infrequent punishment as they grew in age but not always commensurately in wisdom and grace, fighting, shouting, breaking limbs and tearing clothes, tumbling noisily about house and garden; of heartbreak as death snatched them from her arms. Ten children born within thirteen years left Camilla a prematurely-aged semi-invalid. She bore much physical suffering with great patience, but her domestic happiness was tinged with faintly nostalgic regrets for the gay social life she loved, but which had been denied her. Twins - a boy and a girl - born in 1760, lived only a few weeks. There was a gap of six years, after which Teresa, the last of their children, was born.

This child must have been a particular consolation to her par-

---

[2] This is only an approximation of his title. He belonged to the lesser Tuscan nobility, with an hereditary rank of "Bali," and as his title seems best translated by "Chevalier," Sir appears to be the nearest English equivalent. In extant letters he is frequently addressed as "Your Grace," but was certainly not of ducal rank. Probably his status was about equal to that of a baronet.

[3] There were thirteen, four of whom died in infancy, and one at the age of four.

ents. Born two years before Anna Maria's death, and seemingly named after the Carmelite sister she had never seen, the little girl possessed many of the traits and developed a number of the customs and practices her parents remembered in their eldest daughter.

"You see her? That is just how my little Anna used to behave!" Camilla told Father Ildefonse on the occasion of a visit he paid to the Villa when Teresa was four or five.

Francis Xavier, almost four years her junior, seems to have been closer to Anna Maria than any of the others, and apparently he was her favorite brother.[4] "Cecchino," as she always called him - even as an adult clinging to the affectionate diminutive of childhood days - remembered his eldest sister well, for she was constantly with the children. As new babies absorbed more and more of Camilla's time, she would leave Anna to supervise the older ones, knowing they were in capable hands, and indeed, in some ways the quiet, serious girl seemed even more mature than her pleasure-loving mother. It is, however, rather too easy to do Camilla the injustice of writing her off as a superficial and frivolous person, all the more so when one regards her beside her unusually serious and devout husband and daughter. One would certainly not expect Sir Ignatius Redi to choose a light-headed social butterfly for his wife.

Anna Maria disliked rowdiness, and if the games degenerated into a bedlam, she would bribe the noisy ones to be less rambunctious by promising them little gifts, her favorite reward being a holy picture, of which she seemed to possess a limitless supply. One day Cecchino joined his brothers, who were indulging in an unusually boisterous rough-and-tumble in the hall. Being still quite small, and apparently unable to hold his own in the melee, he clambered to safety up a short flight of stairs, and came upon Anna Maria sitting quietly in the window seat. Her eyes were intent on the stocking she was knitting, and apparently she was oblivious of the uproar around her.

---

[4] He entered the Society of Jesus in 1770, the year of Anna Maria's death, and after the suppression of the Society was made a Canon of the Cathedral of Arezzo. He died in March, 1820, after testifying at the beatification process of his sister conducted in 1818.

Cecchino sat there watching her, but she gave no indication of having noticed him, and he became aware of her air of deep absorption which the simple knitting she was doing did not account for. Cecchino stayed for a long time, but Anna Maria did not move, and suddenly it dawned on the child that she was thinking of God ("praying, as I now realize," he said later). This was the first indication of the spirit of profound recollection which was to develop in the girl until it became almost a habitual attitude.

"How good she is," thought Cecchino. "She is just like a little Madonna."

Peace, simplicity, and the practical exercise of the Christian virtues dominated the atmosphere of the household of Sir Ignatius Redi, whether in residence at the family home in Arezzo, or living more informally at "Ortagli"[5] their summer villa some miles from the city on the road to Casentino. Life had a purpose, and seriousness underlay the happy, carefree existence, for as both Ignatius and Camilla were good-living, generous, and pious, their home life was founded on deep religious convictions and principles; and in this atmosphere of warmth and piety, in a setting of orchards and vineyards and great natural beauty, enjoying greater freedom than was possible in the more formal routine observed in the town house, the children grew up healthy, happy, habituated to a daily round that included family prayer and the various acts of piety. In the morning Anna Maria accompanied her mother to Mass, walking across the fields to the nearby Capuchin church; later, when her mother was no longer well enough to make the journey, Ignatius escorted his daughter.

Although Sir Ignatius had inherited a comfortable living and was moderately prosperous, the children were all well trained in habits of thrift and industry. The rudiments of the domestic arts and crafts were early instilled into the girls, who were taught to knit and sew, and as they grew older, they were expected to employ their leisure moments not merely frittering time away, but using their fingers while they

---

5 "The Gardens of Redi"

chattered and laughed, discussing plans for the future or pleasures of the past.

The household was run on conventional lines broadly laid down by their status and the accepted mode of life of the country gentry of the time: refined, courteous, hospitable; the gentle rhythm of order and harmony flowing imperceptibly, because serenely, on.

Had Camilla only her own wishes to consult, the Redi Villa would undoubtedly have been the scene of many lighthearted parties, a rendezvous for her elegant and fashionably dressed contemporaries. But Ignatius' tastes ran along very different lines, and while not in the least sanctimonious, would have had little patience with mere time-wasting or insincere conventional exchanges, and none whatever with anything savoring of gossip. Ignatius himself was essentially a family man, and he was not the person to be tied down by slavish conformity to social traditions. But he was affable, friendly, a good neighbor, and was always glad to welcome his friends and acquaintances. Still, on the whole, he preferred simple entertainment for his children, and probably extended their residence at the Villa, where much of the social life of Arezzo could be avoided. The Redi's recreation was confined to the family circle for the most part. Wholesome home life, the give-and-take necessary in a large family, provided the training and atmosphere for the development of several future religious vocations,[6] and occasional visits to the homes of their friends with informal entertainment of them in return, was the simple, happy framework of this contented and united family, which frolicked and prayed and grew in unstudied, unaffected simplicity, piety, and love.

When Anna Maria was seven, she made her first confession at the Capuchin Church near the Villa, and, although according to the

---

[6] Gregory, the eldest son who succeeded to the family title, was the only one of the eight surviving children who did not become a religious. Francis Xavier and Diego entered the Society of Jesus (after its suppression both, were Canons of Arezzo); Joseph was a Theatine; Anna Maria a Carmelite; Cecilia, Eleanor, and Teresa became Benedictines at St. Apollonia's where they were educated.

regulations at that time, it would be four years before she could receive Holy Communion, she began the practice of frequent confession. She prepared herself diligently, seemingly greatly impressed by the dignity conferred by sacramental grace.

The "coming to the use of reason" is that stage in a child's life when he begins to distinguish between moral good and evil, and to make responsible decisions in that area. In an attempt to gain some practical guide, it is usually placed at seven years of age, with the understanding that this is only an approximation. Some children attain to it earlier, perhaps at the age of five or six, or even younger. Anna Maria appears to have been one of those who reached that level of development rather early. Father Ildefonse later testified that she had reached the use of reason at an earlier age than is usual, and thus was well aware of the moral responsibilities of her small world. Although tending always to gravity, she was charmingly unaffected, and her simple, serious outlook delighted Sir Ignatius, who seemed to realize that, although so young, his favorite child was the recipient of some very particular graces. He began to watch more carefully over the development of her spiritual life, and while never trying to anticipate grace, or force her along a path of his own choosing, he always had the time to answer and discuss her childish questions about the truths of the faith.

It was not always easy to meet the demands of such insatiable curiosity and desire for knowledge. To her question: "Who is God?" she still had not received an answer that completely satisfied her. "How is the goodness of God manifest?" she would ask her father. "What is grace? Who is Jesus Christ?"

One morning when she was about nine, Ignatius accompanied her from the Villa to the church for Mass as usual, their path running through a field full of flowers. Anna Maria was silent, apparently intent on the beauty around them.

"How rightly confession is called the sacrament of peace!" she exclaimed suddenly. "Could anything make us realize how we should be at peace and in charity with others more than pondering the great condescension of God! Truly, we will never be asked to forgive anyone the great offences God freely pardons in us."

"Well, my little Anna, and what heinous crimes has the good God forgiven you?" asked Ignatius with a smile, recalling the absence of peace that was sometimes very evident among his vociferous small fry.

"I have been thinking about the text that was preached on Sunday, the unforgiving servant. We come to the great King of Heaven with empty hands, in debt to Him for everything: life itself, and grace, and all the gifts He lavishes on us. Yet all we can say is, 'Have patience with me, and I will pay thee all I owe,' while all the time we could never pay anything towards the remission of our own debts, if God did not put into our hands the means to do so. And then, how often do we go away and refuse pardon for some slight fault in our neighbors, withholding our love, remaining aloof, or even nursing a grievance against them, and building up grudges that cool charity."

Sir Ignatius was surprised. Accustomed as he was to his daughter's piety, and indeed to hearing her expound some precocious views, he had not expected that the sacrament of penance would impress her so deeply. What did she know of the peace of soul that comes from sin confessed and forgiven, she who was so innocent in her sheltered and supervised life?

But one does not have to be a repentant sinner to understand the love and mercy of God. Some time or other in most lives there comes the awareness, often a blinding revelation, that the love of God has come voluntarily to meet the soul, offering a gift which he would never have presumed to hope or ask for. It seems that a conviction of this sort had suddenly burst into bloom in the heart of the child. After such a realization has completely penetrated one and its implications gone home, how can we ever really fail to understand our fraternal obligations to our fellow men? The little slights and misunderstandings, the trivial differences of opinion and temperament, the failure in small courtesies, and the jealousies, envy, anger, that are at the roof of most of the strife and discord of this world, all stem from pride. But these offences, great or small, which wound, embitter and estrange us, are inconsiderable in comparison with their malice as sin, a rebellion against the infinite goodness of God. Yet some of the most petty disagreements, which would be laughable were the results not so tragic, split society into discordant groups, emanating ill will and clamoring for vengeance, which live on after the original disagreement cannot even be remembered. If the peace of soul that should be ours when we realize that we are forgiven our infinite transgressions were to be translated into action on the level of daily life, if we could gain the self-knowledge necessary to see ourselves as God sees us, then we would spread around us the peace that St. James calls "the seedground of holiness; and those who sow peace will reap its harvest."

Anna Maria continued to expatiate, and for once there were no questions. Indeed, such profound and unexpected remarks astonished Sir Ignatius, who felt more certainly that God had laid His finger on his eldest daughter. This conversation marked the beginning of a new and even more intimate understanding between father and daughter, a lasting confidence and spiritual affection that deepened the bonds of natural love which already bound them so closely together. From that time, Anna Maria's queries and Sir Ignatius' answers increasingly assumed the character of true spiritual direction. This influence became more and more predominant as Anna Maria absorbed and took to herself some of the guiding principles that had shaped her father's piety and spiritual life, and it was from him that she first learned devotion to the Sacred Heart, which was to grow into one of the pivot forces in her life.

It appears that there is something unique - almost surprising - in this turning of the young girl to her father for spiritual guidance. But actually it is the most natural thing in the world. It is to our parents that we automatically look for the solution of our initial perplexities about "Who made me?" and "Why?" What is it that renders it difficult or embarrassing, as children grow older, for them to seek enlightenment from their parents on the unfolding of the vistas of the spiritual life which their original explanations of the fundamental principles of God's love for man have prepared? Or is the hesitancy on the part of the parents, who doubt their ability to fulfill this role? The sacramental grace of matrimony is there to aid the discharge of parental duties, one of the principals of which is the spiritual guidance of their children.

Perhaps again one feels surprise that it was not from her mother that Anna Maria sought enlightenment. But the Redi children were all accustomed to having their father rather than their mother supervise their religious education. Possibly Sir Ignatius deliberately assumed this responsibility, feeling that Camilla's own spiritual life was not sufficiently deep and solid to impart the necessary training to the children, which made it imperative for him to do so; but it is more likely that, because of his deeply religious nature, the children sensed his greater interest as well as his superior knowledge, and automatically looked to him for guidance. Ignatius has described his wife as a woman of "spotless morals," and Father Ildefonse calls her "a lady of irreprehensible ways who kept God before her eyes, and who suffered much from corporal infirmities which she bore with great patience." Francis Xavier testified: "My mother was an honorable lady, but not an outstanding person."

Sir Ignatius, then, was the one to whom Anna Maria turned for advice and the solution of her problems, and it was he who guided her first tentative footsteps, teaching her to respond generously to the action of grace in her soul. So well did he perform this task that later she was to say, "So great was the good my father has done to my soul that I can truly claim that he has been my father twice over." And when on one occasion she was asked why it was that her affection for her father seemed greater than for her mother, she did not deny the fact, but replied simply, "It is because his soul and mine are in such complete accord."

His own intense devotion to the Sacred Heart was quickly absorbed by this impressionable child, and as Ignatius spoke of the human and divine love of Christ, that infinite love became a torch to kindle mind and heart. For now Anna Maria felt herself to be moving a little nearer to the solution of the question she had been asking for so many years. Now, in the Sacred Heart, divine love no longer appeared remote or abstract, something beyond her grasp and comprehension; it was in warm, pulsing human love that the child began to "see" that the Heart of Jesus is at once the symbol and source of infinite love, and for her the word "love" already held deeper connotations than it conveyed to most children of her age.

She had been surrounded by love and affection all her life, and returned it wholeheartedly. She dearly loved her father, her mother, the little brothers and sisters - indeed she would have found it difficult not to do so, with such a warm, impulsive nature as was hers. But children have a knack of accepting the most sublime truths in a completely matter-of-fact way, and where the very simplicity of a concept might baffle or dazzle a more complex mind, the candid, uncomplicated gaze of a child can contemplate with complete confidence, almost casually, some staggering divine reality.

"This King," says St. Teresa of Avila, "only allows Himself to be taken captive by one who has completely surrendered herself to Him."

The unaffected, humble love of the child went forth, unafraid, unhesitatingly. Love had wrapped and cradled her all her life. She was familiar with its simplicity and its beauty. But love is also sublime, and she would never be satisfied with less than infinite love.

Already Anna Maria Redi knew where she was going.

2

To Appear Just Like All the Rest

O little lark, you need not fly
To seek your Master in the sky,
He treads our native sod;
Why should you sing aloft, apart?
Sing in the heaven of my heart;
In me, in me, in me is God!
(Anna Bunson)

While Sir Ignatius Redi's circumstances were comfortable, he certainly did not possess unlimited wealth, and expenses mounted sharply as his family continued to increase. He had two large houses and their staffs to maintain, and as the years passed, more than once he found it necessary to review his finances very closely. One interesting anecdote remains to bear witness both to his straitened circumstances and to the generosity with which he discharged his obligations to his children.

After Anna Maria's ninth birthday, it was decided that she and her education should henceforward be entrusted to the care of the Benedictine nuns of St. Apollonia's in Florence.

Gregory Redi, the eldest of the family (Anna Maria's senior by a year) was already a boarder at the Jesuit Cicognini College at Prato. Now Anna Maria's turn had come; soon the others would be reaching an age when their formal education must be considered. Realizing that this would be beyond their means unless a strict economy was practiced, Ignatius and Camilla resolved that anything in the nature of luxuries and non-essentials must henceforth be ruled out. The first of these to go was the family coach. This represented no small sacrifice for Sir Ignatius, not only in the matter of convenience, but also of status in the community.

It impressed Anna Maria deeply. When they visited Gregory on their way to Florence, she related the incident to him, exclaiming admiringly over their father's generosity, and doubtless taking the opportunity to exhort her brother to work hard so as to repay their dearest Papa for what he had done for them.

The separation from her mother and the rest of the family, so closely united in affection and interests, was a wrench to the girl, although she wished to attend the school, and had herself asked to be permitted to do so. Under the slow and difficult transport facilities of 1756, the distance from Florence to Arezzo must have given the prospect of a long absence something of the appearance of an exile, since at that time it was not customary for the students to return home for holidays. Frequent visits would be ruled out, for the road was long, and apparently a chain of mud and potholes. Still, she desired to attend school, and faced the parting serenely, while Sir Ignatius never begrudged the heavy expenses of educating his four daughters, so often regarded by many better off contemporaries as a sheer waste of money.

In November Anna Maria and her father set out from Arezzo, traveling in a hired coach, and arrived in Florence on the 23rd of that month. They drove directly to St Apollonia's, and Ignatius handed his child - never so close or so dear to him as now when he had to face a long separation from her - to the care of the nuns. It was a difficult moment. The new intimacy that had developed between them in the past months made the prospect of parting painful, but he did not want to upset Anna Maria by any display of reluctance or emotion on his part. The Abbess tried to relieve the tension by chatting amiably to him, while Mother Eleanora, the mistress of pupils, took her new charge under her wing.

Sir Ignatius still hesitated, delaying the final moment of farewell. Furtively he stole a glance at the composed face of Anna Maria, only to discover that she was covertly studying him from under her eyelashes. Both shifted their gaze, and a second later their eyes met once more in a stealthy, sidelong glance. Then Anna Maria, realizing that her father was having a struggle to maintain his composure, slipped her hand into Mother Eleanora's. Gone was the healthy, country coloring. Her face was pale and her lips quivered, but she did not weep as the two of them passed through the inner door to the cloister, leaving Sir Ignatius to take his leave of the Abbess.

Anna Maria, just over nine years of age, was for the first time in her life separated from home and the familiar faces and routine that had comprised daily life, with its small joys and trials, plunged now into a new and unfamiliar milieu in which she must make her way solely on her merits, winning friends among her companions and gaining the confidence of her teachers.

A Benedictine boarding school of the eighteenth century was very different from what we understand by the term today, and St. Apollonia's seems to have been conducted somewhat on the schedule of a junior novitiate. The building was plain, its lines simple, and the routine followed within its walls was correspondingly austere and uncomplicated. The corridors were dim and quiet, and there would have been little fresh air or sunlight but for the large courtyard around which the buildings were grouped. It must have represented a startling change to Anna Maria, accustomed to the space and freedom of the Villa, surrounded on all sides by trees and vineyards and the lovely, sunbathed Tuscan countryside. But one enormous advantage, which the canons of modesty then demanded, was that there were no dormitories. Each girl had the blessed privacy of a separate room, and the common dining hall was designed and conducted similarly to the nuns' refectory, with meals taken in silence, apart from the reading aloud from a devotional or improving book.

The various duties of the day were regulated by the sound of a bell: rising, hours of study, meals, recreation periods, prayer. Each time the bell sounded, it marked the beginning of a new duty. The course of studies was not onerous, for the education of young ladies of the better-class families was not for the purpose of inculcating the natural sciences, without which a girl could get along very well. And the public-examination system was a form of torture that as yet lay in the future; nor was there any fixed syllabus.

Girls were not expected to shine intellectually, and bookish girls were not admired; but they must be thoroughly grounded in the canons of social etiquette. In addition to learning to read and write, Anna Maria and her young companions would be instructed in embroidery, music, languages, and elementary mathematics; they would be taught and encouraged to compose essays and graceful, flowery verses, to dabble with paint-brush and pen, and illuminate a capital or produce neat but uninspired watercolors. But most important they would receive drilling in the conventional social graces, and acquire that "finish" which has always been the hallmark of a convent education, so as to carry out into the world the aura of reverence, respect, courtesy and graciousness which religious alone and the atmosphere they engender in their schools, seem able to imprint indelibly on their students.

The change of environment for Anna Maria was abrupt and drastic, and might well have resulted in an overpowering sense of strangeness and homesickness. Suddenly the noisy children, tumbling about or appealing for arbitration in their quarrels were gone; the dim corridors were quiet, the bare walls unadorned save for occasional pictures and images of our Lord, our Lady, or some of the saints. Only at stipulated play periods did the courtyard ring with the sound of unrestrained children's voices, but far from being disconcerted or chilled by the severity of her surroundings, Anna Maria seemed completely at her ease. It was almost like a foretaste of religious life, and she found nothing forbidding about it. In fact, as she had already developed quite a facility for prayer and recollection amid distracting and often trying circumstances, she found the peace and the freedom with which she was permitted to indulge her taste for quiet meditation a cause for delight.

For the first year, Anna strove to master her lessons, and although usually diligent, she seemed to be but an indifferent scholar. She really did try, and worked carefully at the mathematics that held little attraction for her, but with a result that was by no means proportionate to the effort expended. Latin she disliked, and this aversion or lack of interest was not conducive to a rapid progress in its acquisition. Possibly she did not exhibit much zeal or enthusiasm in those subjects which held little charm for her, but she was extremely sensitive to the rebukes she received on the score of laziness or lack of application and tried hard to master her weakness. Mother Eleanora, her mistress, later remarked that Anna Maria was never in any way obstinate or wayward, and that there had never been occasion to reprimand or correct her apart from her school work. But in this field, there was seemingly frequent cause for reproach. However, she certainly made some scholastic progress and learned to write in a clear, legible hand, and to express her thoughts lucidly and concisely in words.

In the meantime, however, Anna Maria had discovered a secret which she was to adapt and develop, making it her own as a unique and complete method of perfection. Indeed, it may be claimed that it summarizes the whole method of her ascent to sanctity: to hide herself, to appear exactly like everyone else, and by never indulging in any singularity or attracting attention by seeming to be either conspicuously good or bad, to pass unnoticed. So great did her self-control become and so singular was her success in this field, that even the watchful eyes of her teachers never completely penetrated the veil of obscurity which the child drew around herself. "Gentle and well-adjusted," they considered her, "but similar to all the other girls," and certainly she was never regarded by any of them as a future candidate for canonization.

It is to Father Ildefonse that we are most indebted for a clear and detailed account of Anna Maria's progress, even in her childhood and before he came to make her acquaintance, for it was only in the last few years of her life that he became her confessor and spiritual director. But shortly after the death of the young Carmelite, when the fame of her sanctity was already spreading, Pope Clement XIV expressed a wish for some details of her life. This first account was provided by Father Ildefonse, at a time when Anna Maria's parents and contemporaries were still alive, so that he was able to complete his own intimate knowledge of her soul with the testimony of those familiar with all the earlier phases of her life and development. Of her school days he says, "Being placed as she was in the school, she immediately saw the necessity of exterior conformity in everything to the directions of her mistresses ... and the practices of the other students; this she firmly resolved in her heart. But, on the other hand, she did not wish to change one iota of the method she had adopted to foster a recollected interior spirit; she intended to progress as much as she could, but always without giving the slightest indication of it."

Most of the nuns had not the least inkling of the spiritual life that was developing under an exterior that was extraordinary only in lack of application to her studies. Not for many years were they to learn that the simple, pleasant manners, the graceful natural charm of the fresh-complexioned country girl were not the outcome of merely innate courtesy, but the manifestation of supernatural grace at work in her soul. One day, after her death, when the reputation of her holiness was being spread abroad in Florence, the nuns at St. Apollonia's, recalling their pupil of but a few years earlier, were to exclaim in astonishment, "Good, yes. But holy - never!"

Meanwhile the date for Anna Maria's first Communion had been set for the Feast of the Assumption, 1757, exactly one month after her tenth birthday. She had been confirmed in the previous February, and to prepare for the "first awakening of Jesus in her heart" she strove harder to correct her many imperfections, making very particular resolutions about diligence in class.

However, her zeal outran her discretion. Feeling that she should devote more time to prayer as a preparation, and knowing she would not be given permission to do so, she naively took the matter into her own hands. She had read in a biography of St. Aloysius Gonzaga how he had been accustomed to rise from his bed when the palace was asleep and its halls deserted, and, prostrating himself on the bare floor, pray through the long, silent hours of the night. This practice seemed, further, to be much admired by her mistresses, but it did not, apparently, occur to them to stipulate that it was not for imitation, at least by schoolchildren. The thought no sooner entered her head than Anna Maria decided: "I, too, will dedicate some hours of the night to prayer." She managed somehow to wake, and thought that in the privacy of her room her nocturnal devotions would pass undetected. But either she made a slight noise, or something else disturbed Mother Eleanora; possibly it was the additional guardian angel which all schoolgirls are convinced are allotted to teachers and monitresses. Whatever the reason, the mistress looked into Anna Maria's room. There, in the full light of the moon shining through the half-opened window was the culprit, caught red-handed as it were, kneeling at her prie-dieu. It is more than likely that Mother Eleanora was very much less enchanted with this evidence of excessive piety than many biographers would have us believe. It was probably to cure such a precocious taste for prayer - which might have seemed to them somewhat abnormal - that the nuns put Anna in charge of some of the smaller children. Their claims not only eliminated any chance of taking extra time for prayer during the day, but often encroached on her routine prayer time. This is the standard corrective for the piously self-centered, who usually react by bitter resentment at the curtailment of an exercise from which they are deriving considerable enjoyment. But Anna Maria's piety was of the genuine mettle. She resigned herself to the deprivation, realizing that she could please God in no better way then the careful performance of her duty, and the incident was forgotten.

Her attraction to silent prayer was instinctive, and she never appears to have sought instruction up to this period in the art of formal meditation, or to find it necessary to prop her devotions or ward off distractions by the use of a book. It is tempting to speculate on the form her prayers took. How did a child of ten spend those hours which, far from being a burden, seemed to pass all too quickly for her? Did she make a formal discursive meditation, and on what subjects? Undoubtedly the Sacred Heart played a large part in it, and after her first Communion, the Blessed Sacrament became inextricably joined with this devotion. But it seems unlikely that hers was a formal prayer of methodical considerations and resolutions, colloquy, and various acts in a rigid or conventional frame-work; more probably a simplified form of recollection and loving abandonment, for Anna Maria's whole spiritual orientation and attraction was towards the silent, loving gaze of the contemplatives. As a young child, she had no doubt merely "talked to God," putting before Him whom she knew to be intensely interested in her and her small problems and joys, the things that filled her day. So, as she grew, the effort of placing or holding herself in His presence and merely gazing at Him, or resting on His Sacred Heart, became an almost habitual attitude. She did have, however, at this stage, a great predilection for pious acts and would make numerous resolutions, prompted by the spirit of the day's feast, such as: "Today, in honor of St. Scholastica, I shall mortify all my senses, and especially my tongue!" These were all dutifully recorded in a journal where, according to the most approved methods of the period, she regularly balanced her spiritual debits and credits.

It seems incredible that a child of ten could successfully initiate and carry out a well-balanced program of the spiritual life, which was singularly free from the excess of misplaced enthusiasm, or the seeking of exemptions from legislated duties to make room for some of the silly practices so dear to the hearts of pious schoolgirls, and which often have about them more of superstition than genuine devotion. Immediately one looks for the sources of her guidance. The reality makes her unique, seemingly, among the saints, in having her spiritual life as well as her temporal affairs directed by Sir Ignatius, who was thus, as she claimed, "doubly her father."

She turned almost instinctively to him for help in a need that had arisen since the time of her first Communion, when she "daily experienced movements of love, impelling her to try and live a more holy life, for God alone." Yet she feared that others would notice it if she intensified her devotional exercises, and her ambition was to pass unnoticed, appearing, as she put it, "just like all the rest." The obvious person to supply the "prudent advice" which she felt she needed, was the confessor at the convent, Don Bertini. He, however, was extremely unsympathetic to all her ideals and attractions and thoroughly disapproved of her particular devotions. In later life she would have accepted the guidance of whomsoever God placed in the position to give it, without seeking compatibility of devotional tastes or temperament with her own. She knew that God can use any instrument as a channel for His grace, and that in giving advice in the confessional, the priest speaks in the name of Christ, who will ratify his counsel even when mistaken, so long as it is offered and received in good faith. But the deep antipathy of this frigid and rather Jansenistic-minded priest was so opposed to every spiritual ideal of Anna Maria's, both by instinct and previous training, that she shrank from speaking to him of so intimate a matter, and confined herself to disclosing only what was necessary for sacramental confession. Besides, she did not wish to hold long conversations in the confessional, which would certainly arouse curiosity in her schoolfellows and lead to the awkward questions and tactless remarks at which they are usually so adept.

Suddenly the image of her father came to her mind. Had she not learned the basic truths of the faith and practical charity from him? Was not all her devotion founded on his instructions, built on the foundations he had previously laid? On his profound yet down-to-earth advice she had fashioned her whole spiritual itinerary. If only she could see him now, speak with him, she felt certain she could explain her conflicting desires to him and find a sympathetic listener and a wise counselor.

But it was impossible! He was miles away in Arezzo, a long and weary journey; besides, he had no means of conveyance, having disposed of his carriage. Still, there was one thing Anna Maria had mastered very thoroughly at St. Apollonia's, and that was the art of penmanship. She wrote a beautiful hand, and words came freely and easily, so that she expressed herself clearly and concisely. Seemingly there was no censorship of the students' letters by the nuns, as is so often the custom in boarding-schools, and so a correspondence began between father and daughter that was to guide her through the whole of her schooldays and must be unparalleled in hagiography - although it should not seem remarkable for a father to indicate the way of perfection to his daughter or encourage her on it.

Her simple, frank letters revealed not only her problems, but laid open her soul to him, and again Ignatius felt humbly grateful to God that this favorite child of his was also favored by God, and already so responsive to the delicate movements of the Holy Spirit. Certain of her questions surprised him by their depth, and he answered as clearly and as comprehensively as he was able. Later he testified that "from that time a special spiritual bond of inexpressible reverence and love grew up between us;" a statement no one would feel tempted to question.

The letters Anna Maria wrote to her father were all destroyed by him immediately after he had read them, and this was done at her own specific request. Most of her biographers have lamented this loss, feeling that such letters would give valuable insight into her development at such a crucial stage of pious adolescence. Even Sir Ignatius himself expressed regret later that he had complied so literally with her instructions, remarking to Father Ildefonse that he had been "too scrupulously faithful" in tearing up and burning each letter as soon as it was read, although this was done at her own explicit request. He would have liked later to refer to them again, for he said, "those letters contained very lofty ideas about God and excellent concepts on virtue and perfection."

Ignatius has given detailed testimony of Anna Maria's progress and dispositions at this period, which is amplified by Don Pellegrini, and to a small degree by the recollections of some of her school companions. However, these letters were, on the whole, as much "in the dark" as the mistresses of Anna Maria's interior life, but Don Pellegrini assumed full control of her direction when she was fourteen. From the evidence of these two who knew her best, it is possible to get a fairly accurate picture of her development, and Ignatius' integrity in acceding to his daughter's specified wishes in regard to her actual letters can hardly be a cause for regret.

Anna Maria's attitude to and search for spiritual direction is one of the most marked emphases of her spiritual life. During the first year at school, the girl continued to follow in her own quiet, unobtrusive way the directives her father had already laid down for her, and she persevered faithfully in observing the methods and practices she had always followed, merely adapting them to the routine of school life. But there was no continuous and specialized direction, and one feels little surprise at this, considering that she was only ten years of age, and had not as yet made her first Communion. One would hardly expect to find an intense or highly-developed spiritual life. But the seed that falls on fallow, well-prepared ground, strikes instantaneously and flourishes perceptibly; and sacramental grace, flooding into so receptive a soul, hollowed out greater capacities and filled her with a longing for higher perfection which, of herself, she did not know how to achieve.

"Until this time," says Father Ildefonse, "she had not opened her heart to any spiritual director, other than what was necessary for the reception of the sacrament of penance" - that is to say, merely mentioning some valid matter for absolution.

For the ensuing five years, the interchange of letters with her father served to guide and spur her on to the greater endeavor she sought; in 1761 when Anna Maria was fourteen, a retreat made under the guidance of Don Pellegrini threw open another door, and yet wider vistas unrolled before her eyes. Even one of her school companions noticed a change in her, and remarked that from the time of this retreat, "Anna Maria advanced in solid piety and applied herself even more to the things of the spirit." Realizing that at last someone had arrived on the scene who could advise his daughter better than he could do, Sir Ignatius suggested that she now seek formal direction from Don Pellegrini.

Actually Anna Maria never seemed to experience the least difficulty in speaking of her interior desires or spiritual problems, usually an agonizing process for shy girls; her ability to manifest her soul was later attested by a Carmelite Father, who said that in all his experience he had only known one other person who made herself so clear as Anna Maria in the confessional. There is, however, one interesting paragraph towards the end of the long and detailed resolutions she later wrote out before making her religious profession: "Knowing that he who listens and submits to your ministers, listens and submits to you, my Jesus, I resolve to conquer that repugnance which I sometimes experience in manifesting my soul and my heart to the one who represents you, and this in order to walk in all security towards perfection, promising to follow faithfully the teaching of our Holy Mother St. Teresa who said: 'To your confessor and superior you will tell all your temptations, imperfections, and repugnances, so that he may give you counsel and a remedy to overcome them.'"

However, of this period of Anna Maria's schooldays, Father Ildefonse writes in retrospect: "Among the other good effects which this openness of spirit with her father produced in her ... is the fact that it caused a facility in her for dealing later with an experienced, learned, spiritual confessor."

Sometime during 1761, Don Bertoni left St. Apollonia's, and the post of regular confessor was taken by Don Peter di Cosimo Pellegrini, the "learned and experienced confessor" to whom Father Ildefonse referred. Anna Maria had by now benefited much from her father's counsel, and finding the new priest sympathetic towards her attractions and devotions, she told him of her various acts of piety, her method of prayer and preparation for Holy Communion, and her numerous little practices. Don Pellegrini on his part was delighted to find what he described as "a deep sense of piety and very good dispositions for the religious life; a great love of God with the desire of pleasing Him completely," and he recommended certain spiritual reading to aid her in her prayer. In particular, a little book on eucharistic devotion entitled *Food of the Soul* pleased her greatly. She studied it carefully, and from this time forward she was permitted by Don Pellegrini to make a regular daily half-hour of meditation in the presence of the Blessed Sacrament in the chapel or in the privacy of her own room.

While she had an intense devotion to the Real Presence, and loved to spend the time in silent adoration of the Blessed Sacrament reserved in the Tabernacle, Anna Maria seemed to have a sound grasp of the essential nature of the Eucharist, as the food and nourishment of the soul, the day's rations for the day's march, and the remedy for all ills and bruises of wayfaring, the antidote for all the small irritations and fatigues of the way.

The presence of God was a practice with which she had long been familiar, and accustomed from her earliest years to seek Him within herself at all times, speaking to Him in her heart, she delighted in the knowledge that by sanctifying grace, God dwelt in her soul. But the Real Sacramental Presence was not merely another dimension added to this communing, nor did she entertain many of the usual sentimental misconceptions about "the prisoner of the Tabernacle." The Body of Christ, whom she received in Holy Communion, is not in space, as she was fully aware, in the usual sense of that term. Nor is Christ moved from place to place, naturally, when the Host is, but only sacramentally - for instance, in the ciborium or in a procession; when the Host is broken, the Body of Christ suffers no division. What is moved, seen, touched, are the sensible appearances, for our Lord is always at the right hand of the Father. But despite the fact that His presence in the Blessed Sacrament does not exist in space or time, the truth remains that His Body and Blood are really and substantially present; Anna Maria had a firm and sound grasp on these essential facts at a period when it was considered preferable to enthrone the Reserved Species in a monstrance than to receive Christ into one's heart.

Don Pellegrini certainly was convinced that her piety was not mere schoolgirl emotion, for he remarked that after he got to know her through the confessional, he was impressed by the extraordinary innocence and candor of her conscience. Not wishing to give the impression that he considered this anything out of the ordinary, he quietly questioned her about her general conduct, and came to the conclusion that God was leading her in a way that was simple yet profound, and that obviously He had special designs on this girl. As it was patent that Anna Maria's progress had nothing to do with extraordinary states or mystical graces, it seemed preferable that she be left in ignorance that in her spiritual life she was not "just like all the rest" of her companions, as she considered herself to be.

"When a person once understands what has been said to him for his profit," says St. John of the Cross, "he needs neither to hear nor to say more, but rather to practice what has been said to him silently and carefully, in humility and charity and self-contempt, and not to go away and seek new things, which serve only to satisfy the appetite in external matters and leave the spirit weak and empty, with no interior virtue."

Don Pellegrini, therefore, avoided any appearance of favoritism, and never encouraged the pious conversations that so delighted Anna Maria, merely giving her what instruction was necessary in the confessional to aid her, as he said, "to soar aloft to God." He spoke as briefly as possible, for few words were necessary to make her understand what was required, and she never had to be told the same thing twice. Thus none of the other girls were aware that he was, in fact, giving formal direction to Anna Maria, nor did she herself suspect that she was receiving different treatment, except in one thing. Don Pellegrini granted her permission - a rare privilege in those days, and one which confirms his confidence in her genuine spiritual advancement and its authenticity - to receive Holy Communion twice a week, just as the nuns did. Nothing could have been better calculated to encourage her in the determination to deepen her love of God and to do everything to please Him and express in some small way her gratitude for this gift of Himself.

Anna Maria was exceptionally fortunate in the spiritual directors who played their different parts in her life, and in the mode of their direction. Many of the saints have sought in vain for a reliable guide, and when one recalls the words of Abbot Marmion, one is struck by the complete absence of self-seeking or preoccupation in all her correspondence on the matter.

"I am not a great partisan of much direction," wrote that experienced director. "In my opinion long and frequent letters of direction do more harm than good ... I hate what is commonly known as *direction*, and directors *à la mode*. There is often very little of God and a lot of ourselves in it."

All too often spiritual direction is sought as a means of gaining sanction for one's own self-willed ideas, and such persons will go from one director to another until they find someone who "understands" them, i.e. who will approve of their doing what they had already decided upon.

"It is best to avoid speaking to one's spiritual director," Anna Maria was later to say to her novice mistress, "except when it is strictly necessary to do so. And even then it should be as brief as possible, lest through self-love it degenerate into mere pious chat. It so often happens that a spiritual conversation begins in seeking God and ends in finding self."

Obedience is always the safe and final criterion of one's genuine desire to be led, and Anna Maria never went out of her way to seek a guide who was merely congenial. Accepting those God placed in her path, and regarding them as standing in His place and speaking with His authority, she illustrates the correct outlook towards a much disputed and sadly abused procedure. In the apostolic letter *Testem benevolentiae*, Pope Leo XIII in 1899 outlined the necessity of spiritual direction within the framework of a stable, well-grounded interior life. Anna Maria is a virtual personification of the correct attitude and response: how one should seek, co-operate with, and profit from direction. It was one of the most dominant forces in her life and rapid development in the ways of perfection.

3

The Voice of St. Teresa of Jesus

I come in little things,
Saith the Lord:
Not borne on morning wings
Of majesty, but I have set My Feet
Amidst the delicate and bladed wheat
That springs triumphant in the furrowed sod.
(Evelyn Underhill)

Loud wails rent the air.

"I won't, so there! You leave me alone!"

Fourteen-year-old Cecilia stamped her foot and glared at her sister. Anna Maria sighed in exasperation.

"How are you ever going to be accepted as a nun someday, if you carry on with these tantrums?" she demanded. "Do you suppose a novice will be allowed to stamp and shriek when anything doesn't please her?"

"Well, I'm not a novice now, so you leave me alone."

It was a year since Cecilia and Eleanor Redi had come to join their elder sister at St. Apollonia's, and Anna Maria, by now one of the seniors and in her last year, was frequently appointed as prefect to the younger children, especially her own two sisters, who made no bones about the fact that they resented her big-sister ministrations. Both the younger girls were one day to be members of St. Apollonia's community, and Anna Maria's zeal for their progress in perfection

33

was not always accommodated to their years or temperaments. Today there had been open mutiny in the air, and now Cecilia, receiving no reply to her retort, decided she had won this round, and flounced out of the room.

Anna Maria headed her off.

"You may not go out to play until you have finished your work!" she insisted sternly. Cecilia wriggled past to the door, and then stopped suddenly, her head singing from a sharp box on the ears, dealt by her guide and mentor. For a moment surprise immobilized her, and then, with a violent lunge, she gave as good and better than she had received.

Her burst of anger did not last long, and she darted for freedom. But somehow she found the game she had been so eager to join uninteresting, and the remembrance of Anna's set face, with four angry streaks that her fingers had left on it, weighed on Cecilia's conscience.

"I must go now," she told her young companion, "I have some work to do."

Sulkily she flung her books into the cupboard and tidied up the room in a desultory sort of fashion. That was the worst of Anna, she thought resentfully; she always made you feel in the wrong without saying anything at all. If she'd shouted back, it would have been all right, and Cecilia would not have been saddled with this sense of guilt. But Anna Maria never shouted back. She just looked at you and made you feel a worm!

"Anyway," Cecilia thought angrily, "she hit me first. She's got no right to be so bossy ..." She had hit Anna much harder though, she realized, and after all Papa had told her to do what Anna Maria said. And Mother Eleanora *had* put Anna in charge, and Mother Eleanora herself often slapped them ...

Supposing Anna Maria told Mother Eleanora about the fight? There would be plenty of trouble in store, Cecilia knew. When Anna Maria appeared at supper, with a slight bruise discoloring her cheek, Cecilia heard the mistress enquire about it and held her breath. But to her relief, Anna passed it off, and managed to divert attention from herself.

Cecilia's anger and resentment had quite evaporated by now.

"Anna's right," she thought miserably. "I am untidy and lazy and don't do as I'm told. I just can't be good all the time the way she is. She's so polite and kind to everyone and hardly ever gets mad or makes nasty remarks. And she doesn't mind being put upon. No wonder everyone likes her; she always turns the other cheek... ."

It was Cecilia who sought her elder sister after supper and apologized. Anna Maria kissed her. "It's all over, and I have forgotten about it long ago," she said. "You do the same. Go and tell the good Jesus you are sorry and think no more about it."

Anna Maria, at sixteen, was becoming more and more preoccupied with a problem that had been slowly developing for many years, but she felt now that she could put off a decision no longer. For months past she had prayed for light and guidance, but the seemingly obvious solution left her feeling vaguely dissatisfied.

Should she ask Reverend Mother if she would consider an application to enter their novitiate when her schooldays came to an end? Anna Maria had long felt quite certain that God wished her to serve Him in religion, to consecrate herself utterly, heart and soul, mind and body, to His service. What would be more logical than that she should do so here, in the house that had been her home for seven years, where she was known and loved, and where she felt certain - despite her many shortcomings and lack of academic distinction - many of the community would welcome her. At times, as she knelt in the tranquil evening silence of the chapel, the scene of so many happy hours and many graces of light and peace, she would feel almost certain, and would resolve to ask Mother Eleanora to make an appointment for her with the Abbess. But some indefinable impulse always held her back, and the request was never made. Later, when her brother Francis enquired why she had not entered St. Apollonia's, she replied that it was because the observance there was relaxed, and as well she had two (later three) sisters there. It did not appeal to her. She felt called to sever completely all the ties of family and attachment and die to herself and all that bound her to earth, in order to live solely and single-mindedly for God.

Anna Maria's stricture on the fervor of the St. Apollonia community is unnecessarily severe. Her opinion that their life was "slow" was merely the expression of a still unformulated conception of a life of total detachment and abnegation. The question was not one of degree, but of kind. It was not their observance but their rule of life that failed to come up to her ideals. She did not know where she was to find the silence and retirement, the "aloneness with God alone" to which she felt drawn; but the routine life and observance in a teaching order did not satisfy her aspirations or fit in with the standard she visualized for herself. To Anna Maria, it seemed almost like an attraction to an eremitical life; but what she was actually seeking without realizing it, was the austerity of a strictly cloistered life, of which she had as yet no knowledge, never having had any contact with it. Possibly she never would have turned her thoughts towards Carmel, but for an apparently chance encounter during her last year at school in September, 1763.

It was customary at that time for a girl about to enter religion to make a series of courtesy visits of farewell to relatives and friends and to pay her respects to other religious of her acquaintance. Cecilia Albergotti, a resident of Arezzo and an acquaintance of Anna Maria through the mutual friendship of their families, was about to take the habit at the Discalced Carmelite Monastery in Florence, and among those to whom she paid a leavetaking call were the Benedictines of St. Apollonia's.

Anna Maria knew Cecilia, who was her junior by a year, but only slightly. She had been educated at the Convent of St. Nicholas at Prato, and they had met casually there, as well as during visits to the family home in Arezzo. But the two were not intimate, and Cecilia's visit was merely a routine formality.

Cecilia was in the parlor conversing with the Abbess and other members of the community, and probably some of the older students, when Anna Maria joined them. The two girls greeted each other, and chatted about trivialities, but, as was natural, the conversation gradually turned towards the subject of religious vocations in general, and then Carmel was discussed and showered with much praise and admiration by the nuns. However, before taking her leave, Cecilia requested a few minutes' conversation with Anna Maria in private. As they were family

acquaintances, this was readily granted; yet surprisingly it never eventu-
ated. The nuns lingered on, and when Cecilia finally rose and made her
adieus, passing from one to the other with a gracious word of gratitude
for their hospitality and request for their prayers, she took Anna Maria
firmly by the hand and looked at her for a long moment in such a way as
seemed to invite her: *Come with me!*

Is it possible that a handclasp or a mere trick of light and shade
as it falls across the face of a casual acquaintance can alter the whole
orientation of one's life? Grace comes in the most unexpected guises,
and can speak to us in the whisper of a breeze or the thunder of a
hurricane, the blinding light of Damascus or the random remark of a
stranger. In the economy of salvation, man is led to God through other
men. In the realm of nature as well as of grace, God makes use of
human agents and secondary causes - except of course in the original
creation. It is the gentle, almost imperceptible prompting, like the prick
of a pin, that moves most of us, rather than the thunderclap that leaves
one blind and dazed by the roadside. We do not feel the great wind of
Pentecost, but a mere impulse, an intuition, no more violent than the
movement of a bough as a bird alights; yet it ushers in our eternal
destiny, which stands in the wings awaiting our summons or dismissal.
For that one significant moment, which comes at least once in each
lifetime, we and we alone are masters of our destiny.

Cecilia Albergotti departed, and Anna Maria walked slowly and
thoughtfully up to her little room. Everything was the same as it had
always been - the plain white bed, the framed picture of the Blessed
Virgin, a small window overlooking the sun-splashed patio - and yet
somehow it seemed that nothing would ever again be quite the same.
Suddenly, as clearly as though a voice had spoken beside her, Anna
Maria distinctly heard the words: "I am Teresa of Jesus, and I want
you among my daughters." She knew nothing of interior locutions,
but somehow felt that these words, seemingly so clear and audible,
had been uttered in the depths of her soul.

"I am imagining things," she said, feeling rather foolish. She
looked around, but there was nobody about, nor was anyone in the
corridor outside. Fearing her imagination was playing tricks, Anna

Maria ran down to the chapel, and knelt before the Blessed Sacrament. What had put the name Teresa of Jesus into her mind? Until she was mentioned by the nuns this afternoon in conversation with Cecilia Albergotti, the famous reformer of Carmel had never had any place in Anna Maria's life.

Suddenly an overwhelming surge of emotion swept over her, and once again she heard the same voice distinctly repeat: "I am Teresa of Jesus, and I tell you that before long you shall be in my monastery."

This was the only occurrence in the brief and outwardly uneventful life of Anna Maria Redi that can remotely be classed as miraculous grace or an extraordinary intervention; and even it is unspectacular enough. But so deeply-rooted was her conviction of the authenticity of the words she heard twice that afternoon, that never would her resolution to become a Carmelite be shaken, nor would she ever entertain the least doubt about the certainty of her vocation. Her lot was cast, the choice was made; from that moment Anna Maria gave the matter no further thought as a problem to be solved, but merely regarded it as a goal towards which to work, conforming her own ideas and spiritual practices to the Carmelite spirit and the contemplative ideal it enshrines.

From that decisive day, Anna Maria became impatient to leave St. Apollonia's. She had several more months still to spend at the school, since Sir Ignatius had arranged to come and bring her home in April, 1764, three months before her seventeenth birthday. But now that her one problem had been solved, and the future, as it were, decided upon - at last to her own satisfaction - she seemed to see no further need for study. Or perhaps it was that realizing how soon she would be leaving them for ever, she desired to return to her parents as soon as possible. For the first time in seven years, she chafed at the delay, even writing to her father, urging him to take her from school.

"I understand from your last letter that you will soon be on your way here to bring me home," she wrote. "How that cheered me up! It seems that I must wait a million years before I shall see you... "

Although impatience made it seem that the hour for departure would never arrive, yet when it finally came she experienced an unexpected but quite natural reluctance to say goodbye to these nuns who had been such good friends and kind mistresses for so long. For almost half of her life this convent had been her home. Here she had learned much more than her letters and lessons; she had grown in the practice of virtue, and her budding religious vocation had flowered. The silent gray walls enshrined many memories, some bad, some gay, but part of her vibrant girlhood's years were so intimately bound up with the place that it seemed almost as though she were parting with something of herself. Most boarding-school girls have undergone this strange conflict: longing to depart, yet surprising everybody when the hour of release finally arrives by practically wading out on their floods of valedictory tears.

"Goodbye, my dear child," said Mother Eleanora, embracing her. She glanced shrewdly at the tall blonde girl whom she had led through this cloister so long ago almost as though she had divined something of her secret decision. "We had expected you would wish to come back to us; but wherever God in His wisdom leads you, do not forget us in your prayers, and we will always remember you, that you may faithfully practice what you have learned here. Then, wherever your path lies, we will be happy that you were once our pupil."

It was April 8th, 1764 when Sir Ignatius Redi proudly handed his daughter, grown now to lovely young womanhood, down from the carriage at their town house in the Corso Vittorio Emanuele. It was to prove no more than a *pied-à-terre* for this girl, already poised on the brink of flight – a brief respite such as the migrating swallow might take before the final lap of its long flight home, forced on by an instinct stronger than itself. Spring was well-advanced, and out at the Villa the green spears of the narcissi Anna Maria so loved were already pushing their way through the brown earth. Soon the family would be moving out to *The Gardens* for the summer months. But in the meantime, Anna found much to fill her time and absorb her interest in the more formal routine followed in the town residence. Two years after her departure, a little boy had been born, followed two years later by twins who had lived only three weeks. But Diego was

now nearing his sixth birthday, and he delighted in the sudden acquisition of a grown-up sister, who was ready to tell him stories or help
him sail his boats, and in general lavish much more time and attention
on him than he could claim from his mother, now a semi-invalid.
Without fuss, and as the most natural thing in the world, Anna Maria
took charge of the nursery, still full of young and boisterous children,
their natural high spirits effervescing at times erupting in rough-and-
tumble commotion like a volcano. It must have been an enormous
relief to Camilla when Anna Maria assumed command, and she gladly
allowed the girl to use her authority in restoring order and generally
to take over the role of nursemaid, supervising the children in their
prayers and instructions, as well as their meals and play.

But nobody was more happy to have Anna Maria at home again
then her father. For Ignatius, his second child was far more than a
daughter. She was a companion whose intimacy was not merely on
the plane of physical relationship, but the deep understanding and
spiritual affinity that comes rarely between two hearts and minds,
however close the natural ties. And when it does exist, it cannot be
weakened by separation in time or place but can be severed only by
death; although even then the bereaved knows how to find his beloved in God.

All things reveal God to the soul who understands how to
find Him in created nature. "If in all things you seek God," says
the *Imitation*, "doubtless you will find God." Anna Maria had
perfected this art by now and possessed a special facility in raising her heart and mind to the Creator by contemplating the beauty
He had scattered about the lovely Tuscan landscape spread out
before her eyes. The smallest things uplifted her to God, and particularly did she love to catch those breathtaking, unheralded
glimpses of His face that are sometimes suddenly revealed in the
mirror of nature. Always flowers, trees, cloud-masses, the dip and
curve of birds in swift formation off light, the colors of the ever-
changing sky, the shadows moving across the garden and the clear
noonday sun, raised her mind to their Maker, of whose beauty all
this loveliness was but a weak echo.

Anna Maria still assisted at daily Mass in the Capuchin church near the Villa, but now she attended the Jesuit church in Arezzo weekly as well. For the first time she put herself officially in the hands of a spiritual director, a Jesuit, Father Jerome Gioni. He required that as far as dress, entertainments, and all exterior domestic or social matters, she be subject entirely to her parents' wishes and conform to their customs, and that her spiritual life should be entrusted exclusively to his guidance. Even this stern taskmaster was later to express his admiration for the fidelity with which she carried out his wishes in this regard, and he remarked particularly on her perfection of hiddenness which is so dominant a theme of her entire life.

"What struck me most," he told Sir Ignatius, "was her intense preoccupation and endeavor to appear like everyone else in exterior matters such as dress and behavior, regardless of any inconvenience, or conflict with her own personal tastes in such matters." Then, after enumerating instances of this docility, he concluded: "These practices were minute and seemingly trivial, but I am convinced that they were signs of great virtue and strength of character. Acts of virtue were always performed with easy naturalness which (whether bestowed by God or acquired by merit) is out of the ordinary, and a cause for admiration. My opinion was simply that here was a girl who responded to the promptings of interior virtue so effortlessly that it appeared as though she was merely acting quite naturally. This indeed required special grace and a very careful correspondence to it."

The first part of Father Gioni's directive should have raised no difficulty, for the Redi family were neither lavish in entertainments nor extravagant in dress. However, Camilla's love of pretty clothes and the opportunities for wearing them sought to find an outlet by immersing Anna Maria in a whirl of entertainments. It was a delight to array in elegant clothes this graceful, beautiful daughter who wore them with unselfconscious ease; but apparently Anna Maria had not wished to initiate herself into a conventional mode of life precipitately, and had intended cloistering herself in the house and dressing much more severely than Camilla approved, or even Ignatius considered fitting. This Father

Gioni adamantly refused to permit. She must take her place in the ordinary social life of the family, dress according to the demands of custom and her father's status, and not make herself singular by trying to behave like a "nunk or nay-woman" - to use Cecily Hallack's expressive phrase.

Anna Maria did not press the point, but took her place with naturalness and grace in drawing room and picnic party, and here again she adopted the same method of "hiddenness" she had found so effective at school: managing to appear exactly like everyone else. Had she dressed in black and regulated her daily routine according to her own preconceived notions of claustral discipline, she certainly would not have achieved this, but rather have come to be regarded as a freak or a harmless eccentric. And because she was neither embarrassing to others by peculiar behavior, nor tactless in an apparent preference for her own company, but was quiet and simple in her manners, adapting herself to whatever company she was in, she was well-liked and popular.

However, her detachment was not always matched by her consideration for others at this early stage, and one incident seems to sum up the somewhat self-centered orientation that is so typical of strong-minded and excessively zealous beginners in the practice of virtue. Usually they tend to interpret somewhat too absolutely St. John of the Cross' counsel to "live as if there were in the whole world but God and one's own soul." Charity, however, demands our acknowledgement of and allowance for those with whom we associate, their needs and their sensibilities.

Hair styling in the eighteenth century was a major operation, and one in which no self-respecting young socialite could afford to be disinterested. Signor Sacchetti, a coiffeur of Arezzo, attended the Villa daily to dress Camilla's and Anna Maria's hair. A true artist in his own sphere, he lavished all his skill and inspiration on the long, thick golden hair, and expected a commensurate appreciation of his efforts. Anna Maria's reactions were so contrary to those his handiwork usually elicited that he could recall and testify about them years later.

"How will the signorina have her hair arranged this morning?"

A shrug exhibited her complete indifference.

"But *Signorina!*" The expressive hands rose in a horrified gesture of protest.

"Oh," said Anna Maria offhandedly, "do it as you have done my mother's."

"But no! You cannot wear a coiffure the same as the signora's. You are young ... it is not fitting ..."

Sighing, Sacchetti took up the comb and set to work, glancing at the face in the mirror opposite from time to time. But Anna Maria's eyes remained cast down, fixed on the hands clasped in her lap, while the hairdresser muttered, under his breath, a speech daily rehearsed but never delivered.

Sacchetti worked doggedly on, until the masterpiece satisfied even his critical eye. "There! Does the signorina not think that is most handsome?" he exclaimed proudly. But Anna Maria remained unmoved.

Sacchetti snatched up the hand mirror lying on the table, and thrust it into her hand, his eagerness for a well-deserved compliment obvious. But she laid the glass down without so much as a glance. "Thank you, but it is not necessary. I know you have done your work well, as always."

"My *work!*" Sacchetti threw up his hands in despair and stamped out of the room. Still, it never occurred to Anna Maria, apparently, that her strict custody of the eyes was a cause of far greater mortification to the unfortunate hairdresser than to herself, and that however great her disinterest in her appearance or her attempts to appear so, consideration demanded a word of commendation and appreciation.

Francis Xavier, giving testimony for his sister's beatification half a century later, remarked that in his opinion it was providential that Camilla was ill when Anna Maria returned from Saint Apollonia's, "because Mother had a gay disposition, and was attracted to frivolities, and would certainly have wanted to take her out on social calls and all manner of entertaining diversions."

However, Camilla was confined to the house, although not always to her bed, and far from being drawn into the perpetual motion of a social whirl, Anna Maria had the opportunity to indulge her taste for penance to a large measure, apparently with her confessor's consent since he had demanded exact obedience to his direction. She had managed to obtain a hairshirt and a small knotted cord, both of which she wore beneath her fashionable clothing when attending soirées and parties. It is difficult, remembering the fashions of the period, to understand how she contrived to wear the variety of instruments of penance she did without appearing strangely bulky, but apparently she arranged things to her own satisfaction, and nobody, not even her personal maid, was aware of the unusual addition to an already cumbersome garb.

Anna Maria now, in fact, blossomed out in a series of penitential practices. Some years before at St. Apollonia's she had noticed that in all the lives of the saints much emphasis was given to the application of a "discipline" or scourge, and she desired to imitate them in this exercise, which she knew to be customary among religious. Her method of obtaining not only information but also the possession of a discipline is very typical of the girl's charm and determination, as well as her ability to inveigle most people into doing what she wanted them to do.

Feeling fairly certain that a direct request, either to Don Pellegrini or Mother Eleanora would meet with a blunt refusal, Anna Maria approached one of the younger teachers, looking as though bent on some prank.

"Please, Sister," she said, "will you be so kind as to let me have a look at a discipline?"

Sister Teresa Louise seemed surprised, and Anna Maria added hastily: "I do not know what they are like, although I have often heard of them, and I would very much like to see one."

Perhaps the Sister was very young, and not as yet experienced in the ways of schoolgirls; perhaps she merely thought this odd request was in the nature of a "dare." For whatever reason, she produced a discipline of knotted whipcord, which Anna Maria examined with gratifying interest.

"I see," she said at length, "but I still do not understand what it is for."

"Why, little wooden-head! It is for chastisement, as our dear

Lord was scourged for our sins."

"Oh! Then how is it done? Would you be so kind as to show me . . ?"

The enthralled attention of her audience apparently removed the last of the Sister's discretion and reserve, and Anna Maria was given a demonstration in how to wield the instrument of penance to good effect. She was an apt pupil, and seemingly she managed to retain possession of the discipline also. What is almost unbelievable is that she obtained permission to use it from Don Pellegrini (who seems thereby to forfeit some claim to the tribute paid to him as "a wise and prudent director"). Certainly he did stipulate that it was to be for a very short space of time, and only if the discipline was made of cord and contained no metal; but even so it seems an imprudent penance for a young girl, particularly if, as most probably, it was used on the back and shoulders. Today the Church does not approve of this method of penance even for adults, because of the risk to health and physique.

Now, however, Anna Maria began to use in earnest the discipline she had formerly obtained by a certain amount of guile; and the cords around her waist were sometimes varied by spiked metal chains - this, also, no doubt, with the sanction of her director. She was no longer tied down by the crowded itinerary of school days, and was able to indulge her attraction for prayer. It soon became known in the family and among the domestic staff that, when her presence was not required elsewhere, she could be found in her bedroom on her knees. She devised all manner of uncomfortable postures, such as kneeling on the sharp corner of a prie-dieu, or with the palms of her hands under her knees, sometimes praying for long periods with her arms outstretched in the form of a cross. Most surprisingly these discomforts did not seem to distract from her prayers by causing undue preoccupation with a mutinous body, clamoring for relief from such harsh treatment. She seems to have possessed a genuine spirit of mortification and as natural an attraction for penance as most of us have for avoiding it.

Probably Anna Maria thought that by adopting all these physical discomforts she would train herself for her future life as a Carmelite, of which she seems to have had little knowledge at the time. In fact, rigid observance of penitential practices is very far removed from the true Carmelite spirit, which is essentially one of simplicity, openness of soul, and freedom from the successively narrowing horizon of multiplied exterior acts.

After the maid had prepared her bed, assisted her young mistress to undress, unhooking and unbuttoning the heavy clothes, and dressed her hair for the night, Anna Maria would pull the soft mattress from her bed, and sleep flat on the palliasse; sometimes on the bare boards of the floor. For a long time nothing was known of these nocturnal mortifications, as she always rose (probably with no regret) early enough to restore the bed to its original condition before the maid arrived, so that nothing more extraordinary was apparent to the servant than that her mistress must have passed a somewhat restless night.

There was no trace of exhibitionism about these performances, for Anna Maria genuinely desired them to be a secret shared by none but God and herself and, in fact, she was obliged to go to considerable trouble to ensure that they were not detected. Nor was there any evidence of the puritanical attitude that must constantly be crucifying itself because it finds something sinful in all that gives pleasure or comfort. The attitude of Anna Maria was a valid love of God, which desires to sacrifice creature pleasures, not because they are evil in themselves, but solely for the love of God. At table she was quite adept, appearing to eat the same food as was served to the others, but actually she avoided drinking wine, and always took the dishes which she disliked, while passing over those more to her taste.

An amusing anecdote in this connection is related of Madame Louise of France, daughter of Louis XV, later Mother Teresa of St. Augustine of the St. Denis Carmel.[1] Having set her heart on the cloister, Princess Louise decided to set to work and overcome her fastidiousness in many directions. Formerly she had been so pernickety in the matter of food that the royal cooks complained of the impossibility of satisfying her; so she determinedly resisted this weakness, deciding

---

[1] She was a contemporary of St. Teresa Margaret's. She entered the Carmel of St. Denis in April, 1770, one month after the death in Florence of Teresa Margaret.

always to eat those dishes which pleased her least. However, while she herself doubtless benefited from the discipline, the poor cooks' tribulations were in no way lessened, for, finding that she would now not touch their most daintily prepared *chefs d'oeuvre,* they considered that instead of being merely difficult, it had now become quite impossible to please Her Royal Highness! Under this imputation of gourmandize the Princess allowed herself to remain, as some sort of atonement for her inconsiderateness in the past. Still, one cannot avoid the conclusion that here "it is mercy and not sacrifice that God looks for," and that a little more charity and consideration for others might have provided her with ample scope for mortification, and at the same time avoided inflicting it on those who tried so hard to please her - an opinion which later the Princess herself would have been the first to endorse. The extremes in penance are a Scylla and Charybdis between which only the most skillful navigators can pass unharmed without the assistance of an experienced pilot.

However, in all Anna Maria's penance, there was nothing morbid or perverted. It is true that she derived joy from these "little sacrifices" not from satisfaction in the discomfort or suffering they caused, but rather because they constituted a self-denial and abdication of self-will for the love of God. Her amiable, serene disposition was evidence of interior balance. There was never anything flaunting or exhibitionist in the manner of their performance; while far from being disagreeable in other ways by irritable and cantankerous behavior, Anna Maria was always remarkable for her sunny disposition, her desire not to cause trouble or difficulty for others, even the servants. She was an ideal mistress, readily forgiving any oversight or shortcoming on their part; while she would find an excuse for any clumsiness or neglect, should her mother or father rebuke them for carelessness or slovenly work, and not infrequently she performed many of the duties her personal maid had forgotten or neglected, so that the girl would not be punished.

Indeed, even accustomed as they were to tolerant and considerate treatment from Ignatius and Camilla, the domestic servants found Anna Maria almost too good to be true. Certainly they thought highly of her, and there is no stronger testimony than that of a valet who regards his master as a hero, or a serving-girl to whom her mistress personifies the virtues of charity and true humility.

Father Gioni says of Anna Maria at this time, when she was under his direction: "She was determined not to give herself the least satisfaction, even of the most innocent kind, outside of what was strictly necessary, or decreed by obedience or custom; on the contrary she wished to embrace out of love for God any occasion which presented itself to suffer a little for His sake."

Having decided that she was to become a Carmelite at the earliest possible date, Anna Maria did not, as many girls would have done, consider that she might "take it easy" in the meantime, coasting along and getting as much enjoyment out of life as possible while there was still the opportunity. Soon enough she would be confined to a very small area, with restricted companionship, living in a tiny cell devoid of comfort. Why not make the most of life for the few months left?

But Anna Maria was one of those souls who never do things by halves. At the moment of her conviction of vocation, she had given herself wholeheartedly to it. No matter where she was, she would live in what seemed to her the most perfect conformity to its demands. She might be mistaken as to what was the most perfect conformity, but not in her intention or desire. Any slight slackness or self-indulgence now, however blameless, would have left some shadows or spots on the limpid surface of the soul that she wished to remain ever turned to the clear rays of love which had so long drawn her.

Sacrifice does not merely consist of suffering or deprivation - although as such it is often loosely used. We speak of a mother making "every sacrifice" to ensure that her son will receive, say, a university education, and usually we mean that she has deprived herself of the comforts and small luxuries she could otherwise have afforded.

Sacrifice consists in the renunciation of some positive good, or suffering from which the will emerges victorious and stronger, a voluntary renunciation for the sake of a greater supernatural gain. There is much suffering among animals, but no sacrifice, which is something that belongs to the will - a deliberate election, of which the initial step is the submission in faith to the eternal, infinite God.

Love and suffering are inseparable. Anna Maria's desire for suffering was not an unwholesome preoccupation with self, but the burning desire to give, and to continue giving while she had the time and the power to do so. For already she seemed to divine that the time would be short, and there was much to be accomplished before "the night cometh when no man may work."

4

"I Shall Be Yours, Whatever the Cost"

Gift better than Himself God cannot give;
Gift better than His God man cannot know ...
God is my gift; Himself He freely gave me,
God's gift am I - and none but God shall have me.
(Bl. Robert Southwell, S.J.)

"Well, my child, and when do you intend returning to St. Apollonia's?"

"But I have finished my schooling."

"Yes, indeed. But you will go back to them, my little one, for I know you will never be happy in the world. You will be a nun."

Anna Maria turned in her chair and faced the invalid, who watched her closely from her nest of pillows.

Apollonia Fabbri's reputation for holiness, won through years of protracted pain borne with patience and fortitude, was such that nearly everyone in Arezzo applied to her for advice in their troubles. Her rooms had, over the years, become an acknowledged rendezvous for the more pious. Anna Maria, who as a child had often accompanied her mother on visits to Apollonia, now renewed these regular calls, and it had not taken the older woman long to sense the hidden stream that ran swiftly and deeply beneath the tranquil, unruffled exterior of the fashionably dressed, elaborately coiffured girl who gave so generously of her time to talk with the invalid.

Anna Maria was so long in replying that Apollonia thought she did not mean to continue the conversation. Then, looking suddenly and searchingly at the emaciated face on the pillow, her own cheeks suffused with hot color, she said in a low, vehement voice: "Apollonia, I have left that convent, and I shall never return to it."

"And why not?"

Slowly Anna Maria answered, the words seeming to come reluctantly. "One day we had a visit from Cecilia Albergotti. You know her. She was about to enter the Carmel of St. Teresa, and she came to say farewell to the Sisters. I was sent for to speak to her." She paused. To nobody else had she ever breathed a word of this experience, not even to her father; and it took effort to formulate in words that inner conviction which had possessed her so suddenly and inexplicably.

Apollonia waited, sensing that Anna Maria was speaking of an experience that had burned itself deeply into her soul. With a sharp little intake of breath she resumed.

"At that time I felt my heart to be inflamed, and I heard a voice within me which said distinctly: 'You must be a religious in my monastery. I am Teresa of Jesus.' Even now when I speak of it, Apollonia, I cannot find words to express the intensity or certainty of what I felt then. I went to the chapel and asked our Lord to show me His divine will. And once again there swept over me a wave of interior exhilaration and certainty which lifted me so far above the things of this earth that all I desired was to leave everything and beg to be clothed immediately in the Carmelite habit. But I could not explain what had happened to anyone else; it was too intimate and sacred to speak about. I have never mentioned it to a soul, and I do not know what I ought to do. I told our Lord I was ready to follow His will in everything, and I felt so strongly that He wished me to serve Him in Carmel that I could never believe I was mistaken."

Apollonia studied the young face, from which the sudden flush had drained, leaving it unusually pale. Then she said gently: "My child, what does Father Gioni say about this? You have told him, surely?"

Anna Maria shook her head.

"Tell him, then. Explain to him all that you have just told me, and ask his advice."

"I will, Apollonia, but not yet. I must wait a little longer."

"Your father... ?"

She nodded. "Yes, but not for the reason you think." A look of pain crossed her face. "Some time ago, my father gave me an express order that I was not to make any decision about my future until I had completed my seventeenth year. That is still a month away, Apollonia. I must be patient just a little while more."

It is most likely that when Sir Ignatius laid this injunction on his daughter, he was speaking only approximately, not wishing her to commit herself to a way of life before she was sufficiently mature to assess the duties and responsibilities, as well as her own capacities of response. In all probability he had not intended such meticulous adherence to the specified date, nor certainly did he intend any prohibition to her discussing her hopes and plans with himself. But, as has been noted before, this fragile-looking, yet determined and resolute young girl, never did things half-heartedly. She adhered faithfully to the minutest prescription, and breathed no word of Carmel or religious life to her parents until the day of her seventeenth birthday.

Ignatius had not failed to observe that Anna Maria's tastes were developing on lines very dissimilar to those of the young companions with whom she chatted in the drawing room, or the sisters and brothers who romped around her when she joined them in nursery or garden. Although she had now an official director to whom she had given her obedience, her father's influence was still a strong guiding force in her life, and his example was a continual spur to her own fervor and devotion.

More than ever during these months when the old intimate relationship was resumed did Ignatius strive to help and guide his daughter. She waited, saying nothing because of her previous promise to him, but the months seemed to pass slowly, for already she knew that her decision had in fact been made, and she felt that she was wasting time that could be better spent in Carmel.

Others thought differently. She was still young, there was plenty of time to become a nun later; was it not her duty to devote some of her youth to her parents? After all, she had only been home from school a few months, and it was possible to love and serve God in the world, while at the same time returning some of the love and affection that her admirable parents had already lavished on her. Her mother was an invalid, and to her father the separation from his favorite child would be almost unbearable. Anna Maria knew all this and faced it calmly and courageously. "God wants me for Himself," she said. His claims were higher than those of any other, even one's parents, and she knew that despite all suffering, her father would understand her desire and be glad at her going, because it would be for God's will and her own happiness. She would not love him any less dearly because she had given the whole of her heart to God.

Perhaps Ignatius had already divined something of her secret, but she never mentioned it, and he did not try to force her confidence. By this time, he was well aware that Anna Maria possessed deep reserves of strength and flexibility, the capacity to respond with generosity and love to the calls of God, and perhaps - knowing her innocence, love for God and zeal for souls - he did acknowledge tacitly that she was already hallmarked and put aside for His service.

In the evening when the family prayers were over and the children all safely in bed, peace and quiet once more descended on the house. This was the hour when, if no engagement prevented it, Ignatius would take Anna Maria to his study, and spend hours discussing with her the affairs of the house, the progress of the children, and various material problems; however, principally their talk was of spiritual matters.

During these tête-à-tête conversations, Anna Maria never made so much as a passing reference to the one thought that occupied her day and night, although she felt no doubt whatever as to the joy with which her parents would receive the news of her decision. One can only wonder at the power of silence this young girl possessed. After her conversation with Apollonia Fabbri, she did discuss the matter with Father Gioni, and the Jesuit agreed with her interpretation of a strict adherence to her father's time limit, forbidding her to announce her intention until the year had expired, although he himself gave his approval of it. Apparently he decided in the meantime to subject her to some of the standard "tests," for he recorded in a letter to Sir Ignatius: "You are aware of how obedient she was to this command, even though she wanted so much to reveal her vocation to Father Diego (her uncle, Ignatius' brother, also a Jesuit) because of his intense devotion to St. Teresa. I proceeded to suggest considerations on the religious life to her, and I adapted them to the life of Carmel. Many of them she had already put into practice even before I proposed them. Everything I counseled she performed carefully, regardless of difficulties, and in fact, if I tried to caution her about the hardships of the life she proposed embracing, she would merely say: 'But I can count on the help of God.'"

The amount of testing and trying that Anna Maria was subjected to seems to us rather ludicrous. After all, was there anything so extraordinary in the fact that a girl who from childhood had found her most absorbing interest in the things of the spirit, and made eternal values her sole criterion, should turn her steps towards the cloister? Or in doing so that she should be mistaken about the validity of her vocation? Apparently she accepted it all with cheerfulness and good grace. Once, obviously to tease her, one of the priests announced that the Florence Carmel was full and could accept no more postulants; that being so, what would she do?

Anna Maria seemed momentarily taken aback. She had never entertained the least doubt on that score since she had heard the words: "I want you in my monastery." She had interpreted this quite literally, presuming that St. Teresa's in Florence was meant.[1]

"Why," she replied, "in that case I shall apply to the Carmel in Parma."

"And if they refuse to accept you?"

---

[1] At that time it was also the nearest. It was not until 1943 that Arezzo had its own Carmel. This was founded from St. Teresa's in Florence, and dedicated to St. Teresa Margaret. The convent was established in the Redi Villa, where its patron saint had spent her childhood - a future use which undoubtedly would have filled both Ignatius and his daughter with humble gratitude could they have had any foreknowledge of it.

"I shall continue to try elsewhere. There must be a Carmel somewhere that will find room for me."

Perhaps Father Gioni considered it necessary to ascertain the lengths she would go in obeying, for he seems to have had a predilection for "blind obedience." St. Teresa of Avila, whose affection for and close connections with the early Jesuits is far too well-known for her occasional flashes of irony in their direction to cause offence, certainly knew how to handle them, able tactician that she was. "It would be no small gain if the Rector (of the Jesuits) at Seville would be good enough to look after you," she wrote to the Prioress there, Mother Mary of St. Joseph. "But these Fathers of the Company expect to be obeyed, and you must accede to them there, for, although occasionally we may not like what they say, it is so important for us to have their help that we shall do best to conform with their wishes. Think out questions to ask them, for that is what they like."

Eventually it was Father Gioni, and not Anna Maria, who informed Father Diego Redi of his niece's decision. "Little Anna wishes to be a Carmelite," he said, "and she will be a great one, worthy of her mother, St. Teresa." And to her father: "You can thank God for having given you so worthy a daughter, and for having called her to Himself."

July 15th, 1764 was Anna Maria's seventeenth birthday. At last her enforced silence was at an end. But instead of rushing to her father to unburden herself of her "secret," she behaved with characteristic maturity and restraint, quietly asking her mother if she might have a few words with her in private.

Camilla looked anxiously at her daughter's face. It had flushed, and then the color fled, leaving her pale and somehow confused, less serene than usual. Her eyes, so clear and candid, were cast down, as though she were embarrassed. What had happened? Was her little Anna in love? Had she come to break the news that after so few months with them, she was contemplating leaving them for ever? She led the girl to her boudoir.

It seems incredible that neither parent seemed in the least prepared for Anna Maria's revelation. They were stunned and grieved. Surely, if she must go so soon, it was not necessary to make so drastic and irrevocable a parting? There were other orders where enclosure was not so strict. Surely she could spare them a little pain, and not cut herself off so completely in a life of utter silence and solitude, withdrawn behind a grille that would separate her from them forever?

Anna Maria never mentioned the matter to her father; Camilla, distressed and dismayed, told him of the decision their daughter had arrived at so independently, and of her absolute certitude about it. It was a particularly heavy blow to the mother. She had grown accustomed during the past months to having Anna Maria's happy, helpful presence around the house once more after the long separation of seven years. Now, within a few months of her return, she proposed leaving again, not for a few years, but for ever. And Florence was so far away. Camilla knew that in her state of health, and with so many young children to care for, she could never hope to make the long journey.

Meantime the extraordinary testing of the girl's vocation continued. Ignatius now joined in. Priest after priest was consulted, and Anna Maria was put through a veritable third degree. Canon Tonci of Castiglioni, the Carmelite Provincial, Father John Colombino of St. Mary, and even the Bishop of Arezzo, all cross-questioned her, and each in turn expressed himself not only satisfied with the genuineness of her desire and call to the religious life, but specifically stated that here was a privileged soul; *"Agnellina"* ("little lamb"), as Father Colombino nicknamed her.

Family approval was not, however, unanimous. Some of her relatives considered Anna Maria far too young and did their best to dissuade her. But Anna had a ready argument for this objection. Our Lady was not too young at fifteen to make a much more important decision, and at twelve, Jesus was old enough to be about His Father's business.

The news rapidly passed down the grapevine of the domestic staff, and a controversy arose between those servants who approved and those who did not. Anna's personal maid allied herself with the latter camp, and took it upon herself to convince her young mistress of the dreadful mistake she was about to make, putting forth every argument she could think of to change her mind. Anna Maria did not snub her, but allowed the garrulous maid to upbraid her. It would have taken more than the reasoning of a chambermaid to shake her resolution. But eventually she had to face the one thing that might succeed in doing so: her father's heartbroken plea.

Sir Ignatius had not spoken of the matter to Anna Maria, despite the fact that it was uppermost in both their minds, since she had approached her mother rather than himself. Each waited for the other to broach the subject, and for the first time in their lives it seemed that an estrangement, a barrier of silence had risen between them as the days passed. One evening, as they sat together in his study, alone for the first time in many days, they both realized that the topic could no longer be evaded. Each sought carefully for the speech especially prepared for this occasion, but the words would not come. The silence lengthened, then became uncomfortable.

Sir Ignatius looked up.

"My child," he began, "I know of your decision. Do you then really wish to become a nun?"

But the sensible, moderate words he had so often rehearsed would not come. Instead, he stammered a few monosyllables, emotion rendering him incoherent. Then, as he said later: "My weak human heart dissolved into tears, and for the time I could say nothing at all."

It was an agonizing moment. Anna Maria realized as never before that her step was going to be even more costly to her parents than to herself. She was giving them up to follow God's call, it is true; but the choice was hers, as would be the consolation of her consecration to Him, the fulfillment of a destiny that would otherwise leave her restless and unsatisfied. For them, the parting was an even greater wrench, and there was no mitigating comfort, no one to fill the sudden void that her departure would leave.

The moment seemed a foretaste of eternity, in that they both thought it would never end. And for its duration, Anna Maria had to cling to every reserve of grace and willpower she could muster in order to prevent herself from running around to her father, flinging her arms about him, and offering to defer the application for a few years more, so as to soften the suddenness of the blow.

"He who puts his hand to the plough and looks back is unworthy of

Me ... He who loves father and mother more than Me is not worthy to be My disciple ... I have come to bring not peace but the sword; to set a man at variance with his father, and the daughter with her mother ... He is not worthy of Me who does not take up his cross daily and follow me ... He who endures to the last will be saved ..."

Probably never in her life did Anna Maria experience so violent a struggle between nature and grace with her own tempestuous heart as a battleground. She rose quickly, and without a word left the room. Hurrying up to her own apartment, she closed the door, covering her ears with her hands in an effort to drown the voice of human affection. But suddenly another voice spoke, and Anna Maria remembered the mysterious, compelling tones which had announced: "I am Teresa of Jesus;" and her own response: "I am ready to do your will in everything."

Quietly she knelt down and reiterated: "Here I am, Lord, ready at Thy bidding." Then the words of the liturgy came to her mind: "Of your goodness, God, *compel us* to be united to you, even in spite of the rebelliousness of our desires."

Calmly and determinedly, Anna Maria affirmed: "Lord, I *shall* be yours, whatever the cost, despite all repugnance."

And one day she was to write those words with her blood.

5

Entrance Into St. Teresa's Monastery

In Youth, when through our veins runs fast
The bright red stream of life,
The Soul's Voice is a trumpet-blast
That calls us to the strife.
(Victor James Daley)

"The Lord gave; the Lord has taken away; nothing is here be-
fallen but what was the Lord's will; blessed be the name of the Lord."
(Job 1:21).

Sir Ignatius, ashamed of his momentary weakness, and contrite
over the additional suffering he had imposed on Anna Maria, expressed
his repentance practically, by doing all in his power to facilitate her
speedy entrance into Carmel.

Such a soul as hers was not made for the pleasures of this
world, and in his heart Ignatius acknowledged it. Silently admir-
ing the uncommon goodness of his daughter, but still cherishing a
faint hope that he might be granted her companionship a little
longer, he decided to enlist the aid of Father Colombino to postpone the inevitable separation. The Provincial, however, took Anna
Maria's part, and promised that as soon as he returned to Florence
he would visit the Carmel to propose and recommend her to them.

"Our Order has every reason to rejoice and esteem her as an
acquisition," he wrote to the Prioress, Mother Mary Magdalene
of Jesus. "You should praise and thank the Lord, for I know that

His wonderful gifts to her have formed her according to the heart of our Holy Mother, St. Teresa."

This was a time of interior suffering for both father and daughter, and the two upright souls made great progress in the ways of God. Anna Maria in her turn realized that she could profit by accepting a delay that seemed far too long for her ardent desires. After all, she only sought admission to Carmel in order to please and serve God. If He permitted these obstacles, then obviously the way to serve Him here and now was by accepting them with patience and submission. Her sole desire was to please Him who had chosen her for Himself, to console His Sacred Heart for neglect and contempt of those who preferred His creatures to Himself. Knowing that the reality of love is proved only by deeds and the consistent practice of virtue, she set herself to imitate the spirit of the Carmelite ideal, in so far as she already understood it.

Anna Maria wrote a formal application to the Carmel in Florence, requesting that she be admitted to the postulancy, and expressing her desire of "being allowed to grow in the love of God, together with the other fervent spouses of Jesus;" a few days later she wrote to Mother Eleanora, informing her and the other nuns at St. Apollonia's of her decision, at the same time offering a tactful apology for not seeking her vocation with them.

"This is something which is not in our hands to decide, and we cannot choose our vocation according to our own likes and dislikes. We must correspond entirely with the divine call, if we wish to attain the desired end. As you know, I cannot act otherwise, since the Lord has made known to me through many means what He desires of me. True, I felt some repugnance at my vocation, but He continued to knock at the door of my heart and shower me with such blessings that I would appear most ungrateful and irresponsible did I refuse to respond with such alacrity as is in my power to His goodness and condescension."

Mother Mary Magdalene replied that Anna Maria had been accepted, and the girl wrote once more, asking this time for a rule of life to be undertaken during the period of waiting, which would serve as a preparation for her new life. In response to this request, the Prioress suggested that, for one intending to enter Carmel, she could think of no better practice than "to accustom herself to mortify her own will in all things, however trifling, and to yield willingly her own rights in order to convenience others, pleasantly agreeing with their opinions, treating all with a genuine kindness, thus making a continual and entire sacrifice of the self to God." And Mother Mary Magdalene later said: "Anna Maria had good will, and carefully followed these counsels. Later, when she was among us, we observed how God possessed her soul and filled it with consolation and peace. Through these practices she found it easier to adapt herself to the more austere abnegation of the cloister itself."

Anna Maria had now, from an authoritative source, the secret of the essential spirit of Carmel: the holocaust of one's will, rather than the rigid adherence to exterior acts and mortifications on which she had hitherto concentrated. This "transformation of the self" needs no set method or framework, and the Carmelite life comprises an ideal setting for a life of "spiritual childhood" because of its utter simplicity, and humdrum, seemingly trivial routine, which nevertheless ensures complete interior liberty. It is not the Carmelite method to work always and in everything on the *agere contra* principle, deliberately sacrificing one's gifts and talents on the altar of renunciation merely for the sake of running counter to tastes and abilities, or forcing oneself into a mould by occupations for which one has neither aptitude nor attraction. "Where the spirit of the Lord is, there is liberty;" and the same freedom breathes through the exercise of private prayer. One is not tied down to conventional forms or methods, but each is free to choose, or find, or continue, that method best suited to her taste and attractions, which draws and unites her to God.

"A smile when I am inclined to say nothing or look bored", "a friendly word", the hundred and one little "straws picked up through love" which were used by St. Thérèse of Lisieux as a vehicle for expressing her love of God and practicing consistent self-discipline, is the usual way to perfection for the Carmelite. By applying herself to follow the recommendations of Mother Mary Magdalene, Anna

Maria was initiating her training in the two fundamentals of religious life: the poverty of detachment and the obedient submission of one's will to divine authority through the delegation of a legitimate superior. Simplicity and detachment are heavily underlined in the religious life, and it is interesting to compare the wise and moderate rule of life suggested by Mother Mary Magdalene with the resolutions of Thérèse Martin a century later, concerning the same phase of waiting before the enclosure door at Lisieux opened to her: "At first, indeed, the thought came to me to throw off restraint and lead a life less strict than usual. But our Lord made me understand how valuable those months were, and I resolved to give myself up more than ever to a serious and mortified life. When I say mortified, I do not allude to the penances practiced by the Saints. Far from resembling those heroic souls who from their childhood use fast and scourge and chain to discipline the flesh, I made my mortification consist simply in checking my self-will, keeping back an impatient answer, rendering a small service in a quiet way, and a hundred other similar things. By means of these trifles I prepared myself to become the spouse of Christ, and I can never tell you how much the enforced delay helped me to grow in self-abandonment, humility, and other virtues."

It is important to note that Mother Mary Magdalene also made no recommendation of any of "the penances practiced by the Saints." Anna Maria was soon to learn that the Carmelite spirit is acquired far more surely by checking self-will, neither complaining nor excusing oneself, keeping back a sharp retort, rendering small, unobtrusive services at one's own inconvenience and expecting no thanks for them, than by "fast and scourge and chain." These things all played a large part in her program of asceticism, and they have their consecrated place in the spiritual life but they are not an essential ingredient of sanctity. Humility, detachment, obedience, and charity are absolutely indispensable.

Before taking her final departure from Arezzo, Anna Maria, accompanied by her father, made a short pilgrimage to nearby Alvernia, the holy mountain where five centuries earlier St. Francis of Assisi had received the stigmata - the imprint of the five wounds of the Savior - in a vision of a seraph under the form of the crucified Lord.

It was a true pilgrimage for Anna Maria, and a genuine "encounter," confirming in her the already crystallizing ideal of absolute poverty and detachment from all things. The personality and spirit of the little poor man of God still lingers over those rocky slopes - Francis who fell in love with Poverty, for whose smile he cast to the winds all possessions, seeming to grudge even the necessary minimum that must be conceded to convention in the rough sack girded with a cord which he wore; Francis who rejoiced to be a fool for Christ's sake, while suffering most of his life from bodily afflictions, "having nothing but possessing all things" and who spent all his days pouring out his gratitude to God for those gifts and blessings that most of us either take for granted or consider as our right.

Here among the high forests where the wind still sings his troubadour songs through beech and pine, amid the craggy, forbidding masses of rock, cliff, and ravine, Anna Maria found the almost tangible presence of God, was aware of an all but perceptible conviction of the triumph of spirit over matter. One could easily picture the shabby, solitary little figure trudging up these rough slopes to commence the long tryst from which he would emerge with body sealed by the marks of the Passion that had so long been branded upon his soul. This was the transformation to which she herself aspired - to reproduce in herself Jesus crucified, not by the martyrdom of the flesh so much as by the silent imitation of Him who was obedient unto death.

She did not speak of the experience, but from her later references to this visit to Alvernia, it is obvious that she regarded it as a highlight in her spiritual life, the occasion of a singular grace and effusion of light.

September 1st was the date fixed for Anna Maria's entrance into Carmel. The family was still in residence at the Villa Ortagli, when Anna took her final departure during the last week in August. Camilla, ill and confined to bed, was unable to travel, and the thought of the coming separation seemed unbearable to her. When Ignatius led Anna Maria, dressed in traveling clothes, to her bedside for the last time, Camilla broke down completely, and could only hold the girl in her arms, weeping inconsolably. Anna Maria drew the dark head, prematurely streaked with gray, on to her breast.

"Dearest Mama," she said tenderly, "for no one but Jesus would I leave you. You know that."

"Yes, my child, but do not ask me to rejoice. You are my first chick to leave the nest."

"No, I will never leave the nest. Here deep in your heart you will always find me close to you, sharing your joys and sorrows. You know that I love you with all my heart, and always shall do so."

Devout though Camilla undoubtedly was, and fully alive to the honor God was doing her as well as her daughter, such considerations could do little to soften the blow of parting or console her in her own loss. She had pinned such high hopes on this beautiful daughter whom she had expected would be able to make a truly brilliant match and thus offer a vicarious recompense for all that she herself had had to renounce in life. It is not difficult to imagine the mother's inner struggle with her own sorrow, and the half-ashamed admission that it was partly selfish, for deep down was the unworded acknowledgement of God's prior claim and her child's first and deepest allegiance.

"Lord, to whom could I give her with greater joy? I had expected to be approached by some man seeking her as his wife, and I would have given her happily, knowing that this was the fulfillment of her natural destiny. How much more gladly and gratefully, then, should I give her back to You, for she was Yours before she was mine, and I am humbly thankful for the' happiness You have given me in her sweet comforting presence all these years. Still, my heart is heavy. The separation is painful, and I know in my heart it is final. I shall not see my child again in this life, and it is a great sacrifice You ask. Grant at least that we may remain united, and ever draw closer in the depths of Your Heart. In You all love grows, becomes refined and perfected, and despite the anguish I feel at the thought that I will never again hold or caress my first daughter, I am truly happy and proud that You have called her and found in our family one worthy to be Your spouse. Through her hidden life of prayer and sacrifice, may much grace come to this sad world. You have blessed our family with numerous children, many griefs, costly sacrifices, and much happiness and love. Draw us all closer to You, that deep in Your Sacred Heart we may ever remain united beyond all separation in time and space."

Anna Maria disengaged herself, kissed her mother gently, and Ignatius, who only with difficulty restrained his own emotion recalled later: "As I watched the grief of my wife with sorrow in my own heart, I marveled at the self-control of Anna, in consoling her mother and restoring her tranquility. Then she quietly signed to me that it was time to depart."

One last embrace, a swift glance upwards at the great mural of the Assumption, and then Anna Maria turned from the memory-filled room, following her father downstairs, through the familiar hall, its wall decorated with frescoes of crusading scenes, and into the waiting carriage. Little brothers swarmed around her, and all the domestic and farm servants were drawn up to wish Godspeed to their young mistress whom, despite the brevity of her sojourn among them, they all esteemed and respected. Young Diego had been examining the interior of the wonderful vehicle with the near-veneration reserved by all small boys for anything on wheels. Now, as his father hauled him out and deposited him on the steps, he set up a loud wailing, for it suddenly dawned on him that Anna Maria was departing and that he could not go with her. Then the wheels of the carriage crunching on the gravel drowned all other sounds, the poplars bordering the drive slipped behind them two by two like silent sentinels, the last hedge was passed, and the horses' metal-shod hooves clipped smartly on the hard-beaten surface of the highway. It was mid-morning, and the countryside was a glory of burnished copper and gold under the late summer sun.

Not quite five months ago, Ignatius recalled, he and Anna Maria had driven along this road on her return from St. Apollonia's. Then the world had been quickening to new life, garden and hedgerow were bursting forth in the full glory of springtime, opening buds a pink blush on the face of nature, birds twittered in the annual excitement of setting up house, and the sun had seemed to pause and smile upon the serene landscape before slipping below the horizon.

Now the promise was all of the coming bareness of winter. Everywhere leaves were beginning to turn russet on the trees, while fruit and flowers deepened towards purple and gold. It was a season that ordinarily filled Ignatius with a satisfying sense of achievement, a heady feeling of things beginning all over again, the turn of the year with the crops harvested and all the frustrations and difficulties of another summer finished and forgotten. Now, however, his heart seemed as dry and light as those rusty, rustling leaves; already he could feel the chilly winds of winter that would whip them away to blow, lost and lonely, along the lanes and gutters, and he knew that when Anna Maria crossed the door into the cloister, something would go out of his life that could never be replaced. It was, he thought desolately, the old sad rule, one of the immutable laws of nature: we rear our children for the day when they have to leave us, as surely as we once left our own parents. Acorns fall from the parent oak, birds fly from the nest. So it has always been; so it will ever be. Virgil had a tag for it long since: *lacrimae rerum,* he called it, "the tears of things... ."

Sir Ignatius stole a furtive glance at Anna Maria, who sat erect and motionless, staring with unseeing eyes out of the carriage window at the vineyards, orchards, and olive groves. She was barely seventeen, and the parting had been harrowing. The future held unknown and sometimes frightening rigors. There would be only one familiar face to greet her, that of a slight acquaintance, Cecilia Albergotti, now a novice, Sister Teresa of Jesus Crucified.

Anna Maria had not wept or given any external sign of the anguish she felt at the moment of leave-taking, and now she wrestled for a long time with her rebellious emotions before she could trust herself to speak. The lovely countryside, the Villa and gardens that had been the scene of so much carefree happiness were left irrevocably behind. She had "put away the things of childhood," and with them the other and deeper ties - her mother, the younger brothers and sisters, even the animals and pets - and soon she would have to part also from her father. She felt the ties of more than natural love which bound them holding her more closely than ever now the time for separation was at hand. That moment can be understood properly only by one who has actually experienced it.

"Then why do it?" people are wont to ask, if the struggle is explained to them. "You are breaking your father's heart and your own. And for what?"

For the simple reason that one is firmly convinced that this is the will of God. Attraction or repugnance are incidentals. One must go forward, regardless of the double grief of leaving those one loves most on earth, and the knowledge that one is thereby inflicting increased suffering upon them, and that very often they do not, cannot understand.

Never had Anna Maria felt more deeply her intense love for her father than now, when the moment had arrived to part from him forever. He realized her struggle for self-mastery, and tried not to add to her suffering by showing his own. Ignatius, no less than his daughter, was about to consummate his sacrifice, and he felt that he now knew what Abraham had been called upon to do, and what must have been the strength of his faith and love of God.

At last the conflict wore itself out, as all storms must do in time. After about an hour had passed, Anna Maria turned to her father, serene and self-possessed once more, and they began to converse quietly and sensibly, as Sir Ignatius later recalled. "She continued the journey with truly admirable tranquility and composure."

Mother Mary Magdalene's exhortations had not gone unheeded. Her postulant-to-be had indeed acquired remarkable self-control and a considerable degree of detachment already. This girl whose lively, sometimes fierce temperament made her naturally impulsive, hot-headed, quick to react to emotional stimulus, had attained a strength of mastery over her feelings and impulses that many an older and more experienced person has not achieved. Then years earlier, when Anna Sisti had departed after a lengthy stay at the Redi Villa, little Anna had clung to her aunt for an hour, refusing to be parted from her, and weeping broken-heartedly at the thought of the coming separation.

But she was soon to learn that stern renunciations bring their own particular consolations, two halves of the paradox that lies at the heart of all Christian sacrifice. We must give all to gain all; the grain of wheat must be cast into the earth in order to germinate and flourish; death is the prelude to life, joy is born of suffering, every resurrection must be preceded by a Calvary. And Anna Maria Redi was to find, like the young Benedictine Gertrude More, that "to give all for love is a most sweet bargain".

September 1st, 1764, Anna Maria and her father stood expectantly in the austere-looking parlor, a large square room with white-washed walls. Sir Ignatius eyed rather apprehensively the barred grille, with its dangerous-looking spikes, heavily curtained from the inside, which occupied most of one wall. Anna Maria's attention was held by the two framed pictures which hung on either side of the grating - one of St. Teresa of Avila and the other of St. John of the Cross - and the plain wooden crucifix above the grille.

Ignatius dragged his eyes away from the forbidding-looking iron bars, and glanced at the two texts lettered on the wall: "Remember that you have only one soul; that you have only one death to die; that you have only one life, which is short and has to be lived by you alone; and that there is only one glory, which is eternal. If you do this, there will be many things about which you care nothing. Teresa of Jesus." It did not augment Ignatius' rapidly-dwindling store of cheerfulness. He glanced at the opposite wall: "Since when thine hour of reckoning comes, it will grieve thee that thou hast not employed this time in the service of God, wherefore dost thou not order and employ it now as thou wouldst wish to have done wert thou dying? John of the Cross."

Sir Ignatius felt thoroughly depressed by now. Good and salutary though it undoubtedly was to keep before one the remembrance of the four last things, he felt he had had more than sufficient matter for meditation on them for one morning, and was in no need of any reminder about the impermanence of life where parting and sorrow are inevitable.

Would the shutter never open? He paced restlessly up and down the bare polished boards of the floor, wondering how Anna Maria could sit there so calmly and imperturbably. She might merely be waiting in the reception hall to greet the arrival of some casual guests. He felt that this was how a criminal condemned to death must feel, if forced to sit and watch the instrument of execution that was soon to end his life. They seemed to have reversed positions now. Having regained her composure, Anna Maria was determined not to allow her inner struggle to obtrude again. Sir Ignatius, who for her sake had so valiantly repressed his own suffering on that day they set out from Arezzo, now seemed unable to conceal the pain he felt at the imminent separation.

Anna Maria, however, in spite of her air of placidity, was also experiencing the suffocating sense of living her last moment slowly and painfully. Difficult as it had been to drag herself from her mother's embrace, she knew it was going to cost her every ounce of self-possession and will-power she could muster to conceal the agony of this second and last parting that would almost be like tearing out a piece of her own living flesh. Her heart seemed to be beating so loudly that she wondered if Papa could hear it. Without raising her head, she watched him from under downcast lashes, while her heart ached as much for his obvious distress as for her own.

They both started at the soft rustle as the curtain over the grille was drawn aside, and suddenly Mother Mary Magdalene was there smiling a welcome at them.

"Everything is ready now," she said, beaming from one to the other. "If you would go to the enclosure door... ."

Anna Maria stood up slowly and faced her father. Without a word Sir Ignatius offered her his arm, and neither spoke as they left the parlor and passed down a corridor to the cloister door. They heard the sound of a bell ringing on the other side, its tone muffled slightly by distance, then the shuffling of rope-soled sandals on the stone corridor, a subdued rattle of wooden rosaries, a low whispered command, and then the heavy, iron-studded door swung back, creaking protestingly on its hinges. The Prioress and Novice Mistress stood on the threshold, their long black veils falling over their faces, hands outstretched to welcome the newcomer.

Anna turned to her father, who held her close for a moment, blessed her with a hand that was not quite steady, and then she turned away, neither of them trusting their voices at this emotion-charged moment. Rapidly she crossed the doorway, knelt at the feet of the two nuns who would henceforth be her mothers in Christ, and was en-folded in their welcoming embrace. Ignatius stood motionless until the door finally swung to. For a moment he stayed listening to the faint click and scuffle of departing footsteps, and, sounding strangely lonely, the solitary staccato tap-tap of Anna's shoes, as they gradu-ally moved down the corridor. Then he turned away. Later he would see her again, but in a postulant's unflattering black dress, and from the other side of the heavy double-barred grating.

Anna Maria in the meantime had passed into the midst of the waiting community, assembled to meet their new sister. Mother Mary Magdalene led her down the room, from one to the other, to be in-spected, embraced and introduced, but the litany of unfamiliar names flowed past without any of them registering very clearly.

"What is her name to be?" was the eager chorus of questions on all sides.

Mother Mary Magdalene looked at the tall, well-groomed girl whose hand she still held clasped in her own.

"Well," she asked, "what do you think we will call you?"

"Anna Maria?"

"No. We already have an Anna Maria. Your mistress' assistant is Mother Anna Maria of St. Anthony. You will have to be re-named."

"Then I should like to have our Holy Mother's name."

"You would? But we have many Teresas."

"Well, if I am allowed to choose, Mother, I should very much like the name Margaret, after Sister Margaret Mary Alacoque, to whom the Sacred Heart made such great revelations."

Mother Mary Magdalene considered this. "Teresa Margaret," she said. "Well, it will do for the present at any rate." She beckoned the Novice Mis-tress. "Take her now, and introduce her to the other novices. They are not likely to get any work done until the suspense is over," she added dryly, dismissing the rest of the community, who promptly took the hint.

Anna Maria immediately felt at her ease among the chattering, excited trio, eager for the first sight of their new companion. Sister Teresa of Jesus Crucified greeted her warmly, with a "Welcome, Sis-ter," and an embrace. It came as a shock to be addressed as "Sister" for the first time, but it reminded Anna Maria not to address her companion as Cecilia. As the other two novices, Sister Teresa Mary of the Immaculate Conception and Sister Mary Victoria of the Trinity were introduced, Mother Anna Maria watched her new charge closely. She felt an irresistible attraction towards this fair-haired, self-possessed girl and suddenly experienced an intense desire to speak with her, for she sensed that her amazing poise was not the outcome of mere natural good manners or polish, but had its roots in a well-grounded habit of self-discipline and genuine spirituality. She suspected that here was one who had already made considerable progress in virtue, and she was impressed by the dignity and simplicity which seemed to emanate from the postulant.

She watched as the laughter and talk buzzed around, and then suddenly she stood up. The chatter stopped abruptly and in silence the novices rose also.

"Now all back to your work," Mother Anna Maria told them. "You, child, come with me."

She conducted Anna over the monastery, through the cloister garth and the open balcony that ran beneath the cells, and into the choir. The grating was shuttered, and Mother Anna Maria indicated the position of the altar on the other side, whispering: "That is where our Lord is." They knelt for a few minutes in silence, and then went out to the sunny garden, with its outdoor hermitages, through the gallery and upstairs to the dormitory. The long corridor with its rows of cells, each one identical with the next, running down both sides, seemed endless to Anna. At last the Mistress stopped.

"This is your cell," she began, then noticing the flushed face she suspected pent-up emotion.

"Your things have not come in yet," she said suddenly. "Would you like to go back to the choir?"

"Oh, yes, please."

"You can find your way? Good. I'll come and fetch you later." Anna Maria knelt on the bare floor and buried her face in her hands. Years later, speaking to her companions in the novitiate, she admitted that at the moment of leaving her father, she felt an almost physical

6

First Months in Carmel

"Every sin and every sorrow
Every ill that life can borrow
In the Cross will gain surcease;
In the Cross, though sore and grieving,
He that humbly seeks relieving,
Findeth refuge, findeth peace. "
(St. Bonaventure)

Anna Maria sat up in bed, her heart pounding, and the shock gradually died away as the noise receded. It had sounded like an avalanche of stones crashing on to the floor outside her door, and as they broke up, gradually rumbling and banging down the corridor, she realized where she was, and that the roof had not collapsed. She was Sister Teresa Margaret now, and this frightful din ripping the morning apart must be the wooden clapper that was the rising signal. She wondered how long it would take to grow accustomed to such a rude awakening, for her heart and pulse were still racing each other.

It was only faintly light, for the hour was 4:30 a.m. Mother Anna Maria had told her not to rise at the first call, but to wait for the bell half an hour later, which would be the signal for the beginning of prayer.

"I would like to come to prayer," she objected.

"Not the first morning. You will not know where to go. When the bell rings, get up and dress, and I will come and show you what to do. Remember it is still the Great Silence until after Prime, so be as quiet as possible."

75

But she could not go to sleep again. There were sounds of sub-dued movements all about her, and a persistent, protracted rattling, which she was soon to identify as a cincture and rosary being girded on. Then footsteps began to pass along the corridor outside. She looked about the room, but the shutters across the window were drawn, and it was still too dark to see anything more than the outline of the brown stained door, and the dark table against the far wall.

The cloister bell began to peal in slow, even strokes, and she heard the soft shuffle of many feet moving unhurriedly past in the direction of the choir. Her own door opened slightly and a lighted candle was placed on the floor; then the door closed again.

Teresa Margaret remembered the warning about silence and tip-toed across to the door with exaggerated care, placed the candle on the table, and dressed herself quickly in the plain black dress and short cape, pushing her bright, abundant hair into the hideous black postulant's cap and veil. Then throwing aside the wooden shutters, she sat down quietly to await her instructress, glancing about her with obvious satisfaction, as she noted every detail of the small bare cell where henceforward she would spend the greater part of her days.

"Each one shall have a separate cell ... (and) shall remain in his cell or near it, meditating day and night on the law of the Lord, and watching in prayer, unless otherwise justly employed." (Carmelite Rule)

Most of her work would be performed here during the day, and she would sleep here at night. She glanced about the room. It was vastly different from the spacious apartment she had occupied in her father's house – a small area, about ten feet square, the plain plaster walls covered with a light wash; a narrow, low door painted brown; a wooden table; and a plain, straight-backed, hard-bottomed chair. A contented smile flickered over her face, as the thought that at least the first step was taken towards her long-pursued ambition. Here, at least, there would be no necessity to remove the mattress from her bed at night! The couch from which she had just risen would be quite sufficiently hard and uninviting - three planks resting on low trestles, upon which lay a straw pallet and heavy, brown serge blankets. Over her pallet was a soft woolen mattress, to ease the first months of the postulant's adaptation, but Sister Teresa Margaret had already planned to get rid of that as soon as the opportunity presented itself.

On the distempered walls hung a plain wooden cross, a large unadorned holy water stoup, and three unframed pictures: one of our Lady and two of Carmelite saints. A work basket and an earthenware jug standing by the basin in which she had just washed herself completed the room's furnishings. A single window with two narrow casements on the outer wall looked straight onto the quiet, peaceful garden. Teresa Margaret gave the contented sigh of one who has at last come to port after a stormy voyage. Here was her cell, that arena which would witness her daily battles with self-love and self-will, until, emancipated from their claims and demands, grace triumphant over nature, she would be free to serve and love with undivided heart and mind Him who had created her for that sole purpose, and waited only the opportunity to inundate her with the graces necessary to achieve it.

The thought of her father brought a shadow to her eyes, and she wondered what he was doing. He, too, she felt certain, would one day share her own contentment, but it would take time. Only God could give him the consolation that belongs to the austere-seeming joy of doing His will. "We are in the hands of the good God and the Father of all consolation," she thought. "Everything that He permits will turn to our greatest good although now we may not understand it."

There was still much progress to be made, and given her generous determination to refuse nothing to God, she was to make it rapidly; however a transformation there had to be, and so gradual was its course, in a sense as natural and unobtrusive as the unfolding of a flower into full bloom, that the metamorphosis took place daily and hourly under the eyes of her companions without their being aware of what was happening.

The nuns were delighted with their new postulant. Already deeply religious, given to prayer, attracted to silence and solitude, she set herself to become such a Carmelite as St. Teresa desired all her children to be.

Always she had been humble and unassuming, but by no means was she a characterless namby-pamby, good and docile only because she lacked spirit to be otherwise. Such gentle natures do, it is true, find their way into cloisters, but as a rule they very soon find their way out again, or if they remain, they do not become canonized saints. Namby-pambies do not practice heroic virtue; they cannot. But Teresa Margaret still had to learn by painful experience how powerless is unaided human nature, to discover just what we are when God withdraws His hand and leaves us to our own resources. "He who hath not been tried, what does he know?" (Ecclus. 34:9)

Mother Teresa Maria of Jesus was officially the Mistress of Novices, but to her assistant Mother Anna Maria of St. Anthony - many years her junior and very much more active - fell the largest proportion of the actual work of training the novices in the externals of deportment, choir duties, manual labor; and she was frequently deputed by her senior to give conferences and instructions to the novices, so that they were in the habit of going directly to her for any need or the solution of their difficulties.

When Teresa Margaret first came to Carmel as a postulant, she was, as has already been remarked, no beginner. She brought such a dowry of grace and generosity with her that, while she was immediately at home and in some sense found her natural level in the cloister, she needed to learn nothing essentially new, but to make many adjustments both in her way of thinking and behaving. Even the community, prepared as they were by the Provincial's enthusiastic recommendation, to meet an exceptionally gifted newcomer, were astonished to find how mature was the spirit of this girl, how seemingly oriented to their way of life. Where had she learned to make such progress? She had been educated by Benedictine nuns, and, except for occasional contacts with one or two of the friars, she had had no previous encounter with Carmel or its spirit.

It is true that Teresa Margaret was gifted both in nature and grace; however this has led some uncritical enthusiasts to assume that she was already perfect. Until now, however, she had performed rigorous penances, living an astonishingly austere régime for a girl of her age and position, had seemed humble to an exaggerated degree in her dealings with servants and inferiors. But in all this she had nevertheless gone her own way, deciding for herself what she would eat and when she would fast, whether to prolong her prayers and devotions, and in what they were to consist. She had, indeed, given her obedience to a director, but he never made the demands on her that a religious superior must exact in the small details of daily life; indeed, her relationship in this matter had rather consisted in seeking his approval - usually granted - for anything she herself wished to do. Speaking of the five months Anna Maria had spent at home after leaving school, Father Ildefonse remarked on the insistence of Father Gioni that she should accommodate herself to her parents' wishes and normal customs, and that she must adapt herself to their routine and not expect them to accommodate their horarium to her devotional tastes. Father Ildefonse added: "She took part in the social interchange customary among her milieu, but she experienced an incredible difficulty and repugnance at having to dress in a manner not conformed to her own taste."

The first lesson Teresa Margaret had to learn was that our Lord still very often repeats to and through us the words of the psalmist: "Sacrifice and oblation thou didst not desire ... it is written of me that I should do thy will; O my God, I have desired it, and thy law in the midst of my heart." For a feast enjoyed under obedience is of more worth in His eyes than a fast undertaken through self-will; one can go further and say with Monsignor Gay that insignificant and even easy and pleasant things are rendered sublime and more meritorious through obedience than an action which is in itself holy, such as receiving Communion, when it is done through self-will and in a spirit of independence.

It is customary in Carmel, and probably in all monasteries, to dispense postulants from the full observance of the daily horarium for a time, partly to cushion the psychological strain, but mostly to soften the shock of the sudden incursion into a world where standards differ so enormously from those to which one has been habituated - even for those accustomed only to a moderate degree of material comfort. For the first weeks she is not expected to rise at the first signal or to come regularly to the night office of Matins; the food in the refectory is usually made somewhat more attractive, if not in preparation at least in serving; she will probably be dispensed from recreation or certain duties in order to write eagerly-awaited letters to her parents. In many small ways she is gradually and imperceptibly eased into her new environment.

This "being let down lightly" is unnoticed by most, but Teresa Margaret had acquainted herself with the régime, and its mitigation did not please her at all. Nothing would satisfy her but that she must immediately undertake the full burden of the common life, rise and retire with the rest of the community, be served the same food in the refectory. The regulation that exempted postulants from sleeping on the hard straw pallet she found most unendurable of all, accustomed as she was to dispensing with any sort of mattress if she so wished. She immediately set about devising means by which she could rid herself of the unwanted alleviation.

Her repeated and insistent requests to come to Matins and to morning prayer were granted, but still that soft mattress remained in her cell. It never occurred to the postulant that there was anything in her attitude that might appear to question the discretion or authority of her superiors; still less did she realize that she was in fact demanding that the Prioress should obey her in meeting her requirements for the standard of rigor she considered should be undertaken.

Teresa Margaret had always been accustomed to following her own attractions in the performance of her various acts of penance - with the approval of her confessor, it is true, but the choice was hers. She had to learn slowly and painfully the value of complete submission of will to another, even in matters where one's desire for mortification appears genuine and meritorious. Although she had come to the monastery ostensibly to do this, she visualized, in the beginning, that perfection consisted in the rigid adherence to each precept of Rule and custom without any mitigation. Nor, seemingly, had she yet grasped the fact that she was not likely to achieve such absolute conformity by setting aside other customs and usages specifically laid down for the treatment of novices. In short, she was actually opting for her own will in preference to that of the superior who ordered the dispensation.[1]

Mother Mary Magdalene had permitted her to join all the other exercises, but she proved adamant on the question of the mattress. Sister Teresa Margaret must continue to sleep on that until such time as she, the Prioress, saw fit to remove it. Teresa Margaret was equally determined. It must go. She bided her time until an opportunity of unburdening herself of it should arise.

It was not long in coming. One of the novices, Sister Teresa Mary of the Immaculate Conception, was slightly indisposed and confined to her bed for a few days. Although this sister was later to become a complete invalid, on this occasion she was probably only suffering from a chill, for she was not sufficiently ill to warrant her being removed to the infirmary. In company with the other novices, Teresa Margaret obtained permission to visit her sick companion during recreation, to brighten the time by their company and conversation.

Sister Teresa Mary was in bed in her cell, and while talking to her, Teresa Margaret's quick eye noted that the novice was lying on the hard straw palliasse, which seemed to her far too uncomfortable for one who had spent some sixty hours continuously on its unyielding surface.

She hurried back to her own cell, and pulled the detested woolen mattress from the bed. Quickly she replaced the blankets, and then

---

[1] This incident of the mattress is a good illustration of the metamorphosis in her attitude towards such "penances" in the five years of her religious life. When she was dying in 1770, Mother Anna Maria wished to change her serge tunic for a lighter linen garment, as is customary for the sick. Considering this an unnecessary concession to bodily comfort, Teresa Margaret resisted; but the moment Mother Anna Maria reminded her it was a legislated custom, and besides, an express wish of the Prioress, she agreed immediately, and tried to help them change her clothing, despite the intense and continuous pain she was suffering.

ran to find Mother Anna Maria.

"Please, Mother," she asked, "May I have permission to lend poor Sister Teresa Mary our mattress?"

"Your mattress? Whatever next, pray?"

"But truly, I do not need it, Mother. And you know how uncomfortable she must be after all this time. I saw her trying to shift her position. And there is that mattress just lying on the bed all day. If she could use it even during the day when I am not needing it... ."

"Very well, then, but take it back before tonight."

But of course it did not go back. Mother Anna Maria permitted it to remain in the cell of the sick sister when she realized how necessary the extra comfort was to her, and Teresa Margaret managed to avoid reclaiming it.

This girl had considerable charm and was adept at getting her own way. It is possible that Mother Teresa Maria, the Novice Mistress, who is usually presented by most biographers as a forbidding, unnecessarily harsh character, realized this more clearly than some of the other members of the novitiate, who, judging only on externals, were rather inclined to eulogize the extraordinarily mortified newcomer. It is true that Teresa Margaret was fundamentally humble and no mere exhibitionist. Any form of pious ostentation was repugnant to her, and she never desired selfishly, as a personal comfort or consolation, any extraordinary interior joys or graces. She simply desired to be in this house of prayer, "among those angels" as she said, realizing instinctively that in the cloister, and particularly in her small, quiet cell, she could keep before her mind the great mysteries of God in a way that would be impossible in the world outside, even in so virtuous and supra-mundane an environment as her own immediate family circle.

However, Mother Teresa Maria set herself to exercise the postulant in solid virtue, in a way which, had she no real belief that it was a necessity, would have constituted a flagrant breach of justice. To the rest of the community, Teresa Margaret appeared exceptionally humble, self-effacing, willing, charitable; yet the difficult-to-please Mistress never encountered her charge without issuing a public rebuke, and with a harshness that the slight - or sometimes imaginary - lapse did not seem to warrant.

Mother Anna Maria's soft heart bled for her darling. She felt an instinctive compatibility with this child, and her duties as assistant Mistress made it easy for them to converse more frequently and intimately than would otherwise have been possible. To Mother Anna Maria, the Novice Mistress' attitude seemed unjustified, yet it was quite impossible for her to express disapproval, either spoken or implied, nor could she countermand the arbitrary directions of her superior. She did what she could to make life easier for Teresa Margaret in other ways, and her efforts were not always appreciated.

Three months after her entry, Teresa Margaret developed a painful swelling in her right knee. Some trouble of this sort is a fairly common complaint among postulants, resulting from the sudden transition to kneeling on the bare floor, and it is usually remedied by the temporary use of a hassock. But Teresa Margaret's trouble was something more than this variation of "housemaid's knee," and seemed to be more in the nature of an abscess. Fearing that the inability to kneel for long periods on the floor might constitute an obstacle to her being accepted as a member of the community, she said nothing of it, but continued kneeling on the ground, concealing with difficulty the increasing pain, until it became obvious to all that something was amiss. By the time Mother Teresa Maria summoned her to explain her awkward posture she had begun to run so high a temperature that even she realized it was vain to hope that the indisposition would simply pass. She explained her trouble, and the expectation that it might correct itself. But the abscess had developed and was growing worse, so that surgical treatment was now required.

This was not the minor matter it would be today. Two centuries ago there were neither anesthetics nor analgesics. Surgical instruments were primitive and their use often more so. Operations were performed in cold blood, until the patient mercifully fainted and thus achieved some slight degree of insensibility.

The doctors and the sisters who were present all warmly praised Teresa Margaret's courage. She herself felt that this was something worthy of being offered to Jesus, and determined to bear the agony of having her knee lanced and the bone scraped without complaint. The sweat stood out on her face, and when a few whimpers of pain escaped her, she reproached herself for lack of virtue. But it was a frightful ordeal, and she came through it with remarkable fortitude.

Of course, she was unable to walk for some time afterwards, and possibly there was need to recuperate more from the operation itself than from the abscess that had occasioned it. Mother Anna Maria devoted herself to nursing her charge, lavishing every possible care and attention upon her. One day, as a surprise, she substituted for the infirmarian, and carried the invalid's dinner to her on a tray. Teresa Margaret, however, merely tasted the dish and put it aside.

"Is something wrong?" asked Mother Anna Maria anxiously, for, as a treat she herself had prepared the meal to tempt the postulant's appetite.

"No, indeed, Mother, it is very delicious."

"Then eat it up. It will do you good."

Teresa Margaret still hesitated.

"Come now. Are you going to allow it to spoil, and waste good food as well as the time and trouble of preparing it?"

"It is because it is far too tasty," replied Teresa Margaret, who was in the habit of applying her own criteria to such problems. "It seems out of keeping with a life of austerity and mortification to eat so daintily."

Certainly the eggs she had prepared with a little spice were no masterpiece, and Mother Anna Maria had to suppress her amusement at this extraordinary interpretation of submission.

"Eat every scrap of it," she ordered. "That is a command, and by doing so you will have the merit of obedience. Besides, you will need the strength, for I am going to read you a lecture directly after you have finished your meal."

She departed and returned armed with a book, noting with satisfaction that she had been obeyed quite literally. Not a crumb remained on the tray.

"Now listen to this," said the assistant Mistress seating herself and opening a copy of the Constitution. "'The sick should try to give proof of the virtues they have acquired in health by bearing their sufferings patiently and endeavoring to cause as little trouble and disturbance as possible.' Now you must understand quite clearly, there are two ways of looking at these things. Had I brought you a plate of stringy old beans cooked without salt or oil, or by chance let a dash of paraffin find its way into them, you would have eaten it with every appearance of relish, because that is just the kind of penance after your own heart. It is no less meritorious to eat something that is tasty, but which displeases you from another point of view, and it is as well an act of charity to the one who prepares it. Here's another point: 'No Sister shall find fault with what is served at table, whether it be little or much, well or badly prepared.'"

Then, noticing her disciple's downcast expression, she added lightly: "Cheer up, the world has not come to an end. There are many great saints who made the same mistakes - our Holy Mother for one. She was obliged to accept a mitigation of the rule of abstinence due to her poor health, and do you know what she has said: 'Once when I was thinking how it distressed me to eat meat and do no penance, I heard these words: "Sometimes there is more self-love in such a thought than desire of penance."' Now do not be discouraged. Perfection is not gained in a day. It is a lifetime's work."

The wound on her knee required frequent dressing, and on top of this discomfort, Teresa Margaret added some additional mortifications of her own devising. She had a great and truly laudable desire to imitate the saints in some of their penances, but in the early stages she set about it in a peculiar fashion, overlooking the fact that the holiness of the model does not dispense one from the necessity of obtaining sanction of one's own superiors before imitating their self-imposed penances; nor does the fact that many canonized saints have undoubtedly ruined their health by imprudence in these matters give one the right to do the same. It was only by chance that the infirmarian discovered that she had arranged her long hair and pinned it in such a way that her head was a veritable pincushion, on which she was lying with extreme pain, and suffering much from a self-induced headache.

Teresa Margaret had to learn in all these small ways that from now on her chief mortification must consist in submitting to the will of another, accepting privations or their alleviation as and when ordered, because such was the expression of another and higher will, wherein lay the merit, rather than in the action itself.

"You have all the mortification you need and more in faithfully observing the Rule," Mother Anna Maria told her. "Don't try to be more Carmelite than that. The penances that are legislated are quite sufficient."

"Yes, but it says at the very end: 'If anyone does more than is herein prescribed, our Lord will reward him in the Day of Judgment.'"

"That," replied Mother Anna Maria dryly, "is the penultimate clause. The 'very end' as you call it, comes after: 'Let him, however, use discretion, which is the rule of all virtue.' Now give me those pins and let me plait your hair. That will keep it out of your way and you out of mischief."

Despite her indisposition and the anxiety it caused her, Teresa Margaret's time of probation passed quickly. The date had now arrived when she must make her formal request to receive the habit, and on January 4th, 1765, according to custom, she knelt before the assembled members of the Chapter. This petition to be admitted to the novitiate followed a set formula. The postulant presented herself before the chapter nuns[2] and kneeling made her request: "My Mothers and my Sisters, I humbly ask you to receive me to the grace of the holy Habit, although I am most unworthy; but I hope, by the grace of God and the help of your prayers, to do better in the future than I have done in the past."

Then, making the customary gesture of humility by kissing the ground, she listened to a brief exhortation from the Prioress on the

---

[2] I.e., the professed choir nuns who are permitted to vote in matters pertaining to the admittance of subjects, their acceptance for profession, election of officials, etc.

grace of a religious vocation or some phase of its expression; this generally ends on some dampening note to the effect that "you are far from realizing the perfection of the state to which you aspire; yet the community, satisfied with your efforts to date, and relying on your determination to refuse nothing to God, is pleased to permit you to receive the holy Habit."

Half fearful that she might be rejected outright because of her great imperfections, to which must now be added a physical handicap - for what use was a novice who became so afflicted by kneeling? - Teresa Margaret awaited the verdict, which of course revealed that the opinion of the community was wholeheartedly in favor of accepting the young postulant.

Teresa Margaret gave a sigh of relief. Despite her knee and all the numerous faults which Mother Teresa Maria found daily in her, they had not refused to give her at least a period of trial.

Joyfully she wrote to Father Diego Redi to inform him of the good news, asking particularly for a remembrance in Mass, to thank the Lord on her behalf for His great favors and blessings. "I feel in my heart," she confided, "such an ardor of divine love that I long to unite myself irrevocably and utterly to Him; nor could I satisfy it with anything less than the gift of myself. I want to be all His, holding back nothing."

In reply her uncle exhorted her to correspond generously with the tremendous graces of a religious vocation, and by steady progress in virtue to become a worthy daughter of her Holy Mother, St. Teresa. "Try to practice true humility, self-effacing prayer and blind obedience. Endeavor to realize the end for which St. Teresa instituted her Reform, and pray continually for the salvation of souls. My dear child, Jesus wishes you not only to be a good nun, but to become a saint!"

Filled with gratitude, Teresa Margaret began her preparation to receive worthily the habit of the Blessed Virgin and to give herself even more completely to Him whom she knew loved her so tenderly. Our Lord responded by working such great things in her soul that at times she seemed almost overcome and unable to control the vehemence of her feelings.

At that time it appears to have been customary to send the postulant back to the world, possibly as a final testing as to whether she really desired to leave it; thus, Teresa Margaret left the Carmel almost immediately after her chapter petition, not to return until March 10th, the eve of her investiture.[3]

It is not clear whether Sir Ignatius Redi returned to Arezzo after leaving Anna Maria at St. Teresa's four months previously. Most probably he did, for a carriage would not be required to make the journey alone. He could easily do it on horseback; and so now he returned to Florence to be with his daughter during the two months she was to remain outside the cloister.

Anna Maria did not wish to return to Arezzo and a family reunion. It could only be of short duration, and the harrowing moments of parting would have to be faced anew. She and her father remained in Florence as guests of Countess Isabella de'Mozzi-Barbolani, who during this period developed a strong affection for Anna Maria, to whom she became a second mother.

The Countess was cultured and aristocratic, widely read, an experienced hostess who moved much in high society circles. She shrewdly assessed the girl's character, noticing that her simple goodness was not merely the outcome of a pious and sheltered home life, or the naive virtue of one who had never experienced any temptation or the lure of material pleasures. She realized that beneath all this docility and delicacy of charity lay the strength and determination of an extraordinarily mature and vigorous soul who had given herself to God and would not come to terms with the world, regardless of what it thought. Only one who has no calculations about how to relieve others of some of their power or property is completely unconcerned as to whether or not the world approves of him. As St. Augustine says: "Perfect love has neither the desire of this world nor the fear of it; neither the desire to acquire temporal things nor the fear of losing them."

---

[3] This practice has never been in force in this country. Until about thirty years ago, the custom was for the postulant to leave the enclosure on her clothing day and, arrayed as a bride, to assist at Mass in the public chapel with her relatives, then return to the enclosure for the investiture. Now, however, the entire ceremony takes place behind the grille. Once the postulant enters the cloister, she does not leave it again.

"Anna Maria was very courageous and careful to give due attention to everything and everyone," said the Countess. "She fulfilled not only the duties required of her, but she also went out of her way to perform little acts of kindness for others." This was no country bumpkin, she noted with approval. While not possessing the polished speech and courtly manners of high society, Anna Maria's extreme simplicity, natural courtesy and grace lent real dignity to her manner and deportment. Later the Countess recalled her admiration for this poise and unassuming graciousness in her guest, remarking that "she was extremely happy and contented with the state she had chosen." The luxury and ease of life in this wealthy home, with servants once more to perform all menial tasks, the pleasure of well-appointed apartments and daintily served food, the absence of the noisy clapper and bell, which roused one so rudely from slumber or called arbitrarily to prayer or work - the relief from all those little hardships of conventual life did not offer her a temporary oasis of comfort, still less did it inspire regret at having to return to the austerity of community life. On the contrary, she eagerly looked forward to the day when the enclosure door would once more - and finally - open to receive her.

Now it was Anna Maria's turn to embark on those protracted visits of farewell customary among her class at that time. When not escorted by her father, the Countess acted as chaperone and companion, and so had ample opportunity of observing Anna Maria under all the different conditions and amidst former companions as well as with complete strangers, both of lower and higher social status than herself. In all circumstances, she said, this girl was habitually quite self-controlled and composed, neither remote nor familiar, but affable and agreeable, while at the same time punctilious in performing all the conventional rubrics of etiquette.

She called on her former teachers at St. Apollonia's, and her two sisters, Cecilia and Eleanor, still pupils there; also other communities and numerous acquaintances. Her father took her to Prato, where they spent four days with Francis Xavier, now fourteen, in the Cicognini College. During this time Anna Maria had a room in the Convent of St. Nicholas, and her father probably lodged at the College. Fifty years later, Francis was able to recall minute details of those last days with his sister.

At midday one day their father sent the two of them upstairs to wash and prepare themselves for lunch. Anna Maria went into the room her father had reserved, leaving Francis on the staircase landing outside. When she reappeared, her face was flushed, and he was surprised at the vehemence of her manner.

"Cecchino, what do you want of God?" she demanded abruptly.

Taken aback, he replied: "Why, to become better than I am."

"Cecchino, do you want to do good for God?"

"As well as I can, sinner that I am," he said. Then Anna Maria brought her face close to his, and spoke with such intensity that Francis never forgot it.

"Love Him, do you hear me. Love God very much, for you know how lovable and loving He is! How precious is His love, and how worthwhile is every effort we make to attain to it!"

Francis, later a Jesuit, gave evidence in the Process of 1818: "I remember this event so clearly, even to the very words she used, that I would readily testify to its veracity under oath."

Back in Florence the round of calls continued, and the weeks sped by in a torrent of sentimental farewells. But Anna Maria was equal to their demands. Feted, greeted, embraced, bidden "goodbye and good luck" under a hundred different forms, doubtless cautioned as to the imprudence of the step she was contemplating and advised by well-meaning counselors to abandon the idea, she went on her way serene and self-possessed. It is a trying period, and one well-calculated to render the privacy of a cell and the tactful restraint of one's sisters in religion more, not less desirable and attractive.

For her last public appearance, Anna Maria donned her most becoming gown and "magnificent, fawn-colored, elbow-length gloves." Arrayed thus, she happened to meet a priest who, aware that she was on the eve of receiving the Carmelite habit, scolded her for vanity and frivolity, declaring that anyone so worldly and superficial was unworthy to become a spouse of Christ.

The remembrance, all these years later, of those luxurious gloves, seems particularly poignant. It is one of those human touches that make St. Teresa Margaret step down from her portrait as a living person. For it is just this kind of trifle that trips the feet of so many of us. A girl may endure heroically all the suffering of parental opposition and refusal to understand or approve her choice of religious life, and then hesitate at the sacrifice of her hair. It is not that her tresses mean more to her than the sympathy of mother and father, but merely that, in assessing our commitments, we make allowance for the great renunciations, forgetting to take into account the costliness of some very small sacrifices. Anna Maria had borne with outstanding fortitude all the agonies of parting from her parents, her father in particular; yet here we see her, like ourselves, dallying with such a trifle as a pair of embroidered gloves.

7

Her Clothing

I have desired to go
Where springs not fail,
To fields where flies no sharp and sided hail
And a few lilies blow.
And I have asked to be
Where no storms come
Where the green swell is in the heavens dumb,
And out of the swing of the sea.
(G. M. Hopkins)

The clothing ceremony was fixed for the 11th of March, 1765, and on the eve, Anna Maria was to return to the Carmel. The Mozzi-Barbolani residence suddenly erupted into feverish activity, as the bridal finery was assembled, and amid the air of festivity, the bride herself prepared her last spiritual adornment. In these final days, Sir Ignatius sought to be with Anna Maria as much as possible, and he felt consoled at the conviction that she was contented and happy, looking forward almost gaily to her return to the cloister. Satisfied on this score, he gave himself up to the enjoyment of her presence for the last time.

The long-awaited morning dawned at last, and Anna Maria, accompanied by the Countess and a group of attendants and friends, entered the carriages that were to take them on the final short journey. Ignatius went by foot to the convent and met them at the chapel, a fact which would seem to indicate that he had no carriage in Florence on this occasion.

Fr. John Colombino, the Carmelite Provincial, and Father Ildefonse awaited the party. When Anna Maria stepped out of the carriage, both of them felt alarmed at her extraordinary pallor. Did she feel ill? Was she about to faint? But seeing her greet all the guests cordially, moving about from one to the other with a gracious word for each, they felt reassured, and Father Ildefonse - who seems to have possessed sharper eyes for such details than most men - stated that all the ceremonies she had to perform and the responses to be made in the chapel and on her way to the cloister door were carried out without fuss or commotion, correctly, and with dignity. "Yet I knew how much she was suffering, because the only one after God whom she loved with all her heart was her father."

At last the door closed behind her, and in the silence of the cloister she was once more surrounded and greeted affectionately by her sisters. But what a difference from her initial entrance six months ago! Now all the welcoming faces were dear and familiar, and as they embraced her, Teresa Margaret felt that she had really come home at last.

During recreation that evening, the conversation automatically turned to the subject of parting from one's family. The three novices each spoke of the sorrow they had felt on that occasion; then Teresa Margaret remarked quite simply, but with words that came from the depths of her heart, "I do not think that it is possible for me ever to suffer greater pain than that which I experienced in leaving my father."

The remembrance of those quiet words troubled Mother Anna Maria.

"I wonder if the child will be able to sleep?" she thought as she closed the door of her cell. Then, on a sudden impulse, she took up her lamp, walked softly down the corridor, and tapped lightly on the door of Teresa Margaret's cell.

She was already in bed, and the room was in darkness. Mother Anna Maria turned up the lamp she was carrying and saw that the girl's eyes were bright with unshed tears. Her face was flushed deeply - a symptom that Mother Anna Maria had now come to recognize - and she realized that it was with difficulty that she was suppressing her emotion.

The assistant Mistress placed the lamp on the table, and knelt beside the bed, taking one hot hand in hers.

"Do not fight back your tears, my child," she said, stroking the fair hair. "It is perfectly natural for you to feel like this. Let them come. They will do less harm out than in."

Suddenly the tears that had been so long held in check began to flow, and Teresa Margaret wept so heartbrokenly that Mother Anna Maria wondered how she had managed to restrain herself all day. She drew the golden head onto her shoulder and said soothingly, "Do you remember what our Holy Mother suffered at leaving her father? She wrote: 'When I left my father's house my distress was so great that I do not think it will be greater when I die. It seemed to me as if every bone in my body were being wrenched asunder.' And later she added: 'No one realized that I had gone through all this; they all thought I had acted out of sheer desire.' You must not try to do violence to your feelings in this way. It would be unnatural if you did not feel grief, but that only adds to the merit of your sacrifice. If it cost you nothing to leave your family, you would have less to give to God. Even the greatest saints have experienced the same thing."

She continued talking gently, feeling as though she had pulled the plug out of a cistern and wondering how on earth she was ever going to staunch the flow, but gradually the girl calmed somewhat.

"It is for your father you are weeping?" asked Mother Anna Maria.

Teresa Margaret nodded. "Yes, only for him. I have no other cause for tears, no other reason for any regret whatever. Were it not for his sorrow, I should be happier than I could ever express."

She lay quietly for a few moments, and then exclaimed, "Oh, my poor father! What he must have suffered as he watched me enter the cloister. I know how much the separation cost him, for we love each other so dearly."

Mother Anna Maria patted her shoulder comfortingly but said nothing. She knew the truth of those words. Although her face had been veiled, she had clearly seen Sir Ignatius and had noticed his stricken expression; his pain had been so great at that moment that he had seemed oblivious of his surroundings, forgetful that he was being observed, and making no attempt to disguise his emotion.

When the tears had ceased to flow, she said gently, "From now on you must say with St. Francis that you have but one father, God. He is enough. And you have the opportunity of gaining much merit in His eyes by triumphing over yourself and your feelings in this matter. It will only add to your father's distress if he sees yours."

"Oh, I shall do it, I promise you I shall. But I beg of you to ask this grace for me from the Lord. I do so want to please Him in everything. Tomorrow when I receive the habit, I shall implore Him to assist me so that the sacrifice may be as perfect as possible, for I fear that I am sadly wanting in detachment. Perhaps I am actually displeasing Him by seeming unhappy at becoming His bride... ."

Mother Anna Maria, satisfied that the storm had blown itself out, rose. Teresa Margaret caught her hand.

"Please, dear Mother, forgive me; and I hope the other sisters will overlook my weakness. I am truly unhappy at this inability to stifle the impulses of my great affection, and I do ask your pardon."

To many in the world, witnessing the Cinderella-transformation in reverse, as radiant bridal white is shed for drab brown homespun serge, it seems that the word *finis* has been written to any hopes of fulfillment or happiness in this life, or any promise that this vibrant youth has shown. They turn from the chapel, to be once more immersed in the cares and pleasures of life, without realizing that the ceremony they have just witnessed is merely the initiation into religious life. The past months have been a time of testing for physical and spiritual fitness, ability to adapt to a new routine, and most of all, good-will; for that is often the most one can be expected to exhibit in so short a time, during which the postulant barely manages to accommodate herself to the externals of a life of prayer, silence, and solitude so different in tempo and rhythm from what she has formerly been accustomed to.

Now, with the donning of the habit, one stage of the trial is past, and the novice begins experimentally to live the religious life.

Teresa Margaret already knew something of the sweetness of joy in the Lord, had tasted the intoxicating delights of Tabor, but it was not for her to build any arbors there. Her path lay through the shadowy thickets of Gethsemane, up the steeper, more rugged hill of Calvary. To him who sets no limit to his love and gift of self, God imposes no bounds to His graces. Already His favors had been so many that, as she herself said, "We swim in them, as fish in the ocean!" Now it was necessary that "deeper caverns" be hollowed out if more were to be received. This hollowing can be done only by cutting and rooting out all imperfections that remain as obstacles - little attachments and preferences, slight shoots of self-love, touchiness and self-will, small failings in humility and charity because of deficiency in self-knowledge. And as one is cutting out her living flesh, this excavation is always a painful and sometimes a violent process. It can never be achieved without suffering or endured without love.

Presumably as Teresa Margaret had left the house of Countess de'Mozzi-Barbolani the previous day, her bridal finery was entirely prepared under that lady's supervision, and thus the rest of the community were deprived of a first-class entertainment; for this procedure is usually the source of much excitement, and even more amusement. As a rule the postulant's ideas on current fashions both in dress and hair-style differ vastly from those of her more conservative sisters, who have long been disinterested - and in any case could hardly be regarded as authorities - about such matters. Those holding definite ideas usually dismay the postulant by insisting on what might have comprised a charming ensemble twenty or fifty years ago, or else sniffing disdainfully at these "newfangled" notions. But a source of even greater excitement for the bride-to-be than her white satin and orange-blossoms, is the preparation of the new habit - the fitting of tunic for length, the measuring and trying on of scapular, mantle, girdle, sandals - and the happy anticipation that soon the black cape and veil will be laid aside for the graceful folds of the enveloping white mantle.

On the morning of March 11th, Anna Maria Redi was invested in the simple brown Carmelite habit and received the name of her predilection. Florence still slept, but despite the cold morning air and the wreaths of mist that curled through the quiet streets, many carriages were to be seen on the road leading to St. Teresa's Monastery. The small chapel, almost empty on week days, was gradually filling, as friends and acquaintances of Anna Maria and her family arrived to witness the simple ceremony.

It was a tribute to the esteem and affection in which this girl, so reserved and silent about herself, was held, for the compass of her acquaintances was small. She had moved only among the restricted society of her family and immediate neighbors at Arezzo; for over eight years she had lived in even closer seclusion at St. Apollonia's, almost as though she had been a member of the community and for a couple of months among an extremely limited circle in Florence. Her charm, naturalness, and gift of friendship made her popular with all, from the servants to the more exacting mothers of her companions and acquaintances. And now they rose at this inconvenient hour, some out of curiosity, perhaps, but mostly to demonstrate their admiration for the likeable and pretty girl who was about to cover her golden hair with the plain white veil of a Carmelite novice and change her gleaming satin gown for the rough serge of our Lady's Order.

This is anything but a mournful occasion, but for many parents it proves almost unbearably moving. Camilla was not there, and at the last moment even Ignatius' resolution deserted him, and he was unable to watch the ceremony. "I did not have the courage to be present," he later confessed. "I stood in a corner of the church where I could not be observed."

As well as her father, other relatives and friends, several secular priests and Carmelite friars were present, including the Provincial, Fr.

John Colombino, who was officiating at the ceremony. For once the heavy shutters and inner grating that separated the nuns' choir from the sanctuary stood wide open, and the floor was strewn with flowers. Only the one fixed iron grille separated the visitors from what was taking place within. All eyes turned towards it as the cloister bell suddenly began to peal, and from the distance the opening words of the hymn from the second Vespers of our Lady's Office was heard faintly:

O gloriosa Virginum
Sublimis inter sidera ...

The volume increased as the community approached and entered, two by two, taking their places at the stalls on each side of the choir, and finally, between the double row of her sisters in their white cloaks, Mother Mary Magdalene walked slowly, leading by the hand Anna Maria in shimmering white satin, the long flowing train spreading out on the dark floor boards behind her with startling vividness. Her face was covered by a diaphanous white veil, and in place of the usual bouquet she carried in her right hand a lighted wax candle. Unhurriedly they moved through the choir to the center of the grille, where Anna Maria knelt on the floor, her skirts billowing out around her, looking like some delicate orchid among the homely bouquet of brown and white around her. The Prioress placed the heavy candle in a holder and retired to the back of the choir, as the priests approached the sanctuary and Mass commenced. Anna Maria knelt, still and straight, a vision of youth and loveliness in her misty white, accentuated by the forbidding bars of the grille which separated her from those in the chapel outside. To them, the criss-cross of the grating superimposed on the kneeling figure, gave something of the impression of a fragile, caged bird.

Remembering the emotional storm of the previous evening, Mother Anna Maria watched her charge anxiously, but to her relief, the girl appeared perfectly recollected and serene. Indeed, so great was her joy on that day that she seemed partly oblivious of what was going on around her, but never did her self-possession falter, as she calmly performed all the prescribed ceremonies.

Mass ended, Father Provincial moved across to the grille, faced Anna Maria, and began the ceremonial dialogue which has remained unaltered for centuries. In firm, clear tones, she made the customary answers, unambiguous words which manifest both the complete freedom of the choice and the strength of the love which has prompted it: drawing her from all things the world considers most worth living for, to remain "hidden with Christ in God" behind the walls of this convent, which for so many outside, epitomize the restriction of all liberty. But the bride of Christ knew that it was truly a liberator, the barrier which would not imprison her, but rather hold the world at bay, so that, without distraction, she might give herself wholeheartedly to the things of God.

"What do you ask?"

Promptly, calmly, and audibly to all in the chapel came the confident reply: "The mercy of God, the poverty of the Order, and the society of the Sisters."

"Are you resolved to persevere in the Order until death?"

"Thus do I hope and desire, through the mercy of God and the prayers of the Sisters."

Mother Mary Magdalene who had approached noiselessly, touched Anna Maria lightly on the shoulder, and as the girl rose from her knees, took her hand and led her from the choir, as the community began chanting the psalm *In exitu Israel de Aegypto* ... "Not to us, Lord, not to us the glory; let thy name alone be honored; thy name for mercy, thy name for faithfulness ... the Lord that gives hope to all who fear him, their only help, their only stronghold."

Outside, Anna Maria was being rapidly divested of her finery. The veil, coronet, and satin gown slipped to the floor at her feet, and over her head went the heavy serge tunic. As the coarse material rasped across her shoulders, she felt a sense of satisfaction and achievement. But there was no time to delay. Another hand was pulling the pins out of her long hair, which tumbled down around her shoulders. A few expert snips and the heavy golden curls lay scattered among the satin and lace, while a coarse linen coif was drawn around her face and pinned under her chin, then covered by a long, flowing white linen veil. The dainty satin slippers were kicked aside, and her bare feet thrust into rough hemp sandals. The candle was placed in her hand once more, and she was led back into the choir to kneel again before the grille. Lying on a stool beside her was the remainder of her habit, and the ceremony of investiture began.

"May the Lord clothe you with the new man who is created in the justice and holiness of the truth."

The ceremony of taking the habit - or investiture - is always impressive, and one can well imagine the varying emotions that possessed the gay company in the chapel, as the aristocratic young girl prostrated herself at the feet of Him to whom she was consecrating her life.

The Prioress and Novice Mistress took each garment as it was blessed. First the heavy leather girdle, with its large rosary attached, was fastened around her waist, with an exhortation to the complete obedience that was henceforth required of her: "When thou wert young thou wouldst gird thyself and walk where thou hadst the will to go, but when thou hast grown old, another shall gird thee."

The Scapular was lifted, blessed, and laid over the shoulders of the novice:

"Receive the sweet yoke of Christ and His light burden."

Finally, the white mantle was blessed and thrown about her, as the Provincial's words reminded her that it symbolized the life of voluntary chastity she was to embrace:

"Those who follow the Lamb without spot shall walk with Him in white garments. Therefore, let your vesture be ever unspotted in token of purity of heart."

Suddenly, he turned back to the altar and intoned the hymn *Veni, Creator Spiritus.* As the voices of the community took up the words, the newly-clothed novice prostrated herself on the floor in the center of the choir, her arms outstretched in the form of a cross, signifying the mystical death to nature that was being undertaken.

"I spread my garment over you. I swore to you and I entered into a covenant with you, and you became mine." (Eze.15:8) Enveloped in the large mantle, the novice, face to the ground, offered her being to God, while the golden ball of prayer to the Holy Spirit was tossed lightly from one choir to the other over her prostrate form, just touching earth on the penultimate of each verse, to be caught up and rebound once more to heaven. Then followed the lengthy prayers for divine protection to the novice, assistance in her voluntary desire to consecrate her youth and her whole life to God, and the graces that she would need to walk worthily in that high undertaking.

The signal was given once more, and the novice rose, her face flushed and radiant. She was led back to the grille, where, kneeling before the Provincial, she heard the announcement:

"Henceforward, you will be known as Sister Teresa Margaret of the Sacred Heart of Jesus."

"How good and joyous a thing it is when brethren dwell united!" As the glad chant rang out, Sister Teresa Margaret embraced each of her sisters in turn; then the notes gradually faded away in the distance, as two by two the community, following the Prioress and the new novice, left the choir. Finally, the voices no longer audible, the curtain of silence once more dropped between choir and chapel, as the guests remained looking and listening. No sound came from the now empty choir, and at last the congregation rose to disperse and resume once more the normal course of their daily lives. They had now bid their last farewell to one who would henceforth tread a silent and solitary path, far removed from their interests and pleasures. Nobody envied her the change she had just effected, nor did they wish to lay aside their brocades and laces for the penitential hairshirt; but, for a brief interim, until the cares and ambitions of mundane life returned to stifle it, there lingered like a fragrance, an awareness that they had just seen one who had given all to gain all; a faintly nostalgic envy that she would, more rapidly and with less difficulty than themselves, find the pearl of great price, for which any merchant with an eye to a bargain would sell all he possessed. And this would be achieved ... by surrendering herself freely and willingly to the truth that alone can make us free.

In the afternoon Teresa Margaret went to the little parlor to greet her father.

"Well, my child. You have made your choice. And are you quite happy in it?"

He studied closely her radiant face, which under the white coif and veil seemed so childlike and innocent that his eyes grew misty as he saw again the small girl who had always run so confidently to slip her hand in his, and who was now forever out of reach. But he did not need her words to reassure him. Happiness and contentment emanated almost visibly from the glowing face and sparkling eyes.

"Papa," she said, "I have found all that I ever desired or ever could desire, and more. I am living in a house of angels."

"I have left a small gift for you, as a memento of the occasion. Reverend Mother will no doubt give it to you."

"But, Papa, I am in need of nothing."

"Nevertheless," he replied with a smile, "unless I am mistaken you will find the little book an inestimable treasure."

"But I cannot accept it even from you, without our Mother's permission."

"So!" Ignatius exclaimed with mock severity. "Must I take a vow of poverty also, that I may not dispose of my property as I please? Do not worry about Reverend Mother's permission. You will have that I am sure, for it was Father Colombino who recommended that I should present you with a copy of the biography of Sister Margaret Mary. I feel certain, as he does, that you will profit much from reading it. Is there not some other little need I can supply by way of a bridal gift?"

"My dearest Papa, I want nothing and have no need of anything. So great is the gift you have given me in permitting me to put on this habit that were I to go down on my knees, or prostrate with my face on the ground, I could not hope to express my deep gratitude to you."

It was not difficult to believe. Sir Ignatius could not but be aware that his daughter was experiencing to the full the peace that the world cannot give, a deep, spiritual joy for which no pleasure of this earth could substitute or compensate.

He left the convent that day with a great peace and thankfulness in his own heart, despite the pain and the still active sense of loneliness.

"It is absurd," he told himself. "I have six other children, and much, very much to be grateful for."

But he knew that none of the others would ever occupy the unique place Anna Maria had always held in his life. It was a sanctuary which henceforward must remain consecrated, a trysting place where he alone could enter and find again the daughter he had lost, yet could never lose, who would remain always undivided in her heart and affection, and although irrevocably parted from him by an insurmountable physical barrier, yet paradoxically closer to him than any other in spirit and in heart.

The community in the meantime rejoiced with and for their new novice. For the one day she was truly the guest of honor, the feted bride. In choir, in the refectory, in processions, she took her place next to the Prioress. Her fellow novices vied with each other to perform small services, prepare her cell, decorate her place at table with flowers, carry out the various chores usually allotted to her. During recreation, for which on this occasion the novices joined and mingled with the community, the room rang with laughter and good humored gaiety, as each one offered some little gift to mark the occasion: a small illuminated text or a pressed flower, according to the tastes and abilities of each, or little spiritual verses set to music which all sang to their sister.

But even in the midst of this holiday atmosphere of festivity, Teresa Margaret remembered her friends outside, and on this momentous day she had the presence of mind to take up her pen and write a note of gratitude to the Countess de'Mozzi-Barbolani for her kindness and hospitality over the past two months. This gesture of thoughtful courtesy on the one day when she might be excused for dispensing herself from its demands touched that lady deeply. Teresa Margaret wrote a longer letter to Canon Tonci, saying: "I have reached the summit of my desires in being clothed with this holy habit, and as you well know, it was a call that I received from our Lord. He has shown me great mercy, and I acknowledge my unworthiness, but now He has given me a sign that I am obliged not only to change my whole life, but also to become a saint, because in this place where I now dwell it is easier to become one than not."

8

Devotion to the Sacred Heart

A sudden rush of glory fills the air
With golden music, after long delay.
Pass not into the silence, O! most rare
Moment of joy, which knows not yesterday.

(Lady Margaret Sackville)

To regard oneself as a little child in the arms of its heavenly Father, abandoning all care to His Sacred Heart, forgetting oneself in the awareness of His power and the consciousness of one's own powerlessness are attitudes that detach us from ourselves, free us from the bonds of servitude, and establish in us confidence and trust - as St. Thérèse expressed it: "...fully aware of our own feebleness, yet confident *to audacity* in the Father's goodness and power to help."

In the work of our sanctification, we can do nothing without the aid of grace. "No man can say Jesus is the Lord, but by the Holy Spirit." (I Cor. 12:3) We cannot even produce one thought that is meritorious. The grace on which our spiritual foundation rests, and upon which the whole edifice depends, is a free, gratuitous gift of God, so far beyond our understanding that we cannot even conceive of its action or perceive its coming and going. Like the wind, nothing is known of the way it came or the way it goes although we can hear the sound of it and see the result of its destructive force.

Sometimes it flows into the soul like a broad, tranquil river, penetrating the senses and filling the soul with a consciousness of its silent, unseen presence; at other times, it crashes in on us like the pounding breakers of a heavy surf, conquering and sweeping all in its path by its strength and irresistible force. Or it is "the gentle murmur of the breeze," comforting and gently caressing; again, it is a blinding searchlight that pours into the soul floods of light and love, blotting out all else, a dynamo under the impetus of which we can do all things thanks to the strength God gives us. In whatever guise it comes, it is at God's time and pace, it is withdrawn at His will. We cannot stay it, hold it, summon it. As suddenly as it comes it is gone, leaving us without strength or the energy, as St. Teresa of Avila once said, to kill an ant if we were to meet any opposition to it.

The action of God is all-powerful. "Where I will I chasten, and where I will I strengthen." Our part is to abandon ourselves to His good pleasure and concentrate solely on the one thing we are asked to do: "Clear the palace of vulgar people and junk," and place no obstacle to His action. His is the task of filling up once we have cleared the necessary space. And this He will do unless we make it impossible by our untimely interference or the stubborn clinging to our own good ideas on the subject.

So far, only passing mention has been made of the devotion to the Sacred Heart which was so powerful an influence in the whole life and spirituality of St. Teresa Margaret, and it seems opportune to pause here while she peruses the biography of Margaret Mary Alacoque - which was to play so vital a part in her life - and consider some aspects and implications of the name which had now been bestowed upon her in religion.

Teresa Margaret was very much in advance of most of her contemporaries with regard to her conceptions of the Sacred Heart and the Mystical Body. We today are familiar with these rich and satisfying doctrines through recent Papal pronouncements, notably the encyclicals of Pope Pius XI and Pope Pius XII. The mystery of the Sacred Heart is so inextricably entwined with the doctrine of the Mystical Body that neither can fully exist, or be clearly comprehended

- insofar as that is possible at all - apart from the other. But these matters were neither well expounded nor widely understood at that time. Even as recently as the First Vatican Council a century ago, Bishops were reluctant to approve the expression "Mystical Body of Christ" as an official definition of the nature of the Church; an unwillingness that seems almost incomprehensible to this generation which has grown up with the term. It speaks volumes for this young girl's clear-sightedness and spiritual perceptions that she was able to envisage something of the vast horizons these later teachings have since opened up. Only God can keep us balanced. Only in Him can we love others without squandering ourselves in vague emotions or an impersonal philanthropy. Because He is the center of the universe, He balances and unifies all things.

Ever since her childhood days, Teresa Margaret had grasped the truth of the Apostle's words: "What have we that we have not received?" But having received so great a gift - God Himself - we, however unworthy, have an infinite gift to offer back to infinite Majesty. "Repeatedly during the day," Father Ildefonse recalls, "she would offer the Precious Blood of Jesus to the Father to thank His divine Majesty for all the benefits which He had granted to us. She did this especially while assisting at Mass."

The Sacred Heart, the Precious Blood, the Holy Name: In Jesus Christ we must live and in His name appear before His heavenly Father. Thus centering her devotional practices in the Sacred Humanity of Christ, she personifies the words of Pope John XXIII: "Nothing is better for enlightening and encouraging the adoration of Jesus than to meditate upon Him and invoke Him in the threefold light of the Name, the Heart, and the Blood... . The Blood of Christ is the highest mark of the redeeming sacrifice of Jesus, which is renewed mystically and really in the Holy Mass, and gives sense and orientation to Christian life." And the Holy Father then goes on to quote from *Haurietis Aquas,* the encyclical of his predecessor Pope Pius XII: "It is clear that in the Heart of Jesus we are dealing not with an ordinary form of piety which anyone may at his discretion slight in favor of other devotions or esteem lightly, but with a duty of religion most conducive to Christian perfection."

Father Ildefonse later said of Teresa Margaret: "She regarded the Sacred Heart as the center of love whence the divine Word has loved us from all eternity. She considered that this devotion was to love our Lord incessantly, in return for His love. She desired to have the Sacred Heart added to her name, understanding by that to be unwilling to live and breathe except by loving Him with all her strength. This is the signification which I find she gave to this devotion, making it consist completely in returning her love."

The burning zeal which consumed her, young as she was, had its roots in the human and divine love of the Sacred Heart, who had drawn her into the focus of His love and His longing for souls, "...setting charity in order in her." It is no cause for surprise that God should shower His graces lavishly on so generous a soul. "Thy measure shall be My measure," said our Lord to St. Catherine of Sienna; and St. Bernard has told us: "The measure of our love of God should be to love Him without measure." If our own love and generosity knows no bounds, neither will His, and as His gift is infinite, we will indeed receive full measure, pressed down and running over.

It was by continually contemplating the mysteries of Christ's sufferings that Teresa Margaret was trained to practice the solidly Christian virtues, instead of losing herself in sentimental reverie, and thus to lay the foundations for a true understanding - in so far as is possible for a creature - of divine charity.

The cult of the Sacred Heart, Pope Pius XII declared: "...is a most excellent act of religion, since it involves on our part a total and unreserved intention of giving and consecrating ourselves to the divine Redeemer's love, to which love His wounded Heart is a living pointer and symbol. It is equally if not more clear, that the principal idea of this cult or devotion is that we should ourselves make a return of love to the divine love."

"You shall draw waters with joy out of the Savior's fountains" (Is. 12.3). With these words Pope Pius XII opened his encyclical *Haurietis Aquas,* in which he pointed out that the Heart of Jesus,

more than all the other members of His Body, is the natural pointer to, or symbol of, His boundless charity towards mankind.

"The lying slogans of materialism are spreading in practice as well as in theory, while the unrestrained indulgence of sensual desire is everywhere extolled. What wonder, then, if in the hearts of many charity grows cold? Did not our Savior warn us 'because iniquity hath abounded, the charity of many shall grow cold'?

"Where are we to seek a remedy? Consider this holy cult of the Heart of Jesus. Could we find a more excellent form of devotion, or one which accords more perfectly with the essential spirit of the Catholic faith, or is more apt to succor the Church and the human race in the needs of the present day? For we are dealing with a cult which is totally directed towards the very love of God Himself as its object. Devotion to the Sacred Heart increases and fosters the charity of Christ in our hearts at a rate that grows each day."

It was her father who had first introduced Teresa Margaret to this devotion while she was still a small child, thus planting the seed that was to grow and blossom into the whole of her wonderful yet simple spirituality. His own love of the Sacred Heart was intense; indeed, it was the strong and central force of his life. In his speech, as well as in all his extant letters, mention of the Hearts of Jesus and Mary recurred constantly, and in the letters Ignatius wrote to his daughter, particularly during her five and a half years as a Carmelite, reference to this devotion and its efficacy abound. Thus, from her earliest years, Teresa Margaret had been led gradually to realize that the Heart of Christ is the symbol and source of infinite Love, from whose pure fount she had already learned to draw waters in joy.

Devotion to the Sacred Heart did not at that time receive the unqualified approval or the place in Catholic spiritual life that it enjoys today. Despite the revelation to St. Margaret Mary Alacoque a century earlier, and her assurance to Father Croiset, S.J. that his book *Devotion to the Sacred Heart of our Lord Jesus Christ* was so completely in accordance with the wishes of our Lord that no alteration would ever need to be made to it, the book remained in circulation for only thirteen years. Published in 1691, the year after Margaret Mary's death, it was placed on the Index of Forbidden Books in 1704[1], from which it was not removed until 1887. In 1729 the Holy See refused the institution of the Feast, which was later permitted in 1765 (the year of Teresa Margaret's clothing) by Pope Clement XIII, who pointed out that he wished to call attention to the Divine Love who became man to redeem us, by approving the symbol of the Sacred Heart.

The cult was attacked on many sides, and indeed the word "devotion" which has acquired unfortunately sentimental overtones is not the happiest expression to denote the worship we pay to the Sacred Humanity of Christ. The Sacred Heart is not a superior Saint, but the second Person of the Blessed Trinity, in whom the divine and human natures are indissolubly united and must not be thought of in isolation from the God-Man. The Holy See has never shown much sympathy for any attempts to "dismember" Christ by permitting individual cults of His Hands, His Feet, His Head, etc. although naturally the Holy Face holds a unique and readily comprehended position.

But while the Heart is most certainly a symbol, our "devotion" does not terminate with the human Heart, for although we are in the habit of speaking of loving someone "with our whole heart," emotions are not seated in the heart. Love, sorrow, and joy are neither placed in the heart nor produced by it. And the present-day cultus of the Sacred Heart which plays so great a part in our Christian lives is simply devotion to our Lord Jesus Christ, together with the desire to make a return for His overwhelming love for man and reparation for the ingratitude of those who neglect or reject that love. This, Ignatius had explained to his daughter when as a small child she would ask him: "Who is Jesus Christ?" We contemplate the divine and human love of Christ for us, and see

---

[1] The Decree of the Congregation of the Index is dated 11th March (which is now the Feast of St. Teresa Margaret)! [in 1964]

how often it is utterly repulsed, and how seldom it is fully appreciated or returned with generosity and gratitude. The Sacred Heart devotion belongs to the doctrine of the Mystical Body, in which we are all incorporated by grace, so that truly "in Him we live and move and have our being."

Therefore, although the Sacred Heart is in a sense an aspect of the divine life in human form, which is readily understandable and attractive to us, it is no less a mystery than the Incarnation itself, and something completely "ineffable" to the mind of the superficially devout, who regard merely the human aspect of the loving Heart which so readily and conveniently forgives all our transgression and spends eternity "turning the other cheek." The Incarnate Word of God is "a great and mighty wonder," and so is the love of His human Heart, so there is little cause for surprise that the cult has been misunderstood and distorted so frequently.

It was under this loving title, Teresa Margaret said, that she "drew courage despite her extreme unworthiness to approach without fear a God who is so great, just, and terrible, because this also tells us He is a Father who loves us, our dearest Father, full of love and mercy."

Once when discussing the words of the Gospel: "No one can come to the Father but by Me," Teresa Margaret spoke at length on the text: "This our God and our loving Father is All. He is the beginning of everything, and this love is God Himself. The mirror we have to consult to arrive at divine union is the Sacred Heart of Jesus crucified. With love, one must return love for love, and what can we do to make a return in kind to God who loves us so much in spite of our great unworthiness? How can nothingness even the balance between itself and infinite plenitude? We can do this much - endeavor to conform ourselves to Christ Crucified and copy as nearly as possible the humility, meekness, and gentleness of His Sacred Heart."

Speaking of Teresa Margaret, whom he canonized, Pope Pius XI said: "It is in her name that we find the explanation of her marvelous secret: it was in the intimacy of her heart with the divine Heart, it was her wonderful devotion to the Heart of Christ; a devotion which was established amidst difficulties which today we should call ab-

surd, but still real difficulties, springing from the cold zeal of a sect
that knew nothing about the love of God because it wished to comprehend solely His majesty and His greatness."

Teresa Margaret had never encountered this attitude at home; it
was a direct contradiction to the warmth of the religious climate in which
she had been reared. Sir Ignatius' deep devotion to the Sacred Heart has
already been mentioned, and the same can no doubt be presumed of his
Jesuit brother, Father Diego Redi. However, at St. Apollonia's, Anna
Maria obviously had some fundamental disagreement with Don Bertoni,
the convent chaplain, and as he was particularly antagonistic to the cult
of the Sacred Heart, it is not unlikely that his attitude was the reason of
Anna Maria's inability to open her heart and soul to the priest when she
felt the need of some spiritual guidance.

When questioned later about the conduct of his former penitent,
Don Bertoni surprised everyone by saying brusquely: "She was an
impertinent little girl, just like all the others."

Don Bertoni obviously was not popular with the student body, and
his is the severest censure leveled at Teresa Margaret during the whole
of her life. It is surely not fanciful to connect the priest's unfavorable
opinion of an otherwise good and docile child with his disapproval of
her intense love of the Sacred Heart, for whenever the revelations of
Paray-le-Monial were mentioned, he would violently attack or denounce
their authenticity. Anna Maria was capable of defending her devotion
vigorously and even heatedly, and it would be no surprise to learn that a
head-on collision had occurred in this connection, where two strong-
minded persons held such conflicting views.

It was the Carmelite Provincial, Father John Colombino, who
knew both Sir Ignatius and his daughter well, who suggested that she
should read the biography of Margaret Mary.[2] It gave an even stronger impetus to Teresa Margaret's devotion to learn how the whole
vocation of Margaret Mary was consolidated in her love for the
Sacred Heart. She decided to adopt the Visitandine as her "nov-
ice-mistress," and from her she learned the secret that was hence-

---

[2] This was not the exhaustive study by Fr. Croiset, S.J., at one time St. Margaret
Mary's director, which at that date was still on the Index.

forth to be the solid basis of her own life of hidden sacrifice: "Suffer and be silent for Jesus, return Him love for Love." This became so completely the leitmotiv of her life that every action was gradually brought into its focus, until eventually all was performed in intimate and personal communion with the Sacred Heart; not in any selfish isolation, but in generous and complete response to the inspirations of grace and the demands of fraternal charity.

A spiritual life based on so solid a foundation could not but be fruitful, for, says Pope Pius XI: "We do not hesitate to affirm that the cult of the Sacred Heart of Jesus is the *most effective* school of divine charity."

St. Margaret Mary's influence on Teresa Margaret is apparent from many of the themes and maxims that are found in the writings and spirituality of her young Italian disciple, but it is more in the nature of confirming an already formed conviction. Teresa Margaret's spiritual growth displays too dynamic and original an orientation to be a mere copying or even adapting of the life of St. Margaret Mary to her own, which differed greatly in externals. Her devotion to the Sacred Heart was crystallized before reading the biography, but the book gave her great pleasure by confirming her intuitions of the merciful love of God and His desire that human hearts and souls should console Him for the neglect of so many to appreciate and avail themselves of His gift; by encouraging her on her chosen path of silent suffering and guiding her as to the norms through which her wholehearted giving was to find its expression and outlet.

Now, with the donning of the habit, she had been permitted to add the name of the Sacred Heart to her own, and in a sudden illumination of grace, the young novice realized that it personified the whole program of her ascent: Love.

"Learn of Me, for I am meek and humble of Heart ... He humbled Himself, obedient unto death, even the death of the cross ..." These texts became her favorite subjects for meditation. "You must not allow yourself to become absorbed in the external occupations which you are obliged to perform," she counseled one of her sisters. "By

9

Living the Hidden Life

I, God, enfold thee like an atmosphere:
Thou to thyself wert never yet more near:
Think not to shun Me; whither would'st thou fly?
Nor go not hence to seek Me I am he.

(James Phoades)

St. Teresa Margaret can almost be named "the saint of the hidden life," so thoroughly did she absorb its meaning and mystery. The life of Jesus and Mary at Nazareth is indeed the model *par excellence* for all religious, but this silent and self-effacing saint penetrated deeply into it, and gave its application such wide horizons that she can really be said to have proposed something essentially original.

Her desire to hide herself from the eyes of others was more than natural reserve; it was not the instinctive withdrawal of a shy and timid nature. Teresa Margaret was lively, and could converse with animation and interest. Yet from her schooldays, she had seemed to divine that grace is a spiritual aroma that loses much of its sweetness when exposed to the heat and dust of the day. Indeed, she often compared the more fragrant virtues to perfumed flowers and once laughingly referred in such terms to the "odor of sanctity." When questioned, she admitted that she associated this with the scent of the narcissi that grew abundantly around her native Arezzo. Years later, after her death, this perfume was noticed about the clothing she had worn, and at the Redi Villa her mother found the aroma clinging around Anna Maria's room and many objects she had used.

Teresa Margaret once said: "She who is silent everywhere finds peace." The secret of her repose in God was expressed by another piece of advice which carried the first maxim a step further: "She who desires peace must see, suffer, and be silent."

Later Teresa Margaret was to express her desire to "hide herself in the Sacred Heart as in a desert," but already, as a young novice taking her first tentative steps, she realized to the full the necessity of hiding herself and her gifts and talents from those around her. She saw that, even above the degree of solitude and recollection demanded in daily life, there were many higher levels of intensity and degrees of perfection. Hidden from the eyes of the world though she now was, she desired a deeper hiddenness "with Christ in God," concealed even from the eyes of her sisters, so that for God and with Him alone would her life be spent.

Yet this solitariness was to be practiced in the midst of community life, with its setting of common duties, daily work and prayer. The method she adopted was so misleadingly simple that it required near-genius to recognize and perfect it and great virtue to persevere in it.

It is a commonplace to use the life at Nazareth as a type of the Hidden Life, because the enclosed religious is completely withdrawn from the world. But in this sense Jesus, Mary, and Joseph were not "hidden," at least not from their neighbors and the inhabitants of Nazareth and its environs. Probably, like small country towns the world over, everybody knew and discussed the least event around the village well, and anything that happened in Joseph's house would be common knowledge, as with everybody else. But where one can claim that their hiddenness was absolute was that while all their exterior activities were watched, and every visitor noted, so well was their interior life concealed from all eyes, that they passed for the most ordinary and unremarkable among a community that was in itself insignificant. The revelation of miraculous powers in Jesus was received with shocked disbelief. They had known him since childhood and could vouch for his likeableness, kindness, generosity, no doubt - but not sanctity, let alone divinity!

This was Teresa Margaret's method of practicing the "hidden life." Everyone in the community saw all she did, talked with her, worked with her, and were warm in their praise of her goodness and charity. But the real depths of her interior life were completely hidden and were one day to prove a revelation and surprise to these intimate daily companions. She passed every minute under their very noses, so to speak, but managed to remain unnoticed, keeping her soul's secret for God alone.

Her "secret" is enshrined in the heart of another paradox of Christianity: that until we have given ourselves completely to God, we cannot give ourselves wholly to others. The more one progresses into solitude with God - alone with Him alone - the deeper grows one's unity with his neighbors and brethren in religion and solidarity with the whole Mystical Body. This fusion is absolutely essential in community life, for without it we are not united, but merely a collection of individuals who happen to live under the same roof and observe the same horarium and its deepest levels are proportionate with our aloneness with God. These depths are plumbed to their very center by few, those who have given themselves utterly to God, and who understand the basic truth of fraternal charity: "That they too may be one in us, as thou Father art in me and I in thee." (John 17:21).

Her program, then, was to imitate Jesus and Mary, appearing "just like all the rest," and it was implemented by the simple means of fidelity to duty. It is not always easy to remain hidden in a small community; the surest way of becoming conspicuous is to make a solitary of oneself, to be absent from recreation or other communal duties. Just as one is unconscious of a single leaf in a forest, so one never notices the silent, willing worker, who is always at his post, anticipating the needs of others and never shirking his own task, simply because he is always where one expects to find him.

As well as a genuine spirit of silence and retirement, this requires true humility. And there is no better model for this virtue than that of the hidden life. Keeping her eyes fixed on Jesus Christ, the perfect exemplar of humility, and drawing from Him not only increase in virtue but ardor of love, Teresa Margaret exclaimed: "This was true humility! This was real virtue and excess of love! How can we ever sufficiently humble ourselves in imitation of a God so humiliated?"

It is depressingly easy for us, as day succeeds day, to lose our sense of proportion, to begin looking at things from an angle where they are distorted out of true perspective, and to work for the wrong motives. Gradually, imperceptibly, our interests become centered in ourselves, our work is done for an end that has its roots in self, and the motive of pleasure or prestige may indelibly mark and spoil what we should be doing solely for God. There are some rare occasions when great suffering or renunciation is so plainly labeled "The will of God for me" that it is wholeheartedly accepted. But such clear-cut issues appear perhaps once in a lifetime, often never at all. Yet in the ordinary routine of daily life, where even the most insignificant act can be performed for God's glory and our own growth in holiness, there are very few thoughts, words, or deeds in which the glory of God is allotted its rightful place.

Who can explain to us how faith is produced within us? Or how the divine and the human are interwoven and work mutually to the single appointed end? We are constantly dependent on grace, and it is because we forget that we have nothing that we have not received, and that all must be done in utter dependence upon God, that so many of our pet projects fail. We attacked them in the full confidence of our own ability; we put into them our best effort and all our energy. And that is precisely the point at which we run off the rails, for it is when we work as faulty tools manipulated by the perfect workman that our efforts succeed and bear fruit. The deep religious faith of simple souls reveals this power and divine operation as much as does the simple faith of the learned.

But, said Father Ildefonse, "her keen sense of her own unworthiness, and the often painful awareness of her imperfections, did not leave Teresa Margaret cowering fearfully beneath the weight of her own recognized weakness. Rather, it caused her to throw herself confidently on the love and mercy of God, gaining daily and hourly a stronger incentive to greater and more virtuous works for His love."

"Of myself I am nothing," she would insist, "but in God is everything, and I can do all things in Him who strengthens me. The poorer and more miserable I am, the richer and stronger I am in Him. He will be the more glorified in His mercy the more wretched and despised I am in my nothingness, my sins, and my weakness."

The fact is that humility must be firmly allied with confidence. To be aware of our powerlessness to do any good, without an equally strong conviction of God's mercy and willingness to help us, would throw us into despair. "Without God we cannot," says St. Augustine, "but without us, He will not." He might very well have bidden us to learn from Him because, He is Eternal Wisdom, Incarnate Knowledge, All Truth; instead He has said: "Learn of me, because I am meek and humble of heart." St. Teresa of Avila, commenting on this, remarked: "I was wondering once why our Lord so clearly loved this virtue of humility ... it is because God is sovereign truth, and to be humble is to walk in truth, for it is absolutely true to say that we have no good thing in ourselves, but only misery and nothingness." Perhaps St. Thérèse of Lisieux has given the most profound description of all, in her simple exposition of spiritual childhood: "It is a disposition of the heart, which makes us always humble and little in the hands of God, well aware of our feebleness, but confident to the point of audacity in the Father's goodness."

There was no hint of introversion about Teresa Margaret's almost exclusive occupation with concealment. On one occasion, one of the sisters remarked on her air of absorption.

"You look as though you are a long way from the cares of life!"

"Oh, I assure you that I am very far from being so," she replied.

"Perhaps," put in another mischievously, "it is her great interior recollection that emancipates our sister from the mundane things of this world!"

Teresa Margaret laughed.

"No," she said, "it is absent-mindedness, no more or less. I am always falling into this fault. Even when I was quite small, Papa would see me standing gazing into space, and call out: 'Now, Anna Maria, come back to earth!'"

Thus she always managed to divert any attention she attracted, appearing simple and quite ordinary. The external actions through which she practiced the hidden life were similar in broad outline to those of any other Carmelite, whose daily routine varies only in the different forms of work undertaken.[1]

Of latter years, there has been much literature, as well as radio and television programs, depicting the routine daily life in a Carmelite cloister, and most readers must be familiar with its general itinerary – choir duties, prayer, housework, manual labor, recreation - and can visualize the various chores and spiritual exercises that filled Teresa Margaret's day. To her the daily round of rather uninteresting tasks: sewing, sweeping, washing dishes, scrubbing floors - was not (as a Catholic author once labeled it) "a life of intellectual suicide, of rough work that blunts the mind." On the contrary, it provided her with countless opportunities for demonstrating her love of God and of her sisters, volunteering for any unpleasant or difficult task, serving God in her neighbor and rejoicing to imitate Him in the faithful performance of lowly occupations.

The failure of the inhabitants of Nazareth to recognize the divinity of Jesus or the sanctity of Mary and Joseph, is explained by the mystery that envelops the supernatural and its external signs. And it is for the same reason that St. Teresa Margaret could pass unknown and unrecognized by most of the religious of her own community, alert as they were for any indications of outstanding virtue or holiness. God performed no miracle to veil the marvels of grace and the rapid progress in virtue that were taking place before everybody's eyes. It was sufficient to leave grace to work in silence, weaving its own fabric which shielded the external manifestations of the super-

---

[1] The most usual are making altar breads and church vestments, printing, painting and illuminating, weaving, and similar forms of manual work compatible with a life of silence, by which one earns one's living; and as well, the necessary labor for one's upkeep, such as gardening, farming, cooking, mending, housework, etc.

natural, until such time as He was ready to reveal them. This is characteristic of the highest development in all chosen souls.

"Work at your tasks with a will," St. Paul exhorts the Colossians, "reminding yourself that you are doing it for the Lord, not for men." The Carmelite Rule places great emphasis on manual labor, not for the sake of the work itself, but because a life of prayer could easily degenerate into selfish and egotistical withdrawal and preoccupation, unless one were suitably employed. "You shall do some kind of work," it legislates, "that the devil may always find you occupied, lest through idleness he may find an entrance into your souls." The danger is no less real in the cloister than it is in the busy thoroughfare, and St. Teresa was as insistent as St. Benedict before her on the necessity for diligent toil and its salutary effects. As Father Vincent McNabb O.P. trenchantly remarked: "There are some people who are prepared to contemplate eight hours a day, provided somebody else does the work." To indulge in idleness under the pretext of contemplation is to lay oneself open to almost every possible abuse. But manual labor is only a physical occupation, and in no way hinders the union of mind and heart with God; indeed, the opinion of many well-experienced in the ways of the spiritual life, (as it was of the Fathers of the Desert) is that manual work is a powerful aid to prayer; and that humble and even monotonous tasks such as sweeping, laundering, digging the earth, or milking cows, can be a real help to interior recollection and prayer, for such occupations do not take one out of the presence of God. Elemental and not demanding intense concentration, they leave the mind free and enable us to unite ourselves even more closely with Jesus and Mary, who occupied themselves with such menial work. Washing dishes or sawing firewood doubtless roughens the hands, but it has no power to roughen or blunt the mind. "In the noise and clutter of my kitchen," declared Brother Lawrence, "while several persons are at the same time calling for different things, I possess God in as great tranquility as if I were upon my knees before the Blessed Sacrament"; St. Teresa reminds us that God walks among the pots and pans as well as the choir stalls. She speaks from experience, having herself been engaged in the unglamorous task of frying fish when she was, on one occasion, carried off in ecstasy.

Sister Teresa Margaret soon learned how to imitate the industrious and productive bee, using profitably every moment of the day. Carmel is often defined as austere rather than penitential in the strict sense of the word, and its severest discipline is not of a physical nature, but of the will. Probably the most difficult, and usually the most trying manifestation of this is the constant change of occupation. One accustomed to any form of creative work, or large output, finds this so disconcerting at first that unless detachment can be substituted for a sense of frustration, she is unlikely to persevere in the life. Hardly has one warmed up to the occupation at hand and gotten into the swing of things than it is time to drop it and begin something quite different. There are never more than two hours of continuous work, and often not more than one. But this in itself is a part of the spirit one sets out to cultivate, and St. Teresa counsels us to "work with your body, for it is good for you to try to support yourselves; but let your souls be at rest." Tranquility and interior calm must be attained; work must be consistent but peaceful, without haste or fuss, which create an atmosphere of distress and tension, disturbing self-control and harmony, making it well-nigh impossible to attend to God.

To become a saint had always been Teresa Margaret's sole ambition, but her ideal was to be a hidden saint, effacing herself among others, passing unnoticed, remaining quietly in the background, working unobtrusively at her appointed task. Having no spectacular deeds with which to prove her love, she concentrated on the little, trivial details of daily life, doing them perfectly and with the utmost love, making of these "nothings" straws with which to feed the flame within.

10

Everything From God

Thoughts hardly to be packed
Into a narrow act,
Fancies that broke through
language and escaped;
All I could never be,
All men ignored in me,
This, I was worth to God,
whose wheel the pitcher shaped.

(Robert Browning)

It is a mistake to confuse humility with self-depreciation. True humility is capable of recognizing and acknowledging its own gifts of nature and grace. The person who is afraid of admitting that he possesses any

virtue or talent, who seeks lowly tasks merely because he believes that his humility might otherwise suffer, is actually pursuing self-abasement pure and simple. The more humble we are, the higher the honors we can attain to without detriment, because we know that of ourselves we are nothing and have nothing and give God the credit for any good that is in us, or that we may achieve.

Teresa Margaret's insistence that she was not fit to live in the company of her sisters was not mock-modesty, "the pride that apes humility," which has been well-termed the devil's favorite sin.

"I am living in a house of angels," she told her father on the day of her clothing; to the nuns she often spoke of her unworthiness to be with them, and she frequently mentioned her desire "to pass her life in the service of all those angels."

One of the most attractive features of Teresa Margaret's deep humility was its spontaneity. She was quite frank, simple, and open, genuinely considering herself full of faults, not only in comparison with the all holy God, but even when assessed in relation to her sisters. To her they appeared so many saints, and she the unworthy one, full of imperfections. Nor was there anything forced in her conviction of her own nothingness and poverty; it was a genuine conviction of her inability to do any good of herself. As she progressed in prayer, the infused light of contemplation made her ever more aware of the vast disproportion between God's sanctity and her own indigence, while her confidence never faltered, relying solely on Him to supply all that she lacked. "Of myself I have nothing, but in God is everything. I can do all things thanks to the strength God gives me." Thus her consciousness of her own nothingness and God's mercy engendered not discouragement, but an ever more generous effort to reconcile this antinomy. Her habitual attitude was one of adoration, which involves to some extent a comparison - our nothingness and helplessness with His plenitude and all-sufficiency. But always she made this comparison unselfconsciously. Rather than continually dwelling on her misery and worthlessness, she merely let all thought of self fall away before the infinite majesty of God; and truly the most profitable and genuine way of despising self is to forget oneself altogether.

"Why is it," she asked Father Ildefonse more than once, "that the Lord does not permit my sisters to see me as I am in His sight, a worthless creature? Perhaps because it would prove a source of scandal to them. Or perhaps it is because they themselves are so very good that they do not know how to think ill of others, even such a one as I."

There was no affectation about this attitude, and it partly explains her real determination to hide herself, lest her sisters, seeing her perform any external acts of mortification, should mistakenly attribute to her a virtue which she herself felt far from possessing. And this is the condition of one who sees himself as he stands before God. For it matters not how we appear - or hope we appear — in the eyes of others. We cannot even view ourselves impartially against the backdrop of people and events that fill our lives. As St. Teresa says: "We shall never succeed in knowing ourselves unless we seek to know God ... self-knowledge is incumbent upon the soul however high a state it may have attained."

"Father," she asked on another occasion, "if you do not fear to disedify the others, please make known my many defects, so that the sisters will know me as I really am ... I consider that they are all saints ... I tremble when I see how unlike them I am, for I am fit only to serve them in the lowliest tasks. Besides, if they knew me for what I am, their charity would move them to intercede for me with the good God."

Father Ildefonse was insistent about the absolute sincerity of these seemingly extravagant statements. "She spoke so naturally and was always so open that it is impossible to question her sincerity. I certainly could not doubt for a moment that this was her earnest conviction, for I knew her through and through down to the least aspiration of her soul."

On another occasion she said to Mother Anna Maria, who, next to Father Ildefonse probably understood Teresa Margaret's interior dispositions better than any other in the convent, "I fear I am a great trial of patience and virtue to those around me, as well as a constant source of bad example. I wonder how our Holy Mother can endure to have me among her daughters?"

Mother Anna Maria stated, "These words came from her heart, for she really believed what she said. She was convinced that all she did was only her duty, and she spoke so vehemently of her mediocrity that she never believed she had made any progress in virtue."

However, self-knowledge unlike self-love does not depress with the sight of one's imperfections. "I can do all things in Him who gives me strength," she repeated with St. Paul, refusing to be downcast. God could and would supply all she lacked, and Father Ildefonse testified: "The effect of self-knowledge did not discourage her, but rather forced her to throw herself on the goodness and mercy of God. She said to me once, 'From myself, nothing; from God, everything ... the smaller and weaker I am in myself, the richer and stronger I shall be in Him ... He shall be the more glorious in His mercy as I am more despicable in my sins and nothingness.'"

This testimony of Father Ildefonse refers to a later period. At the time of her clothing, Father John Colombino was directing her, and shortly after she received the habit, Teresa Margaret wrote to him of her difficulties, explaining some of the scruples she had begun to feel about the genuineness of her vocation, which he dismissed. Despite her almost perpetual sense of misery and unworthiness, Teresa Margaret was not a scrupulous person. Her humility was too deep for the doubts and self-torture which constitute the basis of this spiritual malaise, and her confidence in God's loving mercy was all-embracing. The fantastic scruples which were to prove such an agony during the last eighteen months of her life do not belong to her "natural" equipment, but rather to the supernatural action of God's purifications. However, it was probably to dispel her fears on this score that she sought and obtained from her confessor permission to anticipate her profession by making private vows of obedience, chastity, and poverty, which she pronounced temporarily on the 7th of April, one month after her clothing.

A year would elapse before her religious profession, the public and official consecration of herself to God by perpetual vows.[1] And now she set to work in good earnest, correcting the many faults she saw in herself, determined to spend the interim preparing a spiritual dowry worthy of the bridegroom who was deigning to accept her. Sister Teresa Mary, one of her fellow-novices, gave testimony about her companion at this period, saying that she noticed in particular the efforts Teresa Margaret made to control her speech and movements, avoiding any precipitate action and endeavoring to practice exact obedience to the will of her superiors. Nor did she ever manifest the least evidence of aversion to any of

---

[1] Today neither solemn nor simple perpetual vows may be taken until after a period of at least three years with simple temporary vows.

the tasks she was assigned, or show resentment at the sometimes unwarranted rebukes given in public.

During these months while the girl strove for self-mastery over her naturally volatile temperament, curbing her instinctively quick movements by forcing herself to stop and reflect before she spoke or acted, she wrote a letter to Canon Tonci, in which the cost of this discipline is evident: "You may be sure that I have found far less difficulty in dealing with external matters. Everything can be reduced to interior movements, where the constant exercise of abnegation is essential. But it is impossible without complete liberty of spirits, and this I still do not possess. However, I trust in God's mercy to gain control in so small a matter, for He has already given me much strength and courage in greater things."

The deepest testimony of one's humility has been claimed to be the manner in which humiliations are accepted and borne. "I *welcome* humiliations," Teresa Margaret declared, seeing in them an opportunity of resembling the Sacred Heart, the victim of love whose image she desired to become.

In the externals of the practice of poverty, Teresa Margaret was perfection itself. The oldest, the shabbiest, the least convenient were her choice and ambition, and nothing made her happier than to be allowed to exchange some useful article for one that was faulty or troublesome to use. But it was in her universal detachment and poverty of spirit that she proved that these externals were expressions of the interior virtue and not merely outward conformity to custom or observance.

Once when questioned by Mother Anna Maria on her practice of poverty and detachment, Teresa Margaret framed the following counsel: "Always receive with equal contentment from God's hand either consolations or sufferings, peace or distress, health or illness. Ask nothing, refuse nothing, but always be ready to do and to suffer anything that comes from His Providence."

"To ask nothing, to seek nothing but the will of God, accepting all things from His hand with equal gratitude and love." Gratitude is the virtue proper to those who are genuinely humble and poor in spirit, and Teresa Margaret possessed a grateful heart.

Sister Teresa Margaret was being well-exercised in the virtues she was so anxious to attain, and the fault-finding of Mother Teresa Maria, the elderly novice mistress, continued unabated. No peccadillo, however trifling, was allowed to pass unchecked. A slight delay in going to her work or the least slowness or inefficiency in performing it, a quick or unguarded movement or gesture, an unsought opinion tendered at recreation, any appearance of abstraction or preoccupation during a community act - all were immediately pounced upon. But although such small involuntary failings were in no way proportionate to the severity of the reprimand, the novice never appeared disconcerted, but promptly prostrated herself in the customary manner, kissing the ground for her fault, and quite gratuitously thanking the novice mistress for her charitable correction. Even Mother Teresa Maria, who seemed determined to test her patience and self-control to its furthest stretch, on one occasion told the other novices that they would do well to study their companion and model themselves on her example. "I am aware of the particular merits of each one of you," she said, "but I am grateful to God for permitting me to know Sister Teresa Margaret, because with her rare innocence she inspires in me the deepest admiration."

Certainly the novice mistress chose a most extraordinary method of demonstrating this admiration, and one could reasonably expect a little less zeal in providing occasions for the exercise of the virtue that inspired it. However often the scene was repeated, Teresa Margaret showed no discomposure, apart from the violent blush which she was unable to control. One day during recreation the novice mistress expressed a wish that Teresa Margaret should help with the sewing of some sacristy linen.

"Go and watch Mother Anna Maria. Look carefully at the way she pleats it, and see if you can learn how to do the same."

The order was promptly executed. Teresa Margaret rose and

went over to the assistant mistress, kneeling down beside her so as to observe better how she was handling the material. She was quick, and in a few minutes had taken it in. With the spontaneity which was so characteristic of her, she clapped her hands together, exclaiming, "Let me have it. I know now how to do it."

"*Sister Teresa Margaret!*" thundered her nemesis from the other end of the room. "I really expected more humility from you. Remain where you are, and try to learn a little virtue as well as the work you are given to do!"

The novice immediately kissed the ground and the scolding continued. Finally, being given permission to rise, she went over to the mistress, and in her usual, unruffled manner, thanked her.

Mother Anna Maria in the meantime felt not only intensely sorry for her charge but acutely embarrassed. However, she said nothing, and as Sister Teresa Margaret continued to work and join in the general conversation as though nothing untoward had happened, she relaxed. The bell rang, signaling the end of recreation, and as they rose to disperse, Teresa Margaret whispered, "Pray for me that I may overcome my pride and learn more humility."

Testifying in the beatification process, Mother Anna Maria recalled this incident, saying, "It does not appear to me that Sister Teresa Margaret was ever proud in any way."

Fortunately, Mother Teresa Maria was old and rather infirm, so it is probable that she did not always preside at recreation, for were it conducted regularly on these lines, it would have produced anything but the effect for which it is legislated. With each of the novices under a sword of Damocles, dreading some involuntary gesture or unguarded word that would bring it crashing down on their heads, there would have been little relaxation or diversion about it.

Sister Teresa Margaret bore this seemingly unjust bias in her direction without developing anything in the nature of a persecution complex, but the other novices felt that she was unfairly treated, and they also considered that she bore it with considerable virtue. It was probably one of them, or Mother Anna Maria, who mentioned the matter to the Provincial, Father John Colombino - possibly during a visitation - for Father Ildefonse stated that the Provincial often tried to persuade Mother Teresa Maria to modify her severity towards Teresa Margaret. But her invariable reply was that, were she not convinced of the solid virtue of the novice, or the heights to which she was capable of being led - one is tempted to substitute "driven"! - she would never try her in this way. She insisted that daily experience only strengthened her in this conviction, since Teresa Margaret never sulked, but grew in detachment and liberty of spirit. Seemingly, the novice mistress had the fixed idea that it was her duty to force her charges to the exercise of virtue at the point of a sword.

Those who have experienced this form of "testing" by being singled out for particular attention by an unsympathetic superior all too often meet the situation by merely gritting their teeth and enduring it "for the duration." After all, novitiates do not last very long, and one will eventually be free of the tyranny. But, says St. John of the Cross, those who are going on to perfection proceed very differently and with quite another temper of spirit. Teresa Margaret made a revealing little comment, which showed simultaneously what this constant fault-finding cost her, as well as the extraordinary maturity of her outlook on such matters: "She who does not know how to conform her will to that of others will never be perfect. Our model is Jesus, whose meat was to do the will of His Father, who was submissive to death, even the death of the cross. And I have resolved to resemble Him in all things."

During this year of novitiate, one incident occurred which was treated of in great detail during the process of beatification, and which all who testified were unanimous in attributing to supernatural causes.

Sister Teresa Margaret was server in the refectory at the time, and because of her duties had not eaten her meal with the others, but remained behind to do so after they had departed. A fellow novice, Sister Mary Victoria of the Trinity, was also still eating -

or attempting to do so, for she suffered so acutely from toothache that it took her much longer than the rest of the community to get through her meals. Whatever the nature of her ailment, she had been afflicted with it since the age of eleven, and possibly her teeth were ground down, and the nerves exposed, in which case eating certain kinds of food, such as hot dishes or acid fruits, would be an agonizing process.

Today Sister Teresa Margaret, who had the reputation of never being known to raise her eyes in the refectory, was quietly eating her dinner, when she suddenly became aware that Sister Mary Victoria, sitting near her, was weeping silently. The girl was in such distress that Teresa Margaret broke her habitual rule of "eyes down," and, rising from her place said soothingly: "My poor little Sister, you are in such great pain that you are unable to eat!" Then, before the astonished sister realized what she was about, she kissed her hard on the cheek. Instinctively, Sister Mary Victoria's hand flew to her face, and she gave a slight moan, for the sudden contact had been like a blow to the hypersensitive jaw. But suddenly, all pain vanished. Sister Mary Victoria held her breath, waiting for it to flood back in an excruciating wave. But nothing happened. Minutes passed, and the two novices stared at each other in stunned silence.

Sister Mary Victoria immediately left the refectory and ran in search of Mother Anna Maria, her companion hard on her heels.

"I am cured!" she cried, and her face, usually drawn with pain, was radiant. Mother Anna Maria looked from one novice to the other.

"Have you two been speaking in the refectory?" she demanded, for this was an infringement of regulations she would never have suspected of Teresa Margaret, usually so meticulous about the least prescription.

She scolded the two miscreants rather half-heartedly, but Sister Mary Victoria really had been cured of her affliction. Never again in her life did she suffer from toothache, although she occasionally experienced a slight numbness, but without pain.

Actually Teresa Margaret had on this occasion been guilty

of two small breaches: speaking without permission and kissing the sister. But the overmastering charity which had prompted her action was apparently the decisive factor in the incident, and the major question it leaves in the mind is how this event can be reconciled with Teresa Margaret's genuine desire for complete hiddenness. She who had sought to conceal anything that might appear virtuous in the eyes of others had deliberately behaved in a way that produced results considered to be not merely admirable but miraculous.

It is unlikely that she had intended anything more than comfort and sympathy by her embrace; certainly she did not anticipate that by kissing the sister she would cure her. Probably she managed to avoid all mention of it, or dissociated herself entirely from the effect of her action. At any rate, she did not discuss it with Mother Anna Maria. She merely kissed the ground, asked pardon for her lapse, and offered no excuse of extenuating circumstances.

Not to excuse oneself when accused was a practice St. Teresa constantly extolled as a means to perfection, and her instructions still stand: "Let the nuns take great care not to excuse themselves for their faults except when absolutely necessary. By acting in this way, they will make great progress in humility."

It was in this spirit that Teresa Margaret accepted all the seemingly unjust and unnecessary rebukes of her novitiate days, without even pausing to question whether she was guilty of the fault imputed to her or not. Had she failed to sweep the corridor thoroughly? Was she lacking in humility because she considered she had so quickly mastered a piece of quite simple needlework? It mattered little. She was more than capable of it and had often been guilty of more serious faults. Even when some of the charges against her were the result of others' negligence, and she was aware of the identity of the real culprit, she never protested, but humbly asked pardon for whatever she was accused of doing or failing to do. Was she not in good company? Was anyone ever more faultless than Jesus, who before His judges stood silent and spoke no word in His own justification? "It requires great humility to see oneself condemned, although faultless, and remain silent," says St. Teresa; and these small irritations which can be stumbling-blocks for those who regard them with resentment were to St. Teresa Margaret the sandpaper with which the rough edges of her imperfections were being rubbed smooth. It was not in the spirit of a victimized martyr that she smiled cheerfully through the dis-agreeable process, but with the attitude of David who, when Abisai would kill Semei for cursing him, replied, "Let him curse as he will; the Lord has bidden him to do so, and who shall call him to question for it?"

However, despite all this, Mother Teresa Maria's idea of novi-tiate training left much to be desired. Her treatment of Teresa Marga-ret was not the expression of antipathy or dislike. She has recorded her deep and sincere admiration for the novice and her conviction of the virtues and potentialities possessed by the girl. It was her interpre-tation of her duty, the method she deliberately adopted in training the exceptionally-gifted soul she recognized her charge to be. One might question the wisdom of the method, but not the intention that prompted it. "I would not try another in this way," she said. She was quite aware, apparently, that her rebukes were mostly undeserved, but seemingly she failed to realize how flagrantly she herself was overstepping the limits of authority and offending against justice.

11

The Art of Never Doing Her Own Will

O thou, at whose august decree,
Once heard, creation bends the knee,
While heaven and earth obey thy will,
Trembling before thee, and are still.
(Creator alme siderum)

"Obedience," said St. Gregory the Great, "is rightly placed before all other sacrifices, for in offering a victim as sacrifice, one offers a life that is not one's own; but when one obeys one is immolating one's own will."

By profession of religious vows, one makes a total dedication of self, the most complete sacrifice that a human being can make to God. It might involve great renunciations or intense suffering - or neither. These are fundamental and important aspects of the individual spiritual life, but not an essential element of the holocaust. The essence of this sacrifice is the vow of obedience by which one offers the gift of his own will - the very core of self - and it is also the reef on which many so-called "lost vocations" have run aground. This is the most perfect external act of religion, but it is without effect in religious life unless it is the expression of the internal reality it professes. One may leave home, family, friends, renounce social position and material possessions, detach oneself from every created thing, but unless he dispossesses himself of his own will, the sacrifice is worthless.

From childhood, Teresa Margaret had been obedient and docile, following the commands and wishes of her parents unquestioningly as do all good children, well-trained in their filial obligations. But even later, when she was to a certain extent emancipated from rigid parental control, and especially during the period she lived at home after leaving school, she developed what one biographer described as "the art of never doing her own will." Even in small things which, strictly speaking, did not come within the ambit of parental jurisdiction, she allowed others to choose for her, as a training for the sterner submission to which she must bend her will as a nun. She was well-aware that for a religious, her superior stood in the place of God, that "he who heareth you heareth Me." All rules, orders, prescriptions could be accepted literally as His personal commissions, and it seems to have been in this spirit that she even welcomed the arbitrary commands of Mother Teresa Maria. Whether the direction was unreasonable or merely petty and irritating, she fulfilled it to the best of her ability, and in some cases when two conflicting orders were issued, she carried them both out as far as possible. Sometimes she was given work to do, and half way through told to stop, undo it, and begin all over again. If she failed to defend herself when wrongly accused, she was charged with pride and sulkiness. The fact that there was any inner conflict was only apparent by the sudden flush she was never able to master, and which was always followed by extreme pallor. But she quickly recovered her equilibrium, and her normal healthy color returned, while her expression remained agreeable and her manner unruffled. She managed to smile her way through all misunderstandings and contradictions, accepting them as God's will, even if at times it must have been difficult to reconcile such senseless orders with omnipotent Wisdom! Mother Anna Maria alone knew the struggle the consistent self-control cost her.

But there is no point in trying to develop a drama out of these episodes. There never was any conflict in the sense of a clash of personalities or wills. Teresa Margaret was too intelligent not to realize that what she was being asked to do was an outrage to commonsense, but she did not find that too great a sacrifice, considering who was asking it and why. And if many of us today are unable to accept this, it is possibly because our whole conception of obedience to parents and legitimate authority has been seriously undermined. If one has little experience in obeying just and reasonable commands, one will hardly submit - or understand how another could do so - to the obviously unjust and unreasonable.

One day Sister Teresa Margaret approached Father Ildefonse after confession.

"Father, may I have your permission to write in my own blood a little resolution to Jesus?"

The priest, who knew Teresa Margaret well, sensed some special motive behind this request, and he granted the permission on condition that she draw blood only from her hand or arm, and not in any quantity - actually he stipulated that "no more than two or three lines" were to be written.

Teresa Margaret left and did not ever mention the matter again. Only after her death was found the little card bearing some words in dark, rusty-looking writing, brittle now and snapping from the paper when it was bent. The nuns showed it to Father Ildefonse, who recalled the permission asked years previously, and the condition he had laid down. There were exactly three short lines: "My Jesus, I am determined to be all yours, whatever the cost, and despite every repugnance."

St. Teresa Margaret was no clinging little piece of thistledown with neither the mind nor will to order her own life. She had a strong character and a warm, ardent nature, and she seemed to sense that the conflict between her own rebellious temperament and her desire for sanctity would be resolved by the perfection of her submission - Saints are made, not born, and it is at the cost of much struggle that they learn to conform themselves to the divine will, to which they gradually offer less and less resistance, until by submitting themselves utterly to God's purifying actions, they emerge as we see them, triumphant over nature, true masterpieces of grace. What people often fail to realize is that this humble, amenable girl was not merely agreeable and submissive because it came easy to her to be so. She had acquired her gentleness and kindness by constant vigilance over the instinctive reactions of a hot temper, and repeated self-control that eventually became habitual. Her courage was sustained more by the strength of her love than by her natural strength of mind, and it was in the Heart of Christ, the strongest and tenderest of all human loves, that she sought refuge, desiring to belong solely to Him at whatever cost to nature.

On another occasion Father Ildefonse questioned her about her method of remaining in the presence of God while absorbed in external tasks. She replied, "If we work here through obedience to God's commands, it is impossible that He should destroy His own work in the soul."

"Yes, that is true," agreed the priest. "Nevertheless most people find the degree of attention necessary for the work at least divides the mind, and usually hinders recollection."

"If we live and move in God," Teresa Margaret declared, "I do not think His company or love will desert us when we perform necessary external tasks, let alone constitute any obstacle to them."

"No, it certainly will not do that. Still, it is so easy to believe that we are working for God when in fact we are working for our own satisfaction in many subtle ways."

"Oh, Father, if I relied upon myself I would most assuredly be deceived. But when I place everything in Love, Love will never abandon me. So I in my turn abandon myself to the love of Jesus Christ, with love for love, because His loving Heart desires to rule and reign in me, and of myself I would not know how to behave unless I placed no obstacle to His acting in me."

"And how can you be certain of that?" he pressed.

"It is sufficient to shut out external matters and material concerns, so that the soul and the heart may go straight to their center, which is God; and He who is the principle of every action in us, helps us to act promptly and well, for here in the convent God Himself commands, through the Rule and our superiors. If I obey promptly and observe every prescription, I can be certain at each minute of the day that I am doing His will. And for this reason I have resolved never to ask for any dispensation except in obedience to your wishes or those of our Mother Mistress."

Father Ildefonse spoke on many occasions with Teresa Margaret, and later he testified: "One thing that always caused me to marvel was her readiness to accommodate and conform her will and judgment to mine ... I think it would have grieved her deeply had she ever thought that I had granted her any request, or refused it to her, merely out of consideration for her wishes or inclinations, and not because of my own judgment."

One morning when Sister Teresa Margaret went to the cell of her Assistant Mistress, Mother Anna Maria was busy writing. While waiting for her to finish, the novice walked about inspecting the contents of the room with a freedom that was unlike her usually reserved and rather shy manner. She appeared to be looking for something.

"Mother, may I *steal* this?" she asked suddenly.

"Yes," replied the other without looking up, thinking Teresa Margaret had probably taken a book. When she finished the letter she turned, and saw that the novice was holding a small iron chain.

"What do you want with that?"

"Please, Mother, may I borrow it?"

"Why?"

"I can make good use of it," replied Teresa Margaret evasively, but with a mischievous smile.

"No, certainly not," said Mother Anna Maria, still unaware of her charge's ability to wheedle a desired permission from reluctant authority. Teresa Margaret began to turn the full battery of her charm and persuasiveness on Mother Anna Maria, half-playful, half-teasing, until finally she capitulated and said that Teresa Margaret might borrow the chain.

Three days later she realized that the "loan" had not been restored, and felt some misgivings about the imprudence of the permission that had been cajoled out of her. Not wishing to expose herself to the risk of another defeat, she wrote a note to the novice, ordering her in unequivocal terms to return the instrument of penance at once. Teresa Margaret was not slow to discern the difference between a half-hearted refusal and a command. When

Mother Anna Maria returned to her cell after recreation, the chain was lying on her desk. And, child of her age though she was, and devoted to penitential practices, Teresa Margaret did not take the initiative in such matters again, but followed the counsel of her superiors and directors. She had not gone very far in religious life before she learned the primacy of obedience and the worthlessness of mortifications undertaken in a spirit of self-will.

"To suffer and be silent," and accept uncomplainingly the unsought crosses of daily life was, she found, the surest and safest method of mortifying not merely the body, but also the will. "Be careful never to waste an occasion for mortification by complaining about it or letting others see it," she once said. These words summed up her program of asceticism. In community life there are countless opportunities for practicing this form of self-discipline. Acceptance of the common lot in regard to sleep and food, silence and noise, and the small inconveniences which are unavoidable in the closed society of the cloister, all provide fuel with which to feed the fire of love. Considered separately, each is but a minute opportunity for practicing self-control and consideration for others; however when faithfully and consistently adhered to, they constitute a rigorous program of real abnegation. "Never permit an occasion for suffering to escape, especially if it is a greater suffering, and always suffer in silence, keeping the secret between God and the soul," was how Teresa Margaret defined this game of spiritual hide-and-seek. She refused to wage war on flies or insects, accepting their unwelcome ubiquity as God's harmless creatures, even when they crawled over face and hands. Never did she claim any alleviation from the weather either in winter or summer, or seek permission to drink between meals in the most torrid heat; and when in winter her hands were covered with painful chilblains which broke and bled, she merely wrapped them in a piece of rough serge without bothering to ask for a linen cloth. On one occasion she even ran melted tallow from her candle into the cracked and broken skin so that the other sisters would not notice the condition of her hands or sympathize with her. There are a hundred little items of this kind to be found in her day, as well as those which she deliberately added: praying with her arms outstretched in the form of a cross, putting pebbles in her sandals, leaving her window open in the winter, or the door closed in the summer. On many occasions it was necessary to put a check on some of her activities, as for instance when she began sleeping on the bare boards of the floor. When Father Ildefonse heard of this, he forbade it as imprudent. Always the desire to "do more for Jesus" drove her on, and even when she managed to cajole permissions for additional penances from her superiors, she always felt that she was not doing enough. Gradually, however, she began to shift the emphasis, seeing the value of obedience over penance, and was content to offer her desire to afflict her body, while submitting to the judgment of others, together with the resolution never to avoid or voluntarily refuse any pain or inconvenience of daily life, realizing the greater merit of cheerful acceptance of such God-sent sufferings than in those self-chosen and self-inflicted.

Yet despite the lack of enthusiasm most of us feel about emulating such a program, there was nothing morbid in Teresa Margaret's determination to make herself as uncomfortable as possible. Always such things were accomplished with a childlike candor and simplicity. Her interior mortification was ceaseless, and her struggles to be regular in community and at choir offices often called for real heroism. She was undoubtedly overworked, and had less food and sleep than her still-growing body required; still, as she never complained - but rather volunteered for other duties that were not her responsibility - nobody realized what a strain this was, or the toll it must have taken. She was young and strong and active, but more and more she found herself struggling to remain awake during the night office of Matins and Lauds. This perpetual drowsiness distressed her, for she feared it was merely a weakness against which she should fight, and also that she was offending God by her inattention and lack of recollection during the official prayer of the Church.

She confided this difficulty to Father Ildefonse, and asked his permission to wear clips on her ears. Nobody would notice them under the cover of her coif, she said, but they would help her to break the habit of falling asleep in choir. It seemed a simple request, far less rigorous than some of those she had made, so he agreed.

It was not until after Teresa Margaret's death that the priest was shown the clips, which appear to have been fashioned rather like the modern earring; and most of us know the discomfort it can cause if the clip is too tight. Father Ildefonse described them as "strong, very delicately indented with a sharp pinch, which were capable of splitting the skin after a short time and causing one to faint from severe pain." Then, he added significantly, "I finally understood!" That such a drastic remedy was necessary indicates something of her heroic struggle to be regular in the performance of all her duties, and also her great need of sleep - so much so that a constant irritant was necessary to keep her awake. But on the other hand, about two years before her death, when she found that she could manage not to fall asleep without the continual prodding of these silent vigilantes, she discontinued using them. Despite the litany of "practices" which sound so alien to modern ears, there was a true equilibrium between interior and exterior mortification in her life, and she knew well that the latter is of value only insofar and in proportion as it expresses and issues from the former. The spirit quickens, while the letter kills. In no sphere is this so true as in that of corporal penance.

Implementing an idea found in the writings of St. Teresa of Avila, in moments of weariness or discouragement, when trials or fatigue seemed to weigh her down, she would picture Jesus beside her, falling beneath the weight of the cross, forsaken by all, pushed to the limits of human endurance, and appealing to her for support. "Jesus did not act thus for me," she would reproach herself; and so vividly did she bring home the lesson that it was always effective, enabling her to muster up reinforcements of courage and determination to go on, never declaring, "I can do no more!" while she had strength left to stand.

Always, she would conjure up that picture of the suffering Savior, reminding herself that she had not as yet suffered to the shedding of her blood, or that if Christ had turned back at the first obstacle, she would not have at her disposal His priceless treasury of grace. And in the "now" of eternity in which the Passion is extended over all time, she remained beside Him to offer the comfort of her love and to unite her small sufferings to His infinite sorrow, and thus share in the infinite value of His redemptive sacrifice.

"To suffer and be silent for Jesus" - the maxim of St. Margaret Mary which she took to herself and made her own, giving it new orientation and impetus, is truly one of the dominant themes of her holiness. "Remember what you promised when you entered religion," she wrote on a card which was found after her death. "To express in yourself the life of the Crucified." Many other maxims and counsels in her handwriting are preserved at the Florence Carmel: "I desire to have no consolation from God in this life, but only in the next. I delight in not tasting, because a fast in this life will prepare me for the banquet of heaven." Again: "Dispose of me according to your will, I am content in everything, for that is the way of Calvary, and the thornier I find it and the heavier the cross seems, the more certain I shall be that I am following in your footsteps ... Every suffering is insignificant when we consider that it is a means of acquiring the true and pure love of God. To attain to our God no toil should appear hard. We must never turn back when difficulties are encountered, but embrace all bitterness and every kind of hardship."

Teresa Margaret's life and spirituality bore many and striking resemblances to that of her better-known Carmelite sister, St. Thérèse of Lisieux. There was the same simplicity and childlike confidence, the same love of Jesus and Mary, a similar absence of incident, either natural or supernatural, a heroic fidelity in little things against the drab background of routine convent life, and finally the same desolation and anguish in a spiritual dark night devoid of all consolation.

But there is one significant and important difference. St. Thérèse attracts many of us in this age because of her attitude towards penitential practices. Quite simply, Thérèse decided early in her religious life that these things were not part of her "little way" to God, and candidly and humbly she abandoned them, seeking mortification and renunciation in those trials of daily life that nature and the members of one's community provide so plentifully - the heat, the cold, the lack of sleep, the fidgety neighbor, the unsympathetic companion, the food that disagrees, and all the

12

Christmas In Carmel

*"Lord you have bewitched me with the spell
of desire for you. You have enchanted me with
divine love. Consume my sins in a spiritual
flame and make me worthy to be filled with
your sweetness, that I may glorify you, good
Lord, in both your comings."*
(St. John Chrysostom)

All the novices were now wearing the habit. How different this Christmas would be, thought Sister Teresa Margaret, recalling the confused memories of last year when, still convalescent from the operation on her knee, she had been on the verge of returning to the world, anxious lest the community should not consider her suitable and refuse to re-admit her. The year of her novitiate was fast running out, and early in the new year she must once more present herself before the community, to request their consent to her profession.

One's first Christmas in religious life is something that is never quite forgotten, a memory that constant repetition over the years cannot obliterate or dim. Often it is anticipated with something like trepidation. As it approaches, the novice wonders will the remembrance of other feasts, of the relatives and friends she has left behind, make

147

this essentially intimate family festivity seem austere and barren by comparison with the freedom and gaiety of other years. How can the atmosphere of lighthearted enjoyment be recaptured in this new and seemingly restrictive environment? Will those occasional waves of homesickness gather all their forces and become a tidal wave of nostalgia, pushing everything before it?

"In the sixth age of the world, when the whole world was at peace, Jesus Christ, Eternal God and Son of the Eternal Father, being pleased to hallow the world by His most gracious coming, having been conceived of the Holy Ghost, and nine months having passed since His conception, having become man, was born at Bethlehem in Judah of the Virgin Mary ..."

At the office of Prime on the morning of Christmas Eve, as she knelt with the community in choir, her face bowed to the ground in humble adoration at the solemn announcement of the Nativity chanted by the reader of the martyrology, Teresa Margaret knew with certainty that for the first time she was really "at home." that it was in the bosom of her own family, of which she was now a member for time and eternity, that she would this year celebrate the anniversary of Christ's birth.

Among the messages received by Teresa Margaret that Christmas of 1765, the one that gave her the most pleasure was a letter dated the 30th of November from Francis Xavier - her beloved Cecchino - still at the Cicognini College, telling her of Cecilia's decision to remain at St. Apollonia's and take the Benedictine habit as a member of the community. "Thank our Lord who has also chosen her for His spouse, and beg Him too to guide me about my own vocation, for I still await an answer to my question: Lord what wilt thou have me to do?"

She herself sent a short note to Cecilia, enclosed with a letter to one of her former teachers of St. Apollonia's, asking her prayers "that I may fulfill in every way all that God asks of me. This is my only desire ... I am very well, and through His mercy continue in excellent health and spirits."

During the day she busied herself with her companions erecting a crib in the novitiate, decking it with yew and fir, holly and ivy, and finally, with loving hands, she placed the little wax figure of the *bambino* in the nest of straw prepared for him.

"It's too soon," cried Sister Mary Victoria in protest. "He's not born till tonight."

Teresa Margaret looked up, her forehead wrinkled in perplexity. "But we'll be in choir at midnight."

"Just the same, you can't put Him in before," agreed Sister Teresa of Jesus Crucified.

"I know!" suddenly Teresa Margaret clapped her hands delightedly, and ran over to the cupboard where the linen was kept. The other novices watched, as she returned with a fine, lace-edged sacristy veil, which she draped carefully and tenderly over the sleeping figure in the crib. "There! After Lauds when we come to sing our carols of welcome, the first one in can light the candles, and our Mistress will unveil the new-born Savior."

The evening was dark and quiet. The stars glittered coldly in a frosty sky. On this night there was no Great Silence, but since most of the older nuns required a little rest in preparation for the unaccustomed and strenuous midnight services, Mother Teresa Maria had given the novices a short but stirring exhortation on charity. Consideration for the needs of others, she pointed out, must never be lost sight of, particularly in moments of festivity or high spirits and they were left with a strict injunction that there was to be no talking or singing outside the confines of the novitiate, where they could enjoy themselves without disturbing those who were in their cells.

The novices chattered happily and excitedly, for although by nature Teresa Margaret was serious and inclined, when alone, to relapse into meditative recollection, she was nevertheless gay and could at times be a very lively companion. At recreation she always put herself out especially to entertain others, making impromptu rhymes and verses, joking and making them laugh at her mimicry, so that as she once admitted, "the sisters continually take delight in making fun of me, and they declare that I am a regular trickster."

However, tonight she felt an overwhelming desire for solitude. After a little time she excused herself, slipped quietly away from her companions, and stole noiselessly along the corridors, brightly-lighted for once, and decked with gay wreaths of holly and graceful trails of ivy. Entering the silent choir she saw that nobody else was there, and went right up to the open grating, kneeling in her favorite corner, where, withdrawn into the shadows, she could watch the tabernacle without being observed by anyone in the chapel outside. But at this hour it was deserted. The still peacefulness of this "silent, holy night" wrapped around her like a cloak, and she opened heart and soul to the joyous expectation of the coming commemoration, as she tried, by her love and gratitude, to prepare within herself a soft cradle into which she would soon welcome her God, become man in poverty and discomfort for love of her. She knelt on, not noticing the cold, lost in prayer and oblivious of other figures who stole in and out from time to time.

It was almost 10:30 when the sudden chimes of the cloister bell brought her back to her surroundings with a start. Rising hastily she left the choir, making her way through the ranks of the sisters, most of whom were already assembled in the ante-choir, wearing their mantles, waiting for the summons to move in procession to the choir for Matins. Quickly Teresa Margaret donned her white cloak and took her place with the other novices at the head of the procession as the bell began to peal once more, and Mother Mary Magdalene gave the signal for them to enter the choir, now ablaze with light.

Christ is born for us; come let us adore Him. The announcement was made, and the voices, high and unhurried, took up the antiphon and the slow, even rhythm of the psalms. As Matins progressed, despite the heavy curtains drawn across the grille, soft regular shufflings and scrapings from the chapel on the other side indicated that it was gradually filling with worshippers for Midnight Mass. Finally the last jubilant note of the *Te Deum* faded away - "In thee, O Lord, I have hoped; let me not be confounded for ever" - merging with the mellow tones of the great bell pealing out for the beginning of the Holy Sacrifice. The priest approached the altar, and the choir intoned the words of the Introit: *Domi-*

nus dixit ad me: filius meus es tu, and kneeling around the grille at right angles to the altar, the prayer of all was, in spirit if not in actual words, that of St. Ambrose: "Let us guard with vigilant care, Jesus Christ in the crib of our hearts, that He only may rest there and sleep."

The last words of the final antiphon and prayer had hardly died away when the choir was astir. Mantles were quickly laid aside and all approached the Crib, gathering around the prioress before the figure of the *bambino,* now peacefully sleeping in His nest of hay where, unnoticed, He had been gently placed at the end of Mass. Once more the house resounded with words of love and welcome, this time in the mother tongue, as all sang greetings to the newborn Prince of Peace.

Come, come to the manger,
Children, come to the children's king,
Sing, sing, chorus of angels,
Stars of morning o'er Bethlehem sing.

And it seemed to Teresa Margaret, almost carried away by the floods of sweetness and devotion that had swirled around her through the inspired words of the Nativity office, that the very stars twinkled as they took up the refrain. "They were called and they said: Here we are. And with cheerfulness they have shined forth to Him that made them." (Baruch 3:35)

As soon as they could gracefully do so, the novices dragged Mother Anna Maria off to see their crib. Mother Teresa Maria had left after Mass and retired already, so Teresa Margaret called the Assistant Mistress to preside at the unveiling ceremony. Sister Mary Victoria darted ahead, and when they entered, the room was dark but for the pinpoints of candlelight flickering about the Crib. As she removed the veil, the novices once more broke into a carol.

"There," said Mother Anna Maria after she had admired their handiwork, "see that those candles are all safely out and then off you all go to the refectory and have a hot drink. Then into bed as quickly as possible."

But nobody wanted to bring to a close this enchanted night which comes only once in the year. Finally, however, prudence prevailed, and reluctantly all left the crib, dispersing to cells, while the winking lights and the faithful, immobile shepherds remained to keep watch over the Babe and His mother.

The Feast of the Holy Innocents is especially dedicated to the novitiate. The senior novice replaces the Mistress, and for the day fulfills her duties, giving her companions an exhortation, proposing various little pious "games" and striving to re-kindle in them fresh zeal and ardor for perfection. Sister Teresa Margaret was the novice on whom this office fell, probably because Sister Teresa of Jesus Crucified, who was the senior novice, had refused the somewhat dubious honor.

On this day the novices take over many of the house offices, and in choir one officiates as subprioress, often with disastrous results. Another is supposed to deliver a conference to the community, but this privilege is usually declined with great firmness.

Not, however, by Teresa Margaret. It really distressed her that on such a glorious feast the sisters should have no preacher to address them with words that would inflame their fervor and gratitude to God for the gift of His incarnate love. She decided she would avail herself of the Holy Innocents' privilege, and speak to her sisters of the love and humility of God. With none of the anticipated self-consciousness or nervous giggles, she stood beside the Crib, her face aglow with her own love and joy, and spoke simply and unaffectedly, with an intensity of fervor, and expressions of such lofty sentiments, that the older nuns - prepared as they were to be entertained rather than instructed - wondered at the astonishing self-possession and piety of the eighteen-year-old novice. She merely drew a word picture of the tableau before their eyes: the young mother and the divine child, the protecting Joseph, the angels and the shepherds, Mary's arms that first fondled the eternal Son of God, dressed Him lovingly and laid Him gently in His poor cradle. How mean the exterior, how glorious within! A stable or a cave - what did it matter, when the God-Man received the love and adoration of the only two hearts on earth worthy or capable of offering it? He would have been in poorer circumstances far, by comparison, had He been surrounded by obsequious attendants, lacking nothing of warmth or comfort, amid the luxury and lovelessness of a palace, and for homage receiving flattery of a temporal court.

"Jesus was born in a stable in poverty and discomfort. During His public life He had not where to rest His head. That is what He asks of all who would be His true spouses, whose lives must be a sacrifice of love. 'If thou wilt be perfect, go, sell what thou hast and give to the poor, and thou shalt have treasure in heaven; and come, follow Me.' Follow Me from the poverty and humility of Bethlehem, through the obscurity and labor of Nazareth, to the complete oblation of Calvary. Sacrifice yourself, as I did, on the altar of my Father's will.

Thy sacrifice, O love divine,
Is all for me."

"What a spectacle of poverty!" she concluded. "What an example of sacrifice and detachment has not this great God given us!"

The sisters were amazed, more by the complete unselfconsciousness with which the homily was delivered than by the content of it. Later she confessed that she had obtained her sermon from her brother Francis, "paying" for it by illuminating some texts for him. But the words were so much her own that, even if she used Cecchino's ideas, she certainly clothed them in her own language and metaphors. Evermore she sought to conform herself to this "spectacle of poverty and detachment," seeing that no sacrifice of hers could ever approximate the self-emptying of God in taking upon Himself our human nature.

"How could we ever sufficiently humble ourselves," she exclaimed once, "before a God so humbled? How can we even speak of humiliations when we compare our lot with the humiliations endured by our Lord who is God?"

It was this supreme example of obedience, regularity, and meekness that she sought always to imitate, seeing the trials of life as little in return for what Jesus had suffered for her. When on occasion weariness or distaste seemed to be more than she could master, she would force herself to look again at the Crib, reminding herself of what our Lord had done for her, thus exploiting trials or difficulties as levers for "spiritual elevation." Instead of becoming preoccupied with herself and her own troubles, she would immediately raise her heart to God, offering "this millionth of Thy gift" and asking that He accept it for souls and for the Church.

Such a reorientation enables the most humdrum life to yield innumerable opportunities for giving little things to God, and from the time of her clothing, Teresa Margaret had determined to use them to the fullest advantage. On that occasion she had framed a resolution, which gives us a glimpse into her gradual change of emphasis from strictly external penances to the more fruitful discipline of heart and will. This she submitted to her confessor for his approval: "I resolve to use every possible means to be present at every community exercise without exception, never unless health or obedience command it, seeking any dispensation or alleviation from the burden of the common life."

There is no shorter or surer path to perfection for a religious than regularity in silence and the spirit of faith, which are precisely the means of Jesus Himself from Bethlehem to Calvary. This was the route chosen also by His faithful follower. And at this Christmas feast, while she put the final touches to her spiritual "trousseau" in preparation for her now-imminent profession, Teresa Margaret steadfastly and irrevocably set her course along this short but rugged way, the unseen warfare where nature finds nothing for herself.

13

Her Profession

By those heights we dare to dare
By the greatness of our prayer,
Ever growing loftier, reaching
To a royaller beseeching
By the olden woes washed painless,
white and stainless
In the tears of bitter price,
By the strength of our assurance to endurance
Of the need of sacrifice.
(Sir James Rennell Rodd)

The time had now arrived for Teresa Margaret to kneel once more before the assembled chapter and make a petition as before; this time, however, to be received not to the habit but to profession, to be permitted to consecrate herself completely to the service of God within the walls of this cloister.

There was yet another change from the previous years ceremony. The triennial elections had been held a month earlier, on February 14th, when Mother Victoria of the Holy Family was elected Prioress in place of Mother Mary Magdalene. And now, to the distress of the novice, the swelling which before had proved to be the beginning of the painful abscess reappeared on her knee.

Was this recurring disability, coming each time immediately before the moment of decision about her fitness for the life, a sign from God that He did not destine her for the life of a Carmelite, or that He was dissatisfied with her preparations? And, if accepted, would it entail a postponement of her profession? The latter likelihood caused her great anxiety, for she felt it was due to her unworthiness that God seemed so unwilling to accept her self-oblation. Then she turned to the Blessed Virgin, and with an act of complete confidence and abandonment, asked her to give a clear sign that God was not displeased with her efforts by curing her of the ailment without the necessity of further surgery. Within a few days, all sign of the abscess had disappeared.

Seeing what appeared to her to be an opportunity of acting upon her avowed desire to become as far as possible a servant to her sisters, Teresa Margaret requested permission to make her profession as a lay sister; but she had completed her canonical novitiate as a choir novice, and this was not granted.

"It does not make the least difference," Mother Anna Maria assured her. "There is nothing to prevent your practicing interior humility, or manifesting it in your work. It is not the task that counts, in the growth of humility, but the way we do it. One does not have to seek lowly occupations in order to be humble."

And Teresa Margaret, who had come far in the past twelve months, realized the truth of this. She was soon to be given the opportunity of serving her sisters in the most humble and demanding of all occupations, that of infirmarian.

All during the past year she had worked tirelessly to acquire that dowry of spiritual gifts she thought would be most pleasing to her Spouse, and during the retreat immediately preceding her profession, she intensified the effort.

"Two days before her profession," Mother Anna Maria said, "I found her so carried away by the love of God that she seemed almost beside herself. I hardly know how to express it, for I myself seemed to catch some spark from the fire that was in her. I was so overcome that it was impossible to continue the instruction, and I had to leave her."

A private retreat of ten days is the usual preparation for profession, and to this Teresa Margaret gave herself up most fervently. She longed for the moment when she would be permitted to make the official dedication of herself in life and in death to the service of her Lord and receive the Church's formal approval of her offering.

Among the notes made during this retreat were some resolutions written out by Teresa Margaret, which express her intense desire to "fulfill in a short space many years," and to progress rapidly on the path of divine love: "Reflecting on the end for which I have been made and called to the religious life, I resolve to renounce entirely my own inclinations, to adhere solely to you, considering the means you have given me for sanctification. In future I am determined to esteem those means more highly, and even in little things to avail myself of them for no other end than for your glory, and to love and serve you in the way that it pleases you to lead me. In this I will not grow weary, because without perseverance there can be no salvation. I am resolved to give complete obedience in everything without exception, not only to my superiors, but also to my equals and inferiors, so as to learn from you, my God, who made yourself obedient in far more difficult circumstances than those in which I find myself."

"Knowing that a bride cannot be pleasing to her spouse unless she endeavors to become what he wishes her to be ... I will always think of my neighbors as beings made in your likeness, produced by your divine love, redeemed at the price of your precious Blood, looking upon them with true Christian charity, which you command. I will sympathize with their troubles, excuse their faults, always speak well of them, and never willingly fail in charity towards them in thought, word, or deed."

Professions are gala days in Carmel, but their graces are treasured jealously as a precious fragrance that might too easily become dulled if exposed to the air. "My secret is my own" and, on this occasion when the soul truly espouses herself in faith, the words in her heart are those placed on the lips of St. Agnes, which are officially reserved for the later veiling ceremony:

"I love Christ, into whose bridal chamber I will go, whose mother was a virgin, and whose Father knew not woman ... when I love Him I am chaste, when I shall touch Him I am pure, and when I shall take Him to my own I am a virgin. I am wedded to Him whom the angels serve, at whose beauty the sun and moon wonder."

Originally St. Teresa had legislated that professions were to be made at the grille as is customary in most religious orders, but later she revised this, a decision for which her daughters have always had good reason gratefully to bless her. "It is well to conceal the King's secret." A Carmelite makes her profession in the Chapter Room, in the hands of her Prioress, without the presence of prelate or priest, and with no witnesses except those members of the community who are already professed. It is an intimate family-feast, this betrothal, in which only the members of the religious family circle participate. No relatives or acquaintances are invited on this day, which the newly-professed consecrates entirely to Him to whom she has declared her undying loyalty and undivided love, He who has chosen her and "led her into the wilderness, there to speak to her heart."

The whole atmosphere of the convent is festive, the usually bare corridors decked with gay little impromptu oratories and flowers. For the past twenty-four hours they have been trickling in, as the garden has been despoiled to pay tribute to the bride of Christ. The previous night, the novice, in company with the rest of the community, has kept vigil before the Blessed Sacrament, and the first streak of dawn reminds all that the great day has finally come. It is difficult for the young and irrepressible to curb their high-spirited excitement sufficiently to observe the great silence, but somehow it is achieved, and after Prime the novices prepare the chapter room. A large brown cloth is pinned in the center of the floor, and decorated with flowers. On this day only white, symbol of purity and virginity, is admitted to the decorations. They are massed on the altar, with the large wax candles rising out of them, and also on the altar are arranged all the relics of the saints which the convent possesses.

Finally the bell rang for Mass. The novice, for this day given priority of place, knelt beside the Prioress. When the time came for Communion, she was led to the grille by the Prioress, to receive her Lord first. Mass over, after a short thanksgiving, the novice was taken from the choir, to return clad in the brown serge tunic and flowing white veil, as for her investiture, and holding a large wax candle. The cantors intoned the hymn *O gloriosa Virginum*, and as the choir took up the melody, two-by-two they left the choir in procession for the chapter room. Mother Victoria, with Sister Teresa Margaret's hand in hers, came last.

The ceremony was short but of moving simplicity. The Prioress had taken her place at the Gospel side of the altar, which was gay with lights and flowers and the simple but precious reliquaries. Teresa Margaret knelt before her, and once more she was questioned in the name of the Church:

"What do you ask?"

Again she affirmed: "The mercy of God, the poverty of the Order, and the society of the Sisters."

The Prioress then made a brief exhortation to the kneeling novice on the privileged but weighty responsibilities attached to the obligations she was about to undertake. The vow of obedience, which excludes all question, choice, or individual action, governing the mind and submitting it to another and higher will than one's own; which must be cheerful and willing in imitation of the perfect submission of Jesus to His Father's will, renouncing her liberty, all right to dispose of anything, even herself, submerging her will into that of another, returning to the state of spiritual childhood and utter dependence on another, resigning the exercise of her own will and retaining only its sacrifice ...

The vow of chastity makes of her body a living holocaust to God. By it she renounces forever those legitimate pleasures of human love, motherhood, and family life, while not imprisoning the heart in a narrow or egotistic sterility based on self-esteem. This vow allows her to embrace freely and gladly that state of life which permits her to lavish her love on her neighbor, the Church, the whole world. Any soul consecrated to God by the vows of religion has responsibility of extending the saving mission of the divine Redeemer who is her spouse and her strength ...

The vow of poverty requires a detachment ever more absolute than her renunciation. The abandonment, not only of all worldly possessions, but of the desire, hope, and power to possess anything, even those necessary articles which she uses as her own, imitates her Spouse who had not where to lay His head. This detachment makes her content with the needs and demands of daily life, helping her to give to others that which is not necessary or commanded by obedience, leading her to cast her cares on God's providence to provide for the unknown future, in sickness or in health, "for what doth it profit a man if he gain the whole world and suffer the loss of his own soul?"

Then, at a signal from Mother Victoria, Teresa Margaret moved forward until she was kneeling immediately in front of the Prioress. She joined her hands, with the little billet on which she had written the formula of her profession held between them, extended to be taken into the strong clasp of her superior, while in a low but clear and firm voice, she recited her promise, brief in words, but eternal in consequence:

"I, Sister Teresa Margaret of the Sacred Heart of Jesus, make my profession, and I promise obedience, chastity, and poverty to our Lord God and to the Virgin Mary of Mount Carmel, to the Reverend Father General of the Order of our most Blessed Lady of Carmel and to his successors, according to the Primitive Rule of the said Order as it is without mitigation, until death."[1]

"Offer a sacrifice of praise to the Lord," said the Prioress, "and

---

[1] The form used today is changed very little from the above: "I, Sister N.N., make my solemn profession, and I promise obedience, chastity, and poverty to God, to the Most Blessed Virgin Mary of Mount Carmel, to the Superior General of the Order of Discalced Carmelites, and to you Reverend Mother Prioress and to your successors, according to the Primitive Rule of the said Order and our Constitutions, until death."

fulfill your vows to the Almighty."

"I fulfill my vows to the Lord in the sight of His people, and in the courts of the Lord," was the steady response from the kneeling novice.

The Prioress then proceeded to perform a similar investiture as at the clothing ceremony. Once more the newly-professed novice was girded with leather cincture and rosary, the Scapular placed over her shoulders, and finally enveloped in the ample folds of the white choir mantle. But this time, as she prostrated herself on the flower-decked carpet prepared for her, it was the Church's great hymn of thanksgiving that the Prioress intoned:

"Te Deum laudamus..." The words were taken up by the choir, as the bells began to peal in joy and triumph, and the novices who had not been present at the ceremony entered at their signal to join in the chorus. "We praise thee, O God, we acknowledge thee to be the Lord ... make us to be numbered with thy saints in glory everlasting."

A crown of white flowers was placed on her brow when she rose from the ground, and the sisters gathered around affectionately to embrace and congratulate their newly-professed sister. For the day she was truly the queen in the community, all vying to serve and honor her, as they partook in the immense grace of her profession.

The final act by which one becomes a fully-fledged member of the community is the official reception of the black veil. This, being a public ceremony, is usually separated from the profession by some days at least. Sister Teresa Margaret's veiling ceremony was on April 7th, 1766, almost a month after her profession.

She still wore the white veil of a novice, which meant that the final seal remained, to complete officially - at least in outward appearance - her consecration. The black veil, symbol of sacrifice and complete dedication, is placed on her head by the officiating priest, in the presence of her friends and relatives in the chapel, and once more Sister Teresa Margaret knelt before the open grille as Mass was celebrated. On the altar lay the veil ready to be blessed during the ceremony, while the community sang the words *Amo Christum:* "I love Christ, into whose bridal chamber I will go ..."

Now the celebrant was moving towards the grille.

"Veni Sponsa Christi" he intoned, and the choir took up the words, singing the antiphon: "Come, bride of Christ, receive the crown which the Lord has prepared for you from all eternity."

Sister Teresa Margaret rose from her knees, and standing in the middle of the choir made her response: "Receive me, O Lord, according to thy word, and let not my expectations be confounded."

Mother Victoria led her to the small communion grille which stood open, and again she knelt. The priest approached, then extending his hands through the grating, placed the veil on her head, saying: "Receive the sacred veil, the emblem of holy reverence and continence; carry it before the judgment-seat of our Lord Jesus Christ to gain eternal life and to live for ever."

Enveloped now in the large black veil which completely covered her face, Sister Teresa Margaret returned to the middle of the choir, standing before the large grating, and replied: "He has set His seal upon my countenance, so that I allow no other love but Him."

Again she prostrated herself on the ground, with arms outstretched in the form of a cross, while the jubilant ringing of the bells mingled with the human voices to glorify God once more in the exultant words of the *Te Deum.* Through the hymn and the long prayers and blessings she lay, her heart overflowing with joy and gratitude, and an ever-deepening determination to refuse nothing to this Lord who had taken possession of her only to give more fully of Himself. "Mine are the heavens and mine is the earth ... all things are mine and for me, for Christ is mine and all for me."

"The consecration and elevation of Christian womanhood through virginal chastity," writes Father Ferdinand Valentine, O.P., "is given a quasi-liturgical expression in the traditional ceremonials of religious profession. These are not only more elaborate in the case of religious women, as one would expect for other reasons, but strikingly different ... Judging from the prayers conferring these sacred symbols, it would almost seem as if this union - the mystical wedlock of chastity - were something essentially different in the case of the religious sister in view of her sex. This is of course not so ... But the outward ceremonials and signs of the religious profession of women must mean what they signify, so that this mystical and divine union of charity confers on the woman a characteristic function consonant with her nature, as helpmeet of Christ in His Mystical Body, insofar as this is the special prerogative of virginal chastity."

"There!" exclaimed Mother Anna Maria, kissing her favorite novice warmly. "That is the last ceremony until we bury you. In the meantime, all you have to do is continue dying to yourself, until the day when the good Lord sees the work is finished, and says: Arise, my love, and come ..."

Looking at the glowing young face, alive with health, youth, and happiness, no suspicion crossed her mind that that day was not far off.

Genuinely though she felt that now all her desires had been granted and that she could from henceforward give herself wholly to God, Teresa Margaret was no disembodied spirit, but a human being, and one endowed with a lively, affectionate nature. Against her deep spiritual joy, the voice of nature did not lose any opportunity of reminding her that she was taking an irrevocable step which, for the remainder of her days, would demand a steadfast crucifixion of the flesh and its claims. But she was determined to be His "despite all repugnance" of nature, to die daily for the sake of Him who had died for love of her. There was no self-delusion or the least trace of hysteria in the calm yet joyous spirit with which she set out to meet the future voluntarily chosen by herself and so long the goal of her striving.

Undoubtedly the most delicate of all forms of asceticism is that which must be brought to bear on the emotions.

"For all persons thou shalt have equal love and equal forgetfulness, whether they be thy relatives or no, withdrawing thy heart from these as much as from those; more so, indeed, in some ways, from thy kinsmen, lest flesh and blood quicken with natural love, which is ever alive among kinsfolk, the which thou must ever mortify for spiritual perfection. Hold them all as strangers to thee; in this way, thou dost serve them better than by setting upon them the affection which thou owest to God."

This is St. John of the Cross' first "caution" which, he says, "anyone who would be a true religious and would quickly attain to perfection must needs bear in mind," and it is regarded by most as one of his typically "hard sayings."

"Leave thy country, thy kinsfolk, and thy father's home, and come away into a land I will show thee." God's invitation to Abraham has rung down the centuries, echoing in the heart of each man and woman called to the religious life. Fidelity to this call requires the severance of all human ties, but only to find them again at a deeper level. On every plane, the religious state witnesses to the great paradoxes of Christianity - dying in order to live, losing one's life that one may find it, having nothing yet possessing all things. The separation from family demanded by religious consecration does not imply a hardening of one's heart, the denial of all affection for our relatives or interest in their concerns. We need only look at the lives of two of the best-loved and greatest saints of the Discalced Carmelite Reform: St. Teresa of Avila and St. Thérèse of Lisieux. The love of their fathers was a central point in the whole life of each, and while this affection became refined and spiritualized, it deepened rather than lessened over the years.

Like both these better-known saints, Teresa Margaret's deepest personal relationship had always been with her father. He had been the recipient of all her most intimate confidences, he had advised and guided her, and the farewell to him was without doubt the costliest of all the renunciations she had made when entering the cloister - probably the most painful of her whole life.

Now, about to seal her consecration officially, she wondered whether the strong attachment that still bound her to her father, the deep natural love she bore him, might be an impediment to the union with God that she desired, and which she knew could be affected only by total detachment from all creature affections. The bond was particularly strong, being compounded not only of natural love, but spiritual compatibility and union of souls and minds, which welded the heart's affection into an intimacy that made it seem at times as though the same spirit animated them both. Sister Magdalene of St. Francis testified to this tenderness of affection, which had been deepened and purified by the supernatural character of their association, recalling how, whenever Sir Ignatius visited his daughter in Carmel, she would write a little note to be delivered to him after he had said farewell at the grille, in order to soften the grief she knew he felt at being unable to embrace her in taking his leave.

Sister Teresa Margaret spoke to Mother Anna Maria about the intensity of her affection, fearing that it hindered or detracted from the completeness of the self-oblation she desired to make.

"What shall I do?" she asked.

"First of all," Mother Anna Maria replied briskly, "you must make quite certain that your attitude towards this matter is supernatural. It is a grave mistake to believe that one becomes a perfect religious when she has managed to crush and suppress all human feelings."

"I feared I might be lacking in the absolute detachment or self-discipline that I feel God is asking of me."

"My child, what we are asked to do is not to crucify our natural affections but to purify them. And that, with vigilance and prayer and the help of God's grace, is possible. Do you think Mary did not love her Son tenderly? Or that there was anything lacking in His affection for her? Or St. Joseph's for them both? Do not ever make the mistake of thinking that those who love nobody are necessarily on the road to loving God. That is not the example the Holy Family gave us."

"Yes, that is true. I see it quite clearly. And yet I do not know how to set about acquiring such discipline, for you know also how strongly attached I am to Papa. I feel for him and with him in every joy and sorrow as though they were happening to me."

Sir Ignatius himself was to resolve the seeming conflict.

"When the time for her profession drew near," he said, "she wrote me a letter expressing her gratitude towards me, her promise of prayers on my behalf, and her desire for complete detachment from everything, even from me, in order to belong completely to Jesus."

So often in the spiritual life, God treats us as He did Abraham, demanding a seemingly impossible renunciation, but actually requiring only our willingness. Once He sees that we are determined to refuse Him nothing, however costly the gift demanded, He is satisfied, and often returns our capital with interest. The complete sacrifice she felt was required of her seemed to Teresa Margaret of such magnitude because it involved not only her own affections but those of her father; and she would willingly have borne any suffering herself to spare him the least pain. Was she entitled to demand of him a similar renunciation?

Yet it was in making this heroic act of abandonment that Teresa Margaret learned the real meaning of detachment. It is not a cutting out of one's heart, a refusal of all human affection; rather, it is to love more deeply and tenderly, but in Christ and for Him, free from the taint of self-interest and self-seeking that resides in so much sensible affection. When we love a person because of the pleasure we derive from the relationship, it is actually ourselves we are loving. And from the pain of her voluntary renunciation, a new and closer bond developed between these two souls who both sought nothing but the will of God.

"In her letter," said Ignatius, "she also mentioned, among other things, the solicitude she had for the good of my soul, and her desire of forming a perfect and indissoluble pact with me. Each evening, before retiring, she would seek me in the Heart of Jesus, and she expressed a desire that we help each other spiritually."

Sir Ignatius rose to the occasion with a generosity that matched his daughter's. "God has called you," he wrote in reply. "May He be blessed a thousand times. Go ahead with this act you propose, for I can see that He wants you completely for Himself. I hope that, in

His mercy, He will make you a saint to be eternally blessed in heaven. Let only love for Him move you to make your profession. May it inspire your every thought, work, and word during your whole life. My child, you embarrass me by thanking me for the good which I have done you. Whatever good may be in me is solely the work of God. You are temporarily separated from me; I accept this through love of Jesus and offer you to Him anew without reservation. With His help I too shall separate myself from you temporarily, for your example has encouraged me. Yes, dearest daughter, I desire to visit you spiritually; in the Heart of Jesus, where you love to dwell, I shall always find you."

With a heart overflowing with love and gratitude, Teresa Margaret laid her holocaust on the altar with no slightest reservation to mar or cast a shadow on its completeness. Her dearest father had not been wounded or felt that she loved him less; now there could never be any separation or estrangement between two who know that always and at all times they could make tryst with each other in the Sacred Heart, whose burning love had communicated something of His ardor to their own.

Our Lord did not say that anyone who loves a parent deeply cannot be His disciple. He said: "He who loves mother or father more *than Me is* unworthy of Me"; we must love Him above all else on pain of not loving Him at all. But one who did not love mother or father would be unnatural, and as such could hardly qualify for God's intimate friendship. We do not place an obstacle in the way of our love of God by loving our parents. On the contrary, to fail in this filial duty would be more likely to do so.

One day when her father and Francis Xavier were taking their leave after a visit, Mother Victoria joined them to thank Sir Ignatius for some gifts he had made to the convent. Teresa Margaret was chatting with her brother, while Sir Ignatius paid his respects to the Prioress.

"Are you not sad at saying farewell to dear Papa whom you love so much?" Cecchino asked.

His sister replied with some spirit.

"Having made that sacrifice to God, do you expect me to take it back again?"

But on another occasion, although she managed to conceal from her father the sadness she felt at his departure, it was noticed by one of her companions at recreation, who commented upon her great love for Sir Ignatius.

"Why is it that you seem to have a deeper affection for your father than for your mother?"

"That is not so. I love my mother dearly, but Papa and I are more intimate, because his soul and mine understand each other. Between us there is complete confidence and understanding."

"But does it not cause you pain to have to say goodbye to your father when he returns home?"

"You do not understand," Teresa Margaret replied. "Do you know the words of St. Augustine: 'He loves thee less, O Lord, who loves anything else together with thee'? It is a different kind of love." And with that she deftly steered the conversation back to safer and more general topics.

In a note to Mother Anna Maria at this time, the young Carmelite said: "You may be sure that I admire the loving designs of our good Master, who has led me to this holy mountain of Carmel. I thank God that He made me the victor, freeing my heart from so many petty attachments that might have led to a deviation from the sole objective, which is to belong wholly and entirely to Him. Though I am still far from such a goal, yet may I ever live annihilated to all things in His Sacred Heart. I beg you make this request to Him on my behalf."

14

Living in the Presence of God

Enter His presence and there find happiness;
He will give the shelter of His arms.
So, rejoicing, you will drink deep
From the fountain of deliverance.
(Pastiche - Pss. 33, 40; Is. 12:3).

From a very early age, as has already been noted, Teresa Margaret had been drawn and encouraged to center her devotion around the Sacred Heart, symbol and source of the love of God, and had learned to approach this "fount of love" and drink from its spring of living water, for where would one seek to know and be united with the God of Love more surely than in His Sacrament of Love - "our heaven on earth" - as she used to describe the Blessed Sacrament. "It is," said Pope John XXIII, "the source at which everyone can find strength to overcome daily difficulties, the courage to profess firmly his faith, generosity in the practice of love and the service of his brothers." And in his encyclical *Haurietis Aquas,* Pope Pius XII stated: "Without any doubt a burning devotion to the Heart of Jesus will foster and advance our reverence for the holy Cross especially and our love for the august Sacrament of the altar." He might have been referring specifically to the development of this awareness and devotion in St. Teresa Margaret.

The Sacred Humanity of Jesus, the humility of God who condescends to stoop to man, opened for her the vast mysteries of the hidden life, which she desired to penetrate and share insofar as that was possible. Jesus was the model she sought always to imitate, the perfect exemplar of abasement and effacement, from His Incarnation to His death. Not content with preaching and teaching humility, our Lord has left us innumerable practical examples to meditate and imitate, in His hidden life, public ministry, His passion and death, and this virtue He still continues to teach and demonstrate from the tabernacle, for in His eucharistic life, He is the model *par excellence* of condescension and submission. St. Paul expresses this theme with characteristic vividness. To him, God did not demonstrate His humility by being born in lowly conditions, but in becoming man at all, "dispossessing Himself, taking the nature of a slave." To Teresa Margaret, the mystery of the Incarnation was indeed "a great and mighty wonder" - how could any creature ever humble herself sufficiently to match the self-emptying of God, who has stooped even to dwell with us?

While at St. Apollonia's, Teresa Margaret had been permitted by Don Pellegrini to receive Holy Communion as frequently as the nuns - that was usually twice a week - a rare privilege in those days. Always she approached the altar rails as often as she was allowed, and with the years her devotion intensified, so that she would sometimes appear quite radiant on the days when she had received Holy Communion. In Carmel, the Real Presence in the Tabernacle exercised a powerful attraction for her, and she formed the habit of turning her thoughts - and if possible her body - as frequently as she could to Him who dwelt there in solitude and hiddenness for love of her, keeping in mind all that Jesus had done and suffered during His earthly life.

Many of her sisters' testimonies contained little incidents that illustrate how her practice of the presence of God evolved around the Blessed Sacrament preserved in the tabernacle. She was frequently observed to genuflect in any corridor or room that adjoined choir or sacristy, and whenever possible, would work in such a position that she faced towards the chapel. On several occasions during the siesta hour, instead of retiring to her cell, she would sit on a wooden bench near the chapel, resting her head against the wall, thus observing the stipulated rest period, and at the same time keeping her Eucharistic Lord company. One day

Mother Anna Maria, after looking for Teresa Margaret in her cell, found her keeping this solitary assignation.

"Truly," Teresa Margaret told her, "God is here. I dwell in the very house of Jesus in the Blessed Sacrament. We must keep our eyes cast down and our hearts raised up to God!"

St. Bonaventure gives a list of the motives which urge us to receive Holy Communion. Beginning at the lowest rung, of those who have sinned so much and so often as to have nothing to offer to God but the divine Victim, or who have no other means of avoiding violent temptation and refraining from further sin, he enumerates various degrees, until the final and most perfect motive of "generous souls influenced by true desire of loving our divine Savior (who) receive Him in the adorable Sacrament of the Blessed Eucharist in order to be still more inflamed with His love." In this last category her sisters' evidence places Teresa Margaret, and they were frequently witnesses to the ardor of this "further inflammation" on days when she had communicated.

She seemed to perceive some indefinable taste and perfume in the Blessed Sacrament, a sensation she always associated with the consecrated Host, but which for some time she thought to belong to it as a result of transubstantiation, and therefore experienced by all. Once she spoke of the matter to Mother Anna Maria, but when she perceived that the assistant Mistress did not understand her, she would not explain herself any further. Several times Mother Anna Maria brought the subject up again, trying to discover what was the "odor" Teresa Margaret referred to, but evasively she replied that it was "the perfume of holiness." When pressed for an explanation of this, she replied that she did not know how to express herself, but that the nearest description she could give was to the scent of the narcissus.

Realizing that this "odor of sanctity" was not apparent to others, Teresa Margaret was careful not to mention it again, until one day when speaking to Father Ildefonse she asked him:

"Why is it that the taste of the Lord which one experiences at Holy Communion is sometimes greater and sometimes less?"

Father Ildefonse hesitated a few moments before replying, surprised by the question and the implication that Teresa Margaret was accustomed to perceiving some kind of sensible sweetness of taste and smell in the consecrated Host.

"In what does it consist, this taste you speak of?" he asked cautiously.

She seemed confused.

"Why, I do not know how to explain. It is the savor of Jesus Christ, I suppose, as the psalm says: 'Taste and see that the Lord is sweet.'"

"That is not a necessary effect of the Sacrament," Father Ildefonse told her. "You know what St. Thomas says in his hymn: 'Seeing, touching, tasting, all are here deceived.' And in the lesson for the Feast of Corpus Christi, he says: 'The accidents subsist without a subject, that there may be room for faith, when we receive visibly that which is invisible and hidden under an appearance not its own. Thus the senses are kept free from deception, for they judge of accidents known to them.' Now you know well enough that the unconsecrated wafers which you handle daily have neither perfume nor sweet flavor, being merely made of flour and water. And you know that after the Host is consecrated the accidents do not change. It is still a wafer of unleavened bread, and the words of consecration which accomplish transubstantiation do not bestow anything that the senses can perceive, such as taste or odor."

Teresa Margaret pondered this, and seemed a little embarrassed at having spoken of a matter that had appeared quite natural and logical to her. For although she was aware of these facts that Father Ildefonse pointed out, still there seemed nothing extraordinary in accepting that the Host, becoming the Body of Jesus, should also assume "the good odor of Christ."

"God can grant such favors when and how He wills," Father Ildefonse continued, "and if you receive them, it should be with humility and gratitude. But I would like you to refrain from speaking to anyone else of such things. The degrees 'greater or less' which you mention could well indicate more or less fervor in the reception of Holy Communion."

Sister Teresa Margaret was well aware of the true nature of the Eucharist as food of the soul. But her greatest joy, after being permitted to receive Communion, was to spend her free time in silent adoration before the tabernacle. Sundays and other feast days would usually find her kneeling in prayer in choir or oratory, drawn back into the shadows whence, with the grating open, she could see the Tabernacle without being observed by anyone in the chapel.

Her duties did not always permit her to indulge this attraction unhindered, and more and more she came to realize that there is no better way of serving God than in the person of one's neighbor. As she willingly relinquished the pleasure of her own private devotions to answer the summons of duty - or very often to anticipate it - so more and more did God's illuminating and inspiring graces lead her deeper into the heart of charity: the incredible mystery of God's predilection for man.

She accumulated a quantity of small pious practices, which seem trivial and rather naive, but which did require constant recollection and advertence to the presence of God, and to which she adhered faithfully through the years: small, insignificant glances such as pass between lovers, becoming fraught with meaning and tokens of the gift of one's heart; always genuflecting when passing in the vicinity of the Blessed Sacrament; sitting, when working, so that she was turned towards the Tabernacle, and if possible doing so on her knees; and before going to sleep each night, turning once more to face the chapel.

However, all these devotional exercises did not have the effect of cluttering or stifling her spirit - such as the multiplication of vocal prayers often becomes - but primarily interior movements of recollection and love in the presence of God. "When two people love one another," she said, "they naturally think of each other." Having given her heart completely to God, her thoughts instinctively returned to Him in every circumstance and frequently in the course of her occupations. In all, there was no constraint, no special effort, for instance, to formulate an act of love at given periods. Such mechanical regulation is not necessary; a simple interior glance suffices.

The various practices she employed were only a means by which

Teresa Margaret ensured a habitual remembrance of that Presence, and
to recall her mind at regular intervals should it have strayed from the
focus within which she desired to move always. Father Ildefonse confirms this: "The visible things of creation always had the effect of raising
her mind and heart to God with a wonderful facility. In her prayer, the
mysteries of the life, passion, and death of our Lord, as well as meditation on His Sacred Humanity, all led her to a lofty contemplation which
was often profound and absorbing."

Ecstasies and visions are not necessary for this. The simplest
things of daily life can be used as a lever to lift us to God; a bird,
dipping and soaring, or filling the air with its triumphant announcement that winter is over and gone - the awe-inspiring crash of thunder
or the unnoticed breath of wind - Rupert Brooke's litany of the homely
gifts of God beginning with the simple

> ... white cups and plates, clean-gleaming
> Ringed with blue lines; and feathery, faery dust;
> Wet roofs beneath the lamplight; the strong crust
> Of friendly bread, and many-tasting food ...

God is always found when He alone is sought. He surrounds
us in His creation as well in His real presence on our altars. "I do
not envy the angels in heaven," Teresa Margaret once said, "apart
from their enjoyment of the beatific vision. Do we not have God
dwelling in our midst... ?"

Her particular attraction to the Sacred Heart is inextricably bound
up with her devotion to the Eucharist. Long before she had been of an
age to make her first Communion, Teresa Margaret had learned from
her father to understand something of the human and divine love of the
Heart of Jesus and grasped that the tabernacle truly contains not merely
the symbol of that love but Love Himself, so that she would often exclaim, "May the Sacred Heart of Jesus in the Blessed Sacrament be
praised, loved, and worshipped in all the tabernacles of the world. Ah,
what continual irreverence He receives from man in His own house! In
His humility He deigns to dwell in our midst, yet how often is He ne-

glected and forgotten, left in empty churches, while in His turn He never grows weary of this lonely vigil. Truly 'Love is not loved!'"

It was in the months following her profession that she began more assiduously to apply herself to the practice of the presence of God, and during this time she was put in charge of the linen office and appointed first as assistant sacristan and later given the full responsibility of that office. It was a source of great delight to her to handle the altar linens and sacred vessels. Several of the sisters commented on how meticulously she performed every duty, never speaking to anyone in any of the rooms near the Blessed Sacrament. She particularly loved arranging flowers for the altar, and saw to it that they were never lacking. Flowers always spoke the language of the spirit for her, symbolizing charity, purity, generosity. She loved to tend them; even as a child they helped to raise her heart and mind to God, and later she naively associated perfumed flowers with the most fragrant of the virtues, while "the odor of sanctity" was inseparably linked in her mind with the elusive perfume of the narcissi which she seemed at one period also to perceive in the Blessed Sacrament. The unusual grace of experiencing scent and taste in the Host receives, perhaps, some sort of unofficial confirmation in the manner by which this particular "odor of sanctity" was later to be linked with her own incorrupt body, so that it has become a part of herself, the "hallmark" one might say of this pure little "lily of Florence," itself "the city of flowers."[1]

"In everything," Father Ildefonse later recalled, "she set herself a very high goal, and her disappointment was keen whenever she failed to reach the level she aimed at - which in the early days she often did, as her ideals were lofty. It was that which was to constitute the whole of her interior sufferings and cause such detailed examinations of conscience. Whether in her spiritual exercise or duties as infirmarian and sacristan, she always saw herself falling below her goal."

---

[1] Florence derives its name from the iris or flag lily. There our Lady is honored as *La Madonna del Fiore,* who holds an *iris florentina.* This is symbolized in heraldry as the *fleur de lis,* which is the emblem of Florence, so the play on names is singularly appropriate here.

This is a condition, as well as one of the agonies, of spiritual progress. There are countless souls who set their aim at a medium mark, and are happy to attain it, well-content with the comfortable level of mediocrity. It was St. Hilary who warned that in pursuing "infinite things" we must resign ourselves to the frustration of never achieving our goal. In this life we must press forward, but "infinite desires" can be realized only in eternity. The penalty of shooting for the stars is the continual and sometimes discouraging experience of seeing oneself constantly falling short of the target, at times not even coming within range or focus. If one does not become disheartened, but rises and aims once more for the ever-fixed mark, the time will arrive when one finds oneself in orbit.

15

Toward the Transformation of Union with God

Not by dreaming but by using,
Not by claiming but refusing,
Then shall dawn on eyes unsealing the revealing
Of a self that knows and grows.
And the stream of thy devotion find the ocean
When its meaning overflows.
Rennell Rodd *(In Excelsis)*

It goes without saying that no work can be successful if it is not based on love, nor will it be fruitful unless it is animated by prayer - the personal prayer of the individual members of the body as well as the communal prayer of the body itself.

The Christian concept of love of God cannot be separated from love of neighbor. "The man who loves God must be the man who loves his brother as well ... if a man boasts of loving God, while he hates his brother, he is a liar."

The charity of one who neglects the needs of her neighbor to devote herself to long private devotions must always be suspect. "You cannot do anything for me," our Lord said to St. Catherine of Sienna. "But you can help your neighbor. You cannot give back to me myself the love I demand, but I have put you beside your neighbor, that you may do for her what you are unable to do for Me. Whatever you do for your neighbor, I consider as done for Myself."

Love must show itself in deeds. As St. Teresa says, we cannot be certain that we are loving God; on the other hand, we are never in any doubt as to whether we are loving our neighbor, for we know quite well in what that consists: service. And there is one particularly illuminating little incident related about St. Teresa Margaret that well sums up her attitude to others, which was invariably to seek a favorable interpretation for the actions of her sisters, however outwardly imperfect they might seem, ready to excuse or defend their faults and failings because, as she so often insisted, God alone could see their intentions, while appearances - on which so much rash judgment is based - are usually misleading, always deceptive. Wisely she realized that it was better not to pass judgment, but to commend the matter to God, who alone knew of the good intention and therefore was the only one in a position to assess the matter.

On one occasion a postulant was dismissed because of a physical defect which, for some time, had passed unnoticed by all save Teresa Margaret, who, being placed beside the offender in choir, could not but be aware of her infirmity.

"Why did you not mention this before?" demanded Mother Anna Maria.

"I thought she might be sent away because of it."

"Did you not think you would have acted with greater simplicity had you reported it without comment and allowed your superiors to decide that?"

"No, Mother, I did not. It is so very easy, in speaking of others, to allow prejudice or aversion so to color our words that we convey much more than we actually say. I thought, and still believe, that it is better to leave the matter in God's hands."

"And you would do the same again?"

"Yes, again and again, unless commanded by obedience to give my opinion. And even then I would endeavor to speak impartially. If it is God's will that she leave, then she will do so no matter what I say or refrain from saying. And at least I will not have to accuse myself of failure in charity."

"You have a duty in charity to the community as well as to individuals."

"Dear Mother, I once read in a book this excellent advice: 'She who desires peace must see, suffer, and be silent!' True, there are some things I cannot avoid noticing, and at times they cause suffering. But I lose nothing by being silent about them - that is something that rests entirely with me. And I have tested the truth of the words in practice. I have done that, and I have found peace. I can think of no safer guide in such matters than these words: 'Never meddle in the affairs of others, nor even allow them to pass through your mind, lest perchance you may be unable to fulfill your own task.'"

"And you apply this advice to all things, irrespective of circumstances?"

"Irrespective of all circumstances save obedience. Silence and prayer are my refuge when in doubt. To speak to God about what we want links our hands in some fashion with His divine liberality, just as in consultations between two friends. And while prayer and silence produce total abandonment to God's loving paternal providence, He has made us understand it by the words: 'Cast all your care on Him for He hath care of you.' We do not even have to pester Him with the details of our requests but merely put ourselves before Him and repeat with the Psalmist: 'O Lord, you know all my desires!'"

Love of God, love of neighbor, a sense of humor, and an almost limitless stock of patience - such is the equipment that get us through the ups and downs of community life without too many detours in our own spiritual progress. "There is nothing, however trying," St. Teresa declares, "that cannot be borne by people who really love one another."

All the saints are, and must be, eminent in charity, and in the case of Teresa Margaret such a bald statement embraces a passionate love for God, unwearying devotion and service of her neighbor, and a consuming zeal for the salvation of souls. Charity was the outstanding characteristic of her whole life and devotion, the key that unlocks the secret of all else - her desire for suffering and mortification, the intensity of her identification with the Sacred and Eucharistic Heart in the hidden phases of Christ's life, and the amazing rapidity of her ascent through such unspectacular circumstances as those in which her life was set.

One of the reasons why a woman hides her family background under the anonymity of a religious name is that, in the cloister, no preference or privilege is to be given merely on account of worldly rank or possessions. Carmelite nuns are expressly forbidden to reveal or even speak of their fathers' position - either of wealth or poverty, high or low social status - but such things can never be entirely concealed, and unfortunately they are at times capable of swaying the judgment of those who have a vote in the election of officials. Teresa Margaret lived in a community who were all, by birth, of a higher rank than her own. The Carmel had been founded in 1627 by a noble widow of the Ugolini family and had since then drawn much of the upper strata of Florentine and Tuscan society into its cloister.

The Redi family was old, but not of noble descent. They traced their ancestors back twelve generations from Sir Ignatius to a Spaniard, Leffo del Reda of Madrid, who settled in Arezzo in 1427. Contemporary with Teresa Margaret in the Florence Carmel were many members of Tuscany's most distinguished families, whose names were already old and venerable when that of Redi was first established. Mother Anna Maria of St. Anthony, for instance, was a Piccolomini, a well-known family who had already given two popes to the Church, Pius II in 1458, and the brief reigning Pius III in 1503.

And yet, among all these, Sister Teresa Margaret was conspicuous for her deportment and manner, simply because she had early trained herself to take as a yardstick, not those around her but the criterion of Christ whose kingdom is not of this world. Temporal rank or power neither dazzled her nor gave her any sense of inferiority, for she was as much at her ease in the company of a servant or a duchess. She did not envy her sisters their titles or feel overawed by their connections. Her own title of nobility was the one under which she was known in religion - "of the Sacred Heart." Our Lord had chosen as His closest associates men in whom even the most sanguine could hardly have discerned, at the outset, the raw material of saints and pillars of the Church. They were not of high birth, but on the contrary were all laboring men, rather dull, very ignorant, uncouth, and self-opinionated. They did not appreciate Him in the least. His own relatives considered Him mad and in need of forcible restraint. No, if she would imitate Christ, she would have to make as little of herself and her natural endowment as possible, and remain unconcerned as to whether her companions thought her intelligent, or well-born, striving always to remain indifferent about such things herself.

A superficial reading of the glowing testimonies of Teresa Margaret's practical love for her sisters is apt to deceive one into suspecting that it cost her little. Her naive innocence, the disarming simplicity which saw nothing but good in those around her, and designated her sisters as "angels" or "saints", the fact that never in word or gesture did she betray the least aversion or antipathy, her universal popularity - all seems to point to a natural disposition which made it easy for her to be affable and agreeable to everyone, as it is to some gentle and genuinely humble people.

But, in fact, she appears to have experienced real difficulty in conquering a natural repugnance for some of her companions, and this is all the more remarkable in that she never betrayed her struggles to anyone but her confessors. Two of them gave her express cautions about this matter. In 1768, Father Gregory counseled her to "see God in *every* person without exception, to love Him in all, even those whose defects of mind or body make them repulsive," and to "do good not only before God, but, before creatures also." And the following year Father Ildefonse, exhorting her to imitation of Christ in His humiliations and love of lowliness, said, "Seek the company of those persons who give annoyance by a certain roughness of manner although your natural inclination is to be with the pious and refined ... Be grateful and esteem highly even the least thing that is done for you. Assign the motive of charity to others in all things, and never seek approval whether it be privately or in public."

She was the personification of sympathy for every form of pain and suffering and so had the makings of an ideal infirmarian. Sickness and suffering seemed to make special claims on her charity, and when she was unable to relieve the physical ills of her sisters, they would unfailingly draw strength and courage from her little homilies and counsels, for she was easy to talk to and had the knack of divining others' troubles.

Teresa Margaret was quick to see the scope for the exercise of charity that the office of infirmarian provided. Much was demanded of this sister, but there were also unlimited opportunities for doing a great deal over and above the mere fulfillment of duty. The tasks devolving upon serving the sick are numerous and often far from congenial, and there are heavy calls on one's time, patience, sleep, and freedom. Even the little leisure permitted in the monastic horarium is encroached upon by the needs of the sick. The office of infirmarian is an exacting, never-ending one, and the principal qualification looked for in a candidate is deep, practical charity.

At about the time Teresa Margaret received the habit, the health of Mother Teresa Maria, the fault-finding Novice Mistress, began to decline, so that she was unable to manage without additional care and assistance. It would require little imagination for the young novice to realize how difficult a patient the eighty-year-old-nun would be, yet despite this - or perhaps because of it - she volunteered to act as unofficial infirmarian to Mother Teresa Maria, whose needs were more for a companion than a nurse. Old and partly helpless now, her age and infirmities made her an even more exacting charge than formerly she had been as a superior.

Mother Anna Maria observed Teresa Margaret closely during this time and testified that she was tireless in anticipating the demands of the cantankerous old nun who was almost impossible to please although Teresa Margaret never wearied of trying to do so. She had to assist her up and down stairs, help her to prepare for bed, see to her meals, and perform a hundred and one little services, which she always did without waiting to be asked. Finding that Mother Teresa Maria often needed further assistance during the night, the novice brought her straw palliasse into the cell of the old nun and slept there on the floor, ready at the least movement from the other to be of service. For one so young she must have slept remarkably lightly, for Mother Teresa Maria never even had to call her. As soon as she would begin to make restless movements indicating distress, even in the bitterest winter weather, Teresa Margaret would be on her feet await-ing orders. And yet, even under these conditions the determined old martinet never let pass an opportunity for rebuking and trying the patience of her voluntary nurse whose virtues she praised incessantly to everyone else.

Mother Victoria, the Prioress who had received Teresa Margaret's vows, was also nearly eighty, and partly crippled with rheumatism. She still managed to attend choir regularly, but she could not get to bed without assistance, and in order to render her this service, Teresa Margaret would accompany her to her cell after Matins and settle her for the night. During the winter months, fearing that the Prioress might not be able to sleep, she would wait, sometimes for half an hour or more, to allow Mother Victoria to warm herself thoroughly and then get her comfortably into bed. But here her services did not go unappreciated, and the old Mother could never find words sufficiently warm to express her gratitude for the patience and kindness of the infirmarian whose services far exceeded the obligation of her office.

At the end of 1766, some six months after Teresa Margaret's profession, Mother Teresa Maria died, and normally there would have been no further need for her services in the capacity of extra infirmarian. But in the succeeding winter months, half the commu-nity were down with an epidemic of influenza. One after the other the sisters fell sick, sometimes as many as ten at a time being ill and needing care and nursing. Again Teresa Margaret volunteered her services, and she and a former fellow-novice, Sister Mary Victoria, were appointed assistants to Sister Magdalene, who had the office of infirmarian. After the epidemic had passed, Sister Teresa Margaret was left in the office, a charge she retained until her own death.

Over and above her normal duties, Teresa Margaret had to care for several nuns who, while not actually ill, were old and infirm, and at times difficult to please. She was a devoted nurse, and although her natural feelings revolted sometimes at the dis-agreeable tasks she was called on to perform, she was always smilingly cheerful and ready to do far more than mere duty demanded.

When the English Mother Margaret Mostyn was infirmarian in the Carmel at Antwerp during the penal days, she records that she could only overcome her aversion to some of the services demanded of her by resolving to do all things for the sick in the same manner as she would actually do to the person of Jesus Christ. Our Lord then told her that if she did this, all would become easy. "I have brought you here to love Me and Me only. You must not incline to those for whom you have inclination or contradiction, but behold them all in Me." This was also Sister Teresa Margaret's method and the source of her success.

For some months she had as patients both the Prioress, Mother Victoria, and the former Prioress, Mother Mary Magdalene; and, as well, Sister Louise of St. Philip now passed into her care. This nun had suffered a mental breakdown, resulting in insanity, and she was liable at times to become violent, particularly towards anyone for whom she conceived one of her irrational aversions. There was no way of helping the unfortunate young woman (who was not then thirty years of age) at that time. She was kept in a separate apartment and looked after as well as could be done and to the extent she would permit. During the periods when she had to be forcibly restrained, she was kept locked in her room. No cure or treatment was known or attempted, but she was cared for with a tenderness and devotion that were unknown in that era among the insane, who were invariably incarcerated in public places of detention and neglected in a way that would not be tolerated today in a captive animal; so the kindest thing that could be done was for the nuns to keep her within the convent and look after her as best they could.

Sister Louise was humored as far as possible, but she developed an array of phobias, one of the most violent being in the matter of food. When it was within the bounds of reason, her demand was met, but unfortunately, as so often happens, Sister Louise's tastes seemed to run along lines that were imprudent if not actually harmful, so that her orders were not always fulfilled. Any deprivation of this nature would provoke an uncontrollable outburst of rage, as would any other refusal of her senseless demands. On one occasion when Teresa Margaret was forced to withhold what Sister Louise had asked for, she suggested, "This is the moment to offer Jesus the sacrifice which He expects from you." As one might imagine, such a consideration did little to mollify the other, and all the infirmarian received for her pains was a blow.

"Where words are of no avail," she remarked later - not it would seem without a tinge of dry humor - "the best thing is to have recourse to prayer and silence, and to speak of such things with God alone." She must have spoken very frequently with God about her unfortunate charge who taxed everyone's patience. Even Teresa Margaret's charity was sorely tried at times.

Despite the fact that she longed to be able to give the poor demented creature whatever would soothe and comfort her, she was obliged to follow the instructions of the doctor as well as those of the Prioress, both of whom realized that firmer handling was better for the patient than the indulgence of all her whims. And of course the unfortunate nun, refused day after day what she demanded, became convinced that the infirmarian was deliberately thwarting her. Gradually she developed an intense aversion to Sister Teresa Margaret, who probably appeared to her in the role of a persecutor, the source of all her troubles. One day, verbal protest proving ineffectual, she snatched a heavy dish from the tray and hurled it at Teresa Margaret. However, Sister Magdalene happened to be present and managed to intercept the missile, after which she removed all potential weapons from the room. On several occasions Sister Louise attacked Teresa Margaret, who wore many bruises as the result of blows and cuffs from her patient. Ceaselessly she tried to win the disordered affections of the other, but it was hopeless. The more eccentric Sister Louise's behavior, the more gently did Teresa Margaret treat her. The only result was, apparently, to add fuel to the flames and incite an even deeper antipathy and wilder tantrums.

Orders had been given that no one should remain alone with this sister in case she became quite unmanageable. One day, after the community had finished the midday meal, Sister Teresa Margaret took up a tray to Sister Louise, probably expecting that, as usual, Sister Magdalene the senior infirmarian, would follow her, for she left the door ajar. Sister Teresa of Jesus Crucified happened to pass down the corridor a few minutes later and noticed that, instead of being locked as usual, the patient's door was standing open. She closed it, without realizing that in doing so she had locked Sister Teresa Margaret in with the insane nun who could not endure the sight of her.

It must have been a bad moment for the girl. Had her patient become violent she could easily have killed her, as she was much the stronger physically of the two, and there was no possibility of escape. This incident is revealing in many ways, illustrating Teresa Margaret's practical judgment and commonsense, as well as her charm and power of persuasion. She realized that the worst course of action was to give any indication of alarm. It was the siesta hour, and the house was quiet. Nobody would pass along this way for an hour. Fortunately the patient on this occasion took her food without any trouble, and Sister Teresa Margaret got her onto the bed and settled comfortably. Then with no appearance of fuss or doing anything out of the ordinary, and managing not to attract the attention of the other, she lay down on the floor at the foot of the bed where she could not be seen, to take the midday siesta, without Sister Louise realizing that she had remained in the room.

Nobody missed Teresa Margaret until the bell rang for Vespers at 2 p.m. The community assembled in the choir, but the candles on the altar remained unlit, and the stall of the regular and punctual sacristan stood empty. Where could she be? What had happened?

When she could not be located either in her cell or the infirmary, it occurred to Sister Magdalene to look into the room of Sister Louise, where she found the missing sister, quite serene and matter-of-fact about the adventure. But Sister Magdalene was not.

"What is the meaning of this silly prank?" she demanded sharply. "I thought you were discreet and trustworthy, but as you seem not to be, you are obviously not a suitable person for this task. From now on you will not serve Sister Louise or come into this room."

Sister Magdalene's agitation was obvious. She realized the danger to which her young assistant had been exposed, but she was also annoyed at the needless risk taken, as she believed, deliberately.

Sister Teresa Margaret saw that it was useless to plead her case until Sister Magdalene had calmed down somewhat, so she made no attempt at an explanation, but instead went off to the choir to recite Vespers, having been absent from the community office. Later she went in search of Sister Magdalene.

"You need not worry about me in the least, Sister," she said with a disarming smile, "for I was able to take my siesta as usual."

"It was not your siesta I was worried about, but your life!" retorted the other sharply. Sister Teresa Margaret turned on the full battery of her most winning smile.

"Please, dear Sister," she begged, "will you permit me to continue caring for this poor sister of ours? I am sure you will."

"No, certainly not."

Teresa Margaret continued to plead, but the other remained adamant. From now on, Sister Louise would be no part of her responsibility.

In the evening Sister Magdalene went to the infirmary to prepare Sister Louise's supper. She looked up as the door opened, and her assistant entered softly.

"Sister, will you allow me to take the tray to Sister Louise as usual?" Teresa Margaret asked.

"No, Sister. I told you this afternoon that you were not to go to her room. I do not wish to discuss the matter any further or to hear any more about it."

Teresa Margaret's face fell. She did not consider that she had committed any crime or even a serious indiscretion. After all, it was merely an occupational hazard, an accident that might as easily have happened to Sister Magdalene as to herself. She felt distressed at being refused permission for a charge which, even though it tried her sorely at times, afforded her the consolation of serving God in His suffering members. Being able to tend this very needy person always kept before her Christ's words: "I was sick and you cared for me ... inasmuch as you did it for the least of my brethren you did it for Me." Suddenly the tears began to flow. Sister Magdalene stared at her aghast.

"My dear Sister!" she exclaimed. "Are you ill?"

Teresa Margaret shook her head.

"Then what on earth is the matter?"

"You refuse to allow me to perform this act of charity."

"Well, I offer you instead the opportunity of performing an act of obedience!"

"Oh, my dear Sister, if you only knew... ." Suddenly she dropped to her knees and held out her hands. "I beg of you, for the love of God, forgive me this once, and allow me to serve Sister Louise again. I promise you I shall be most diligent in the future and take the greatest care ..."

Sister Magdalene nodded her head towards the tray. "Very well, then, take it before it gets cold," she said.

"Oh, thank you, thank you ...

Rising quickly, all trace of tears gone, Sister Teresa Margaret took the tray, and with a happy face fled towards the locked room before Sister Magdalene had time to change her mind.

Shortly after this, Teresa Margaret was given charge of the infirmary, and there were few members of the community who did not, at one time or another, have some experience of her solicitude. More and more she was obliged to forego those devotional practices she had so long maintained, and which had been a source of such consolation to her. Spiritual reading and recitation of the rosary often had to be omitted, and in the hurried notes she scribbled to Father Ildefonse, she told him of this, adding the reason: "So many are the duties imposed on me by obedience." No longer could she find leisure to spend hours of free time in visits to the Blessed Sacrament, but more and more she learned to find Christ in His suffering members, and gladly she deprived herself of these consolations in order to give herself more completely to her sisters. There were many occasions when the time she could normally have spent in preparation for Holy Communion had to be sacrificed to the needs of her patients.

On one occasion she was performing some service for Sister Teresa Mary of the Immaculate Conception, and the patient noticed that it was past the hour for Mass.

"You must not stay here with me any longer," Sister Teresa Mary urged her. "It is late. Go now, and prepare yourself for Holy Communion."

But Teresa Margaret continued calmly with her task.

"Don't fret," she said soothingly, I shall be deprived of nothing except perhaps a little leisure. As for preparation, can there be any better than the performance of duties given one by obedience, particularly when it is also serving the sick? Even though I am in your cell instead of in choir, I shall lose nothing, for God is not restricted either to time or place."

On another occasion Sister Teresa Mary had a fainting attack just before Communion and could not be left. While Teresa Margaret was attending her, Mother Anna Maria entered the room.

"If you wish to go to Holy Communion, Sister," she said, "I will ask one of the others to take over from you here to give you time to go to choir and prepare yourself."

The young infirmarian looked up with her usual unhurried calm.

"I cannot think of any better preparation or one more pleasing to God than assisting His suffering members," she replied with a smile.

Mother Anna Maria said later, "I have never forgotten those words or the spirit of charity and tenderness that emanated from her. I always recall them when preparing for Holy Communion, for it never fails to enkindle fervor and recollection in me merely to recall the complete absorption in God which that act of charity affected in her."

One unusual, although not necessarily miraculous, event occurred while this nun was in the infirmary. One day, as Sister Teresa Mary, who suffered from a mild form of epilepsy, seemed much better, Teresa Margaret thought she could safely be left alone. When the bell rang at 5 p.m. to summon the community to prayer, she made her way with the others to the choir, for the first time in many weeks.

The *Veni Sancte Spiritus* was said, and Teresa Margaret allowed the care of the infirmary to slip away, immersing herself in the wordless prayer which had now become habitual with her, enjoying the peace of the quiet, dim choir, and the chance to join her sisters in this spiritual exercise, which had so long been denied her. But suddenly and quite inexplicably she began to feel uneasy, and a strong urge seemed to draw her to return to her patient. She shook it off as a distraction, and applied herself once more to prayer. But the prompting returned more insistently:

"Go to Sister Teresa Mary at *once!*"

For a few more minutes she struggled with it, and then, on a sudden impulse, asked permission to leave the choir, and almost ran to the infirmary. There she found that Sister Teresa Mary, in another epileptic fit - the first in months - had fallen out of bed and was lying unconscious on the floor, in urgent need of assistance.

This incident was submitted to Father Ildefonse by Teresa Margaret for his verdict as to whether she had acted imperfectly in leaving the choir on her own initiative and without a direct order to do so!

Teresa Margaret now had ample scope to make herself a servant to "all those angels," and she was undoubtedly overworked. But she was always so willing, eagerly seeking an opportunity to perform some little gratuitous service on top of her actual duty, that nobody seemed to realize how heavily she was burdened.

She was an ideal infirmarian, attentive to all, solicitous, but without that agitation and fuss that so often creeps in when one has rather more than usual to cope with, and which is particularly trying to an invalid. Seemingly she had the wonderful gift possessed rarely, but which is the outstanding characteristic of a perfect nurse, the reassuring touch of "friendly fingers" - that is, the ability to soothe with a hand laid on an aching head; or a wrinkled sheet or lumpy pillow straightened and discomfort eased. Most of her patients, young or old, found in her ministrations not only relief from physical ills, but great spiritual comfort and profit, a desire and determination to bear their ailments patiently and with love.

"Confidence" the infirmarian would give as her constant advice and principal panacea for all ills, "Have confidence in God!" She sought to comfort them in their troubles, knowing that anxiety was not a good nurse. Her counsels were aimed at true perfection and the merit to be won from sickness. They were never mere condolences of the "soothing-syrup" variety, but advice as to how the cross must be accepted, with love and submission to the will of God, which is the only true source of peace and joy in suffering. Her simple, sincere words touched their hearts and very often met the particular needs of their souls, which to some of them, seemed almost miraculous.

Her self-mastery as well as her self-denial was extraordinary, as during this period she herself was suffering many spiritual difficulties and trials. One day Sister Magdalene noticed the apparent interior conflict with which she was struggling, and which she usually concealed so well. "Why do you not speak of these troubles with Father Ildefonse?" she asked.

"Ah, I must be about my Father's business. So long as I strive to fulfill my obligations, there is no place in my life for the luxury of spiritual conversation and consolations."

She refused nothing that was asked of her. Often she was requested to recite the Divine Office with one of the Sick sisters, although she had already attended the recitation in choir; but with no appearance of reluctance, she would fetch her breviary and slowly plod through the psalms and lessons once more at their pace. Many patients asked her to join them in their prayers, which she gladly did, although very often the particular devotions to which they were attached were singularly unsuited to her own needs and tastes, and as there was not time for both, she willingly sacrificed the hour of silent prayer she had so much looked forward to, in order to recite long litanies and special petitions for this or that intention with some of the old nuns.

One of her most interesting and consoling charges was the eighty-year-old Sister Adelaide of the Cross, who had been bedridden for some years, and whose failing memory was a source of much distress to herself. These two, despite the great disparity in age, were spiritual sisters in the real sense of the word, and between them developed an extraordinarily intimate friendship. The young infirmarian suffered acutely because of the "indolence" or aridity of spirit she often experienced; and she was aware of a similar anxiety in Sister Adelaide. Besides, the resignation of the old nun, her patient suffering and unfailing gentleness, endeared her to Teresa Margaret, who sensed in her serenity a detachment and submission that was the fruit of real virtue and grace. The two conversed at length on the love and beauty of God, exhorting each other to a desire for suffering with and for Christ.

Sister Adelaide had been almost deaf for some time, and even with an ear-trumpet she could distinguish very little of what was said to her. Yet so well did Sister Teresa Margaret understand her that the two could converse and comprehend each other with ease. Indeed, a sort of telepathy seemed to develop between them, and should Teresa Margaret be absent from the infirmary, Sister Adelaide had only to call for her in a low voice, and the infirmarian would come hastening to attend her need. On her side, Teresa Margaret never needed to raise her voice to be understood by Sister Adelaide, who heard others only with great difficulty. They really understood each other's hearts and souls, and a look was often sufficient to communicate mutual thoughts or needs.

Sister Teresa Margaret cared for this patient almost single-handedly, and many of the sisters remarked on the astonishing facility with which she handled the old nun. Despite her seeming fragility, she was strong, but even so the others were amazed at the ease with which she lifted Sister Adelaide without assistance when bathing and dressing her. To them it seemed to transcend natural powers.

One day towards the end of 1769, Sister Adelaide was very ill and expressed a wish to make her confession immediately. A priest was sent for, and the call was answered by Father Ildefonse, who found Sister Adelaide distraught and restless. After hearing her confession, he tried to speak a few words of comfort, but she could hear little. His visit soothed her, however, and she began to breathe more easily and seemed less distressed. Suddenly, in a voice that was barely audible to those in the room, she called: "Sister Teresa Margaret!"

Immediately Sister Teresa Margaret, who was in another room, put down what she was doing and went to the patient. She raised the pillows and eased her position.

"Thank you, thank you. I am quite comfortable," murmured the patient gratefully. "Now speak to me a little about the good God."

Teresa Margaret began to speak in a quiet voice, hardly above a whisper, suggesting acts of faith, resignation, and love. Watching her from the adjoining room, all the onlookers marveled, because Sister Adelaide, for all her deafness, followed the words of the infirmarian and appeared to derive great consolation from them.

"Sister," Teresa Margaret said at length, bending low over the bed, "when you are in heaven, for the love of God I beg you not to forget the promise which you made me."

"Well, Father," said one of the nuns as they accompanied Father Ildefonse from the infirmary, "You have seen our little Sister Teresa Margaret in action. And what do you think of her?"

"Indeed, I think she could teach many priests how to assist the dying. But what is this promise they were talking about?"

"Oh, those two have made a compact. As soon as our patient shall be in the presence of God, she is to ask Him to permit Sister Teresa Margaret to join her quickly in order that she may love Him without hindrance for all eternity and be fully united with the fount of divine charity."

It was Father Ildefonse who related this little incident, which introduced him into a new and hitherto unrevealed aspect of his gifted young penitent. There is no need to look for a preternatural explanation or regard as miraculous the ease with which Teresa Margaret communicated with the old nun. It is quite possible that Sister Adelaide understood Teresa Margaret without difficulty because she was the only person who took the trouble to speak carefully and quietly, in such wise that the old nun could partly read her lips; as is well known, a person who is not totally deaf can often catch softly spoken words, if carefully enunciated, when shouting is quite unintelligible. But it appears that there was more to it than that, or Father Ildefonse would not have been so impressed. It is hardly likely that he himself had been shouting at the old nun whose confession he had just heard, and to whom he had endeavored to give some spiritual counsel. Yet he had failed where Teresa Margaret had succeeded without the least effort.

But what gave him most food for thought was the "spiritual promise" which these two had so artlessly made, and which the young nun obviously expected to be literally fulfilled. It was not the first time Father Ildefonse had noted the desire which was gradually gaining intensity, and this compact seemed to add fresh impetus to it. "It closely resembled the longing expressed by St. Paul: 'I desire to be dissolved and to be with Christ,'" he said later. "Her mind and heart were always drawn towards God, and, she had a truly burning desire for an early death and quick liberation from the prison of the flesh in order to love Him eternally without any obstacle."

Less than four months after this incident, Teresa Margaret was indeed with Christ in God. If the cause of her death actually was hernia, it is more than likely that it was in lifting the heavy, inert body of Sister Adelaide that she strained herself; in which case, it provides a delightful "seal" to their simple pact.

When he was informed of her sudden death, Father Ildefonse expressed no surprise. He had realized for some time, he said, from her interior state and development, that she was rapidly approaching the end of her mortal life in the transformation of union with God, and commented: "Death itself was the final victorious consummation of this hidden fire that burned within her, and to her might very aptly be applied the words of Scripture: 'The Lord thy God is a consuming fire.'"

Little difficulties, great trials, small discomforts or agonizing sufferings - all are meritorious insofar as we unite them to the Passion of Christ. Our Lord once said that often souls are in less danger in time of great temptation than when assailed by petty failings, such as curiosity, breaking silence, and lack of custody of the eyes. These, being regarded as trifling matters, are not guarded against with the same energy as would be expended in the case of a really serious and obvious danger; however, far from being of little importance, these imperfections are in reality a great hindrance to spiritual progress, because less effort is made in regard to them than is the case with more apparent spiritual dangers. And, as the Wise Man tells us, the one who is careless of little things shall gradually fall to his own ruin.

The same rule applies to little acts of courtesy, kindness, charity. Because they are so trifling, we neglect them, instead of seeing in them countless opportunities of proving our love of God. "Force yourself to become like Jesus in humility," Teresa Margaret counseled. "If we want to find God, no way is surer than humility of heart and simplicity of soul. We shall obtain nothing without a struggle, but have courage! We shall not lack the grace and help of the Sacred Heart. Let us not waste time, however, for every moment is precious ... if we want to become saints, we must work and suffer in silence, keeping our souls in peace."

In this spirit, which softens any tendency to harshness or rigidity in so absolute a program of asceticism, investing all with the bright joyousness of a freely-made gift to love, Teresa Margaret found in everything the opportunity of giving to God at her own cost. But what strikes one most forcibly is that all such offerings were made, not as the sacrifices of a stern self-executioner, or in a gloomy spirit of expiation, but with a free, glad spirit, which delighted in pouring out whatever came to hand, as a precious ointment on the feet of Him who was all to her. It was no negative renunciation, but a positive lavishing of her love, expressed by whatever the present moment put in her hand to give. This is the animating motive of all her penances and self-abnegations, transmuting them into a fruitful source of spiritual joy to herself, while at the same time she appropriated to herself no merit from them. Nothing could be further from her thoughts; she was, she considered, doing nothing more than her duty and much less than God had the right to expect of her in strict justice, weighed in the balance of what He had done and suffered freely and willingly for her.

She bore the rigor of her ascetic life with such love that, seeing the tranquil joy of her face and bearing, no one could possibly suspect how many privations or what great interior trials she in fact endured. While herself capable of the highest virtue, she knew how to encourage the weaker, enkindling in them an ardor and determination to advance towards perfection. When she had more to bear than usual and felt oppressed by the load, she would call to mind all that Jesus had done and suffered for her, saying "God has endured so much for me, it is well that I should suffer a little for Him. He would not have acted thus for me, for when He fell beneath His cross it was through weakness of His body, whereas our falls are due to weakness of our wills." Then she would try to think of the eternal glory He set before her, by comparison with which the present difficulties or afflictions would indeed appear light.

It troubled Teresa Margaret to think that she had so little to suffer for God who had suffered so greatly for her, and she continued to seek permissions for additional fasts and penances over and above those legislated. Seeing so much suffering among the sisters whom she tended as infirmarian, she would remark, "Clearly, Jesus treats you as real spouses, allowing you to share His cross; while to me, so ungrateful and unworthy, He sends no suffering, but allows me always to enjoy perfect health." And yet, apart from penances, on the physical plane, Teresa Margaret suffered much from overwork, fatigue, the intense summer heat which caused persistent thirst and discomfort, the biting cold of damp winters in an unheated building. Her constant weariness was a source of both interior and exterior suffering, for she felt it was through lack of fervor that she fell asleep during the choir offices instead of attending to the recitation. Much as the sisters admired her willingness to endure discomfort and mortification, together with her humility in seeking to avoid observation, none save her director ever really knew the extent of her physical sufferings, except on those occasions when concealment was impossible. She endured agony from chilblains every winter, but continued to wash her cracked and bleeding hands in icy water and scrub them vigorously with coarse, hard towels. The flat heel-less sandals do not usually give any trouble to present-day novices, accustomed to sports clothes. But the sudden change from her accustomed footwear caused real discomfort, which Teresa Margaret managed to conceal until her feet and ankles swelled noticeably and she was ordered to do something about it. The Carmelite habit is itself a form of penance, and more so in those days when the materials were much heavier. A loose tunic of rather stiff serge, caught at the waist with a leather girdle, it is neither cool in the summer nor particularly warm in winter, and when one is engaged in heavy manual work, its weight can cause extreme discomfort.

The Rule requires it - God wills it. Those two considerations were quite sufficient for her to overcome all natural repugnance or inconvenience in duties or renunciations that the common life and observance imposed. She genuinely believed everyone else to be better and more virtuous than herself, and it never entered her head that she herself was the most conspicuous example of humility, charity, and obedience in the convent - conspicuous, that is, to us seeing her life in retrospect, but not to her companions. For it is a condition of perfection to pass unnoticed. It was because of her absolute perfection that our Lady lived unremarked and unobserved by her neighbors. The moment anything, even the practice of a virtue, becomes obtrusive, it has veered slightly off the true, departed from the path of genuine perfection.

It is an outstanding tribute to the self-discipline and control of this twenty-year-old girl that she was never regarded as being in any way extraordinary. Her ambition was always to appear "just like all the others," and her natural talents and gifts of mind and heart, as well as those of supernatural grace, were as though they did not exist to herself and to those who lived in intimate companionship with her. It is true they did not notice faults, such as are semi-habitual with most of us, but this is something quite negative. What is truly astonishing is the naturalness with which she subtracted all that was obtrusive from her acts of virtue, so that they too were performed unnoticed at the time. Yet in retrospect they could be recalled so clearly by all as to be deemed really outstanding. This is the perfection of the hidden life, a vastly different thing from perfectionism.

Important as is fraternal charity, it is only one part of the vocation of love. True contemplation must be apostolic, and although the scope of her activity is restricted and her ability to render practical service limited to the few of her companions, nevertheless the cloistered nun's charity goes out to the world, wherever there are souls to be saved. "A Carmelite who was not an apostle," St. Thérèse declared, "would be unworthy to call herself a daughter of the seraphic St. Teresa, who would have given a thousand lives to save a single soul."

Zeal for the salvation of souls holds a vital place in the life and prayers of the enclosed religious, for the aim of her consecration is so to live in God as to be permeated by His Spirit which is love and thus impregnated, to love with His own love all that He loves and to participate in His own redemptive desires. Genuine Christian charity unites love of God with love of one's fellow-men. Without this zeal for the apostolate, the enclosed religious would indeed be failing to fulfill her vocation. And this remains true, despite the fact that the life of prayer and silence does not find its outlet in active apostolic work. Her mission is the apostolate of prayer, the apostolate of love.

This solicitude for the salvation of souls had always exercised the mind of Teresa Margaret, but once she entered Carmel, her prayers and sacrifices were channeled very particularly towards the apostolate. Sister Teresa Mary, one of her fellow novices, said of her: "An ardent zeal for the propagation of the faith literally devoured her. She longed to bring every soul out of the darkness of ignorance. By her prayers she would help priests and all those who were laboring to lead souls to God. She often said: 'Let us never forget that our Holy Mother founded our convents especially to pray for this end. If we are negligent about this point, we are totally lacking in her spirit and can no longer regard ourselves as her daughters.'"

Her zeal in this respect led Teresa Margaret to issue a series of "spiritual challenges" to her sisters. This custom, highly esteemed by St. Teresa as a means of spurring others on to greater efforts by the use of the natural spirit of rivalry, is only to be recommended with reservations. It can easily degenerate into a mere competition for tallying up astronomical scores of aspirations or acts, with little spiritual value, and no other merit than purely natural satisfaction. But with Teresa Margaret it was not merely a form of pious parlor game. She obtained sanction for it from her confessor and officially placed it under the aegis of the Sacred Heart, who was to be, as it were, the recipient of the graces obtained as well as the arbiter of the "challenge."

The various exercises of prayer, mortification, and virtue were the field of their engagements, and the emphasis was to be on the practice of the presence of God. Encouraged continually by the efforts and example of each other, they were to grow and increase in charity themselves and also to obtain similar graces for souls weak in faith or fervor, who were not in a good position to obtain them for themselves. There would thus be no limit to their zeal, which could include not only every soul in this world and in purgatory, but would embrace the whole communion of saints. Observance of the rules of silence and deportment with particular exactitude, voluntary practices of mortification, little curbs on self-will and curiosity, extra care in performing manual work - all such small external activities - became occasions for self-control and self-denial, making fuel for the fire of love in this silent apostolate which, although it might sound trifling, did produce much good for themselves and for others. Father John Colombino, their confessor, encouraged it, and when through illness he relinquished the post, his successor continued to give it warm support. After the death of Teresa Margaret, Father Ildefonse was shown many little notes she had written to her "competitors" which he read, as he said, "with great emotion, because they breathed profound humility, ardent love of God, and zeal for the profit of souls."

Unlike many of the Carmelite saints, Teresa Margaret has left us no written testimony of her doctrine; on the contrary, she was assiduous in concealing her own gifts and graces, so that if possible they should pass unnoticed. For this reason, the detailed evidence of Father Ildefonse, her spiritual director, is particularly valuable. A learned and experienced guide of souls, his sober and carefully-phrased sentences carry the weight of authority, and he knew the soul of Teresa Margaret through and through. He affirms that "it was not difficult to discern where the activity of her soul was concentrated, and out of her all-embracing love was born the ardent zeal, devouring as a flame, that was to consume her life with its own fire. One thought animated her: to use every means, to leave no stone unturned, that could win to the love of Jesus Christ all souls capable of knowing and loving Him. The glory of God and the salvation of souls were her exclusive preoccupations." And this was achieved in complete forgetfulness of self, which characterizes the state of holiness.

The further Teresa Margaret advanced in divine charity, the greater became her longing to see Him loved by all. On occasions when prayers were requested for special intentions, such as the conversion of one leading a sinful life or neglecting the practice of his religion, she would exclaim: "Is it possible that there can be so much evil in the world, and so many offences committed against a God who is so good?"

She exhorted others on every possible occasion to lose no opportunity of offering some little mortification, however trivial, even the mere stifling of an impulse to curiosity, for souls in sin or in danger of losing the faith. On one occasion Sister Teresa of Jesus Crucified had been guilty of some breach of regulations which had earned her a sharp reprimand before the community. The rebuke seems to have been more severe than the offence warranted, and to the novice's distress was added resentment at the seeming injustice. This threw her into a state of confusion and an agony of embarrassment, which her young companion was quick to notice.

"Quick now," Teresa Margaret whispered to her, "this is a fine chance to make your fortune for eternity. Offer this grief to Jesus, and give it to Him as a bouquet. Forget it; excuse it; pardon them! Accept the humiliation in expiation for faults committed by souls consecrated to God."

The value of Father Ildefonse's testimony lies not only in its objectivity, but in the fact that as an experienced director, he was unlikely to be misled by superficial piety. He observed Teresa Margaret closely, always taking care to say nothing to her that would reveal his more than usually close scrutiny and interest. She was completely candid and frank, and he knew her soul, as he himself said, down to its least aspiration. She had, he declared, "reached the most eminent degree of union with God and perfection of virtue. Her recollected bearing, the mortification of her whole being, especially of eyes and tongue, her calm and humble deportment, gave her the appearance of being completely detached from external things and absorbed in deep meditation. It was not difficult to discern where the activity of her soul was concentrated ... now that she was nearing the summit of transforming union. Her love felt the urgent need to communicate love to others and carry them with her in her flight towards God who is Love."

It is as well that these words were penned a century before Thérèse

Martin opened her eyes on the light of this world. Otherwise, it would be easy to suspect that the writer, struck by the similarities between Teresa Margaret's "little way" and that of her Carmelite sister of Lisieux (the hiddenness of their apostolate and the power and strength of their love, the consistent use of little things done with perfection and love, to mention but a few), had borrowed the language of St. Thérèse. In her letter to her sister Marie, on the boundlessness of her apostolic desires and the attraction of divine love, drawing her inexorably towards its consummation, and with her the souls of all those she had loved and who were united with her on earth, Thérèse expresses sentiments which seem to echo Father Ildefonse's evaluation of the apostolic zeal of his own spiritual daughter.

"To acquire the holy love of God," Teresa Margaret once told a sister who questioned her on this subject, "the best means is to live in the presence of God. Just as someone who loves a person often recalls that person to mind, so we too must often remember that God is always present and concerned with doing us good. In love, one must return love for love, and God has loved us and loves us so much in spite of our unworthiness. How, then, can we succeed in rendering Him a similar love, even in part? There is only one way. We must *force* ourselves to become like Jesus, telling Him always in the pains and difficulties we experience: 'I want to suffer everything without murmuring for the love of my God; I fear nothing.'"

16

The Grace of *Deus Caritas est*

Love with Thee no spring had ever,
But summer bright;
Shadow rested on it never,
Nor dawn, nor night.
I, who knew but winter's bareness,
How could I prize,
Earth lit up with springtide fairness
From out Thy eyes?
(Vincent McNabb, O.P.)

God has indeed pitched His tents among men, but He does much more than merely dwell in our midst; He has His abode within the soul in grace. The awareness of the indwelling of the Blessed Trinity was so integral a part of the spiritual itinerary of Sister Elizabeth of the Trinity, that often we are tempted to think of its expression mainly in connection with her life and the accent she placed on it; but it is a facet of the life of grace and progress in holiness in every soul, for as Julian of Norwich expressed it so aptly six centuries ago: "Where Jesus is, there the whole Trinity appeareth."

When God dwells in the soul, nothing, however humdrum, can be trivial. We do not live in those commonplace things that fill our daily life, but above them, in the realm of the supernatural, enclosed, hidden in God. In religious life it should not be difficult to love and to live in love. From morning till night one has rule and customs, as well

as the wishes of superiors which present God's will to him from moment to moment, so that this act of love is rendered quite uncomplicated. When a religious becomes entangled with *minutiae,* is anxious and troubled about material preoccupations or success, he has
stepped out of the supernatural, and, what is more, he knows instantly
that he has done so.

True love necessarily involves imitation of Christ, who is the
way, the truth, and the life. "Nobody can go to the Father except
through Him," and at all stages of the spiritual life, however high its
development, Jesus must be our model and our guide. In the resolutions she made before pronouncing her vows, Sister Teresa Margaret
wrote: "Knowing that a spouse cannot please a Spouse if she does not
study with special care to become like Him, I resolve now and for
always, O Jesus my Spouse, to imitate you and to crucify myself with
you in a more complete mortification of all my powers."

From the commencement of her religious life she had set herself
the ideal of resembling her crucified Savior as far as possible through
obedience, self-denial, and prayer, so as to offer herself to the Heart of
Jesus as a victim of expiation and love for the sins of mankind. In prayer,
the mysteries of the life, passion, and death of our Lord, and all medita-
tions on His Sacred Humanity, lifted her to a sphere of pure love and
profound contemplation, Father Ildefonse said, which often produced a
deep and absorbing recollection that lasted sometimes for days.

When we consider her love of the Sacred Humanity of Christ, "the
radiance of the Father's splendor and the full expression of His being," it is
easy to realize that everything in her very simple life and spirituality was the
logical outcome of that love - her humility and hiddenness, her love of lowliness, charity, and constant desire to "suffer and be silent for Jesus, to return
Him love for Love." More and more she sought, so far as is possible for a
creature, to unite her personal actions with those of the Incarnate Word, and
to imitate ever more perfectly the hidden life of Christ. Her love for God as a
tender Father, through the Son and in the Spirit, was childlike, confident, and
reverent, full of gladness and tranquility, drawing her gradually into the inner
life and love of the Blessed Trinity.

"Do you not understand that you are God's temple, and that the

Spirit has His dwelling in you?" St. Paul asks the Corinthians. "The Kingdom of God is within us! Oh, what a fine temple is ours - what an abode for our God is the soul in grace!" exclaimed Teresa Margaret on the day of her profession, overwhelmed by the thought of the splendor of the soul in its purity and grace of this "second baptism."

The love of the Father flows down to us through the Son, who is the model of our supernatural life of grace. It is only by becoming sons in the Son that we can enter into the life of the Trinity, and our place in that life is a participation in the sonship of Christ. This divine love catches men up in its flood, proceeding from the Father, through the Son, in the Holy Spirit; and bearing us on its tide, ebbs back by the Spirit through Christ to the Father.

But it does not carry us as passengers. There is a condition, St. Paul tells us: "If we would share His glory, we must also share His sufferings." *Ex tenebris lux* is the great paradox of Christianity: the joy out of suffering, victory through defeat, light out of darkness, and life from death. "He who loses his life for my sake will find it"; while "he who loves his life will lose it; he who is an enemy to his own life in this world will keep it, so as to live eternally." Like the grain of wheat cast into the furrow, we must learn to die to ourselves before we can germinate and grow in the spiritual life, the only sphere in which we can truly hope to yield a rich harvest.

We must belong to Christ on pain of being excluded from His kingdom. And if we are Christ's (and Christ is God's), then He will draw us to the bosom of the Father and into that eternal life of love that is the Blessed Trinity.

Every Sunday is, in a sense, a feast of the Blessed Trinity, as is obvious from the liturgy. Sister Teresa Margaret sought to pay homage to the three divine Persons especially on this day by acts of adoration and thanksgiving directed to the Father for His omnipotence, adoring Love as Creator and Giver; to the Son, Incarnate Love in the Sacred Humanity of Jesus, for His wisdom; and to the Holy Spirit as the love consuming her heart. She always prepared for and celebrated the feast of the Blessed Trinity with particular care and devotion. She would honor as distinct each divine Person, entering into a personal communion with Him without however in any way looking past God's essential indivisible unity.

She was always particularly attentive to the doxology, *Gloria Patri, et Filio, et Spiritui Sancto,* repeated constantly at the endings of prayers during the day, and after each psalm of the divine office, recalling that she was invoking the Blessed Trinity and needed to be recollected. Her favorite invocation was a prayer she discovered:

"To you be love, praise, honor, glory,

To you be expressions of deepest gratitude,

O most holy, blessed and glorious Trinity,

Our one God."

Speaking to Mother Anna Maria on one occasion, Teresa Margaret said, "In God the Father there is everything, for God is Love. Through love He made everything, and He is the first cause of everything; and this love is God Himself. We constantly receive countless blessings from God, and we can give Him nothing that is in any way worthy of Him. So let us be content to remain in a perpetual abyss of debts, depending purely and simply on the infinite generosity of the Supreme Giver."

On another occasion, reflecting that we cannot go to the Father except through Christ, and that the way *par excellence is* by imitation of His humility and suffering, she repeated the words of St. Bernard: "Under a Head crowned with thorns, it ill becomes us to have our bodies crowned with roses."

"Remember," she cautioned, "that on entering religious life you undertook to reproduce in yourself the life of the Crucified. The cloister is your Calvary, regular observance the cross, and the three vows the nails that fix you to it." On another occasion she declared that no one could profess to follow a rule of life unless she fully understood every part of it. "Many seculars could give an example to religious by their zeal in serving the princes of this world, for they have no regard for inconvenience or hardship, when there is a chance of doing something for their temporal masters or for material profit."

Father Ildefonse, giving testimony on this matter, spoke of Teresa

Margaret's deep and ardent devotion to the Holy Spirit, the Love of God, who enkindled in her the flame of His own love. All her aspirations, doubts, and needs, as well as her prayers and petitions on behalf of others (particularly for priests and the conversion of souls) she confided especially to the Holy Spirit. He was her "plenipotentiary" - everything, for her, went through love in the Spirit. At times she became so overwhelmed with these desires and her own inability to articulate them, that she felt as though she would explode with the pent-up vehemence she experienced. "I should like a strong faith to break these bonds which hold me prisoner," she said, "but I do not know how. Yet I hope in the mercy of God and in His Love. 'I have run the way of thy commandments, when thou didst enlarge my heart.'" Indeed, it was only by enlarging her heart, deepening her capacity for these graces, that she was able to contain them without faltering under the weight of glory confined in a finite human heart.

The effect of love is to unite and transform, begetting intimacy and likeness between lover and beloved, and the triumph of love is the domination of the soul by the Spirit of Love. Although fidelity to duty, charity, and the external practices of virtue are indispensable at all times, of themselves they are unable to effect this sovereignty which is brought about by a union in the deepest center of the soul as love grows in strength, supplanting all attachments to creature joys. The primacy of love in the supernatural order was at the basis of Teresa Margaret's whole spiritual life, which ever sped towards its deepest center in the Blessed Trinity. Willing charity, kindness, forgetfulness of self, and humility were her outstanding traits. Love drew her towards God, ever seeking the solution to her childish question: Who is God?

One Sunday after Pentecost, on the 28th of June, 1767, when Sister Teresa Margaret was officiating in choir, she read out the little chapter at Terce: *"Deus caritas est."* She had heard these words repeatedly, Sunday after Sunday, for the past three years, but now it seemed as though she understood them for the first time - or rather, her understanding of them was raised to an entirely different plane. The verse struck her with the force of a revelation: "God is love; he who dwells in love dwells in God, and God in him." This dwelling had been the goal of all her striving, seeking as she did to imitate the interior life and hidden operations of Christ. From that day onwards the necessity of proving her love by deeds became so compelling a force that it was obvious to her sisters that some special grace had been given her. "Nobody comes to the Father except through Jesus," she said. "To come to God who is everything and consequently all good, no fatigue must seem to us too great; we must not be put off either by the difficulties we meet on the way, but accept bitterness and welcome every kind of cross with eagerness. By these means, which are precisely those of Jesus Christ, it is not difficult to come to the true God, to live in charity, to walk in love."

Despite her customary reticence and assiduity in concealing any graces or spiritual favors, the fact that something out of the ordinary had taken place on that Sunday morning was apparent to all. For days the young nun seemed quite out of herself, and the sudden illumination that the words had sent flooding into her soul is difficult to explain, because of the seeming triviality of the incident and her own habitual silence about such things. It marked the beginning of a new stage in her spiritual life, as Father Ildefonse was quick to observe. From this time, he noticed that the quiet, self-possessed and reserved sister appeared to withdraw even more into herself, becoming engrossed in a silent, determined, and conscious awareness of the presence within her, and her endeavors to attain to perfect union with Him. However, this withdrawal was a purely spiritual matter, and there was no suggestion of cutting herself adrift from the community, for she continued to give herself wholeheartedly to all, in her services as infirmarian, in companionship and sympathy at recreation, and in never avoiding her share of work on the grounds of seeking more solitude.

Speaking to Father Ildefonse one day, she tried to express to him something of the significance those words *God is love* now held for her, but she became almost incoherent in her emotion. "Just as the soul in the state of grace (which is charity) is in God, God is in her. Just as the soul lives the life of God, so does God in a certain way live

IN her. And so it is that between them there is but a single life, a single love ... God alone! The difference is that God has all by essence, whereas the creature has it only by participation and grace." And, adds Father Ildefonse, "Note that these words came from a simple child who had never studied and knew no theology apart from what her instinct taught her."

On another occasion she ventured the opinion that, after one had passed the whole day in continual spiritual activity, sleep itself ought to be an "occupation of affection and service of the divine majesty."

"Is it not possible," she asked, "to work with the intellect and will while the body sleeps? I mean, cannot one continue to love God while asleep, in virtue of the consistent daily habit of doing so?"

"To be sure the value of our actions depends to a great extent on the habits we have formed," he told her cautiously. "This applies to bad or careless habits as well as to good ones. If, for instance, we are accustomed to looking at all things from the point of view of our own pleasure and advantage, then the evil lies not so much in neglecting to consider the glory of God as the projection, in countless repeated acts throughout the day, of the dominant theme of our own selfish interests. By such daily conduct, although never consciously adverted to, habits of mind are formed, which, from merely being errant or negligent, become ingrained dispositions. It is thus that 'he that contemneth small things shall fall by little and little' as we read in the Book of Ecclesiasticus."

"Then," said Teresa Margaret, "if one is habitually watchful during the day, could not the act of love in which one lives endure even in sleep? Is not that what the Spouse in the *Canticles* intended when she says 'I sleep, but my heart watches'?"

"An act of the will does not destroy a habit of mind. For instance, were there no contrary habits of thinking and acting, the one act of offering made in the morning would consecrate to God every action of the day. But as you know, this is not so. Despite our morning intention of doing everything in God and for Him, we constantly look to our own interest and need to recollect ourselves and renew our offering frequently."

"Ah, yes," she said, "but in speaking of an act of love, I did not mean one formulated such as when we make an act of charity. Is it not the property of a habit to procure its action without the soul's even noticing its particular influence? You say that when we act habitually for ourselves we no longer notice it. Very well, I want to act for God, to live in His love so uninterruptedly that the habit dominates me completely and so thoroughly that I no longer perceive it and can continue to love God and give myself to Him even while my body sleeps."

On that June morning, Teresa Margaret crossed the threshold which marks the final stages of union of the soul with God. There is, of course, no clear or definable line of demarcation, and the expression "threshold" is only by way of metaphor. But now God begins to manifest Himself through His action on the essence of the soul's powers. The two streams - that is the soul's own efforts and the divine action - have not, of course, been running parallel or divided courses but have mingled at all times; but now the intervention of God becomes more tangible and unmistakable, and an experienced director, such as Father Ildefonse, could not have failed to notice and classify it. Vivid illumination is shed on truths already known, and at times the soul becomes aware of the divine Presence as an external and internal reality which floods the mind and heart with sensible delight. Instead of making known to the soul facts about God, He reveals Himself in the most perfect way that is possible in this life. This is what is known as "infused contemplation" in the strict sense, and it is described by St. Teresa in Mansions V, VI, and VII of *The Interior Castle,* also under the Third and Fourth Waters in her *Life.* St. John of the Cross expounds it in the *Spiritual Canticle* and *Living Flame of Love.*

True to her elected program of "ordinariness," however, no spectacular grace such as St. Teresa received to mark the various phases of mystical union, initiated it for her little Florentine daughter. Her soul was transpierced by a shaft of light and love, but all the community noticed was that, during three days following the signal grace, her face and bearing expressed the radiant transport she had experienced, and for once her habitual self-control and restraint of speech and gesture seemed to desert her. Again and again she would repeat the words: *Deus caritas est.*

One day she spoke at length with Mother Anna Maria, who endeavored to probe her on the subject of this experience. Suddenly Teresa Margaret blushed violently with the effort to control her emotion, and as rapidly the blood drained from her face, leaving her pale and exhausted. She laid her head on the older nun's shoulder, seemingly overcome by an upsurge of feeling that could not be expressed in words. On another occasion, in conversation, the words of St. Paul: "It is in Him that we live and move and have our being" were mentioned. Sister Teresa Margaret asked Mother Anna Maria to make a compact with her: to recall often to mind this indwelling, that they lived in God, moved and had their being in Him. They were to repeat the text frequently as a means of reviving the awareness of their union in Him and with each other in Him.

Father Ildefonse had always watched Teresa Margaret closely, and he testifies that from this time the level of goodness and virtue she had already attained seemed to act as a springboard or a runner's block. She now prepared to gather together all her forces and fling herself towards the summits, her sole preoccupation being with the glory of God, the practice of virtue, and the wholehearted giving of herself in charity to her sisters. A decided change had occurred in her spiritual life, confirming her in the strong attraction she had always felt towards making a complete holocaust of herself to the love of the Sacred Heart, and transforming the attraction into a vocation as victim of love and expiation. Her disposition of oblation remained uninterrupted from that morning in 1767, although she was not to make a formal offering of herself until nine months later.

As the late Father Gabriel of St. Mary Magdalene, O.C.D. said: "It is clear that during the choir office of Terce on that Sunday in 1767, the work of her sanctification passed out of the control of her human will, understood in terms of spiritual theology, and became subject to a power infinitely greater because wholly divine. It was obvious that she retained the full and free use of her will, since she continued to live - and to advance - in a community which made many heavy demands upon it, but henceforward, her personal impulses and initiatives were under the complete control of the Holy Spirit."

17

Hidden with Christ in God

So long thy power hath
blest me, sure it still
Will lead me on
O'er moor and fen,
o'er crag and torrent, till
The night is gone,
And with the morn those
angel faces smile,
Which I have loved long since,
and lost awhile.
(J.H. Newman)

Towards the end of February, 1768, Sister Teresa Margaret made a private retreat which was to have considerable influence on her spiritual progress. She seemed now to throw herself completely into the furnace of the Sacred Heart, receiving fresh lights and impulses on her attraction to this devotion. Even though she had always been meticulous in her regularity and fidelity to the common life and her duties, and assiduous in her practice of hiddenness, her companions could not but be aware that from this time forward there was some indefinable change; she had crossed a new threshold, and despite her habitual reticence, the ever-deepening experience of Love could no longer be concealed. Her face and deportment at times betrayed such an overflow of emotion that the patients in the infirmary, who saw her constantly, were conscious of some new phase of growth or orientation.

On February 25th, when Teresa Margaret commenced her retreat, another of the Discalced friars, Father Gregory (who had succeeded Father Colombino as Provincial)[1] wrote to her: "As requested, I am sending you some suggestions by which you might profit during your retreat. If you apply yourself energetically to these exercises, you can become a saint without being forever on your knees, and without performing extraordinary penances."

Enclosed was a sheet of paper on which were enumerated sixteen maxims, exhorting her to the practice of prayer and the presence of God, humility, recollection, retirement, and mortification of the will; recommendations of a variety of acts and ascetical practices to be persevered in, which would lead to detachment and interior immolation, and flower in the love and union with God.

It was only eight months since Teresa Margaret had experienced the contemplative intuition of the mystery of divine love in the sudden and blinding illumination of that *Deus caritas est,* which had opened up to her a whole new dimension in the mystical life. Although she was always docile to the directions of superiors and disposed to adhere rigidly to the program proposed by Father Gregory, her spiritual orientation during this retreat was to develop into something immensely more dynamic than a mere routine performance of certain pious exercises. She was to receive a personal vocation to imitate and participate in the hidden life of Christ, no longer externally only, but as a form of mystic grace and to the fullest extent possible for a mortal to achieve. Although now nearing her goal of union, she herself - faithful to her chosen path of hiddenness - remained unaware of this, and she continued to seek a means to attain what she had in fact achieved. With the intention of following Father Gregory's maxims faithfully, Teresa

---

[1] Early in 1768, Father John Colombino was transferred to another community. After his departure from Florence, Father Ildefonse, whom she now knew well and who understood her soul so completely, became Teresa Margaret's regular confessor and spiritual director. He remained in this close communication with her until her death two years later, as Father Colombino died suddenly in the August of 1768. Thus Father Ildefonse was the one who followed and guided her through these last two years of the final perfection of her soul.

Margaret herself drew up another document entitled "Resolutions of the Retreat of 1768, which I must review every day." At the beginning of this itinerary, she merely implements Father Gregory's suggestions, with a few characteristic variations: "I propose to have no other purpose in all my activities, either interior or exterior, than the motive of love alone, by constantly asking myself: 'Now what am I doing in this action? Do I love God?' If I should notice any obstacle to pure love, I shall take myself in hand and recall that I must seek to return my love for His love."

This form of practicing the presence of God is often termed "habitual examination of conscience": a rapid glance at our interior state and disposition, constantly repeated, by which we become aware of the predominant inclination of heart and will from moment to moment, and recall it the instant it strays from its true focus. Among the many and varied emotions that assail the human heart, there is always one feeling that dominates, gives the heart its direction, and determines, so to speak, its orientation, before it is transferred to the will. This "theme song" can be desire for praise or fear of reproach, suspicion or contempt, resentment or inertia; equally it can be an energetic movement of love for God, a compelling desire to work and suffer for Him, a zeal for His glory, the austere joy of submission to Him in humiliation and self-surrender. After we have identified the theme - love, fear, joy, discouragement, hope - we immediately tune it to the pitch of the melody we wish to play, by means of God's grace.

When one becomes accustomed to referring continually to the master plan in this way, one conserves or restores the powers of heart and will from moment to moment, directing everything to the one end. Nothing escapes its notice, and all is done in accordance with God's will. It is not a habit acquired in a day or a week; but when one has learned to uncover the predominant inclination of the heart at any given moment, he discovers the main wellsprings of good and evil within himself, and is not tossed and torn this way and that by every passing desire, but can ride out any emotional storm in the safe anchorage of God's will.

Teresa Margaret had, in fact, by now passed the stage where

any mechanical computation of acts of virtue was possible. Such exercises, which are the sustenance of our spiritual powers and activity, ought to lead to unity, gradually inhering, expanding, developing, until the acts themselves are simplified and gathered into one all-embracing disposition, directed to the glory of God. Multiplicity and division cease to exist when the means, whether they be specific practices or a too-rigid itinerary, no longer hold primacy, and the end, which alone unites everything, also becomes the way. This Teresa Margaret seemed to have sensed, for she added: "Knowing that if I am to do this, a total abandonment to God is necessary (since I am aware that I can do nothing because of my misery) I give myself completely to you, my only Love, so that you alone can work in me according to your plan. For I desire nothing other than what you wish."

The constant self-examination of motives was too narrow an act for the spaciousness her soul had now achieved. There is no need for continual intellectual stock-taking, efforts of the will, ransacking the memory, for one who truly lives in the presence of God and under the impulse of His Spirit of Love. On the contrary, it becomes an intuitive enquiry, instantaneous and automatic. In a glance, simple and rapid, the soul accustomed to enter into herself sees and hears, without worrying or fretting about details. One does not need to follow or explore the course of a stream when one is placed at the source of its rising.

Teresa Margaret was doubtless unaware that she was not giving literal expression to Father Gregory's counsels, but rather paraphrasing them, expanding a purely ascetical directive by the unconscious application of what she already possessed within herself, giving rein to the liberty of spirit that is characteristic of her; as indeed it is of the whole Carmelite school of spirituality, which is anything but a series of progressively narrowing horizons, confining and restricting the interior spirit. She showed complete liberty in the development of her spiritual life and prayer, and this autonomy is illustrated in her retreat notes.

"Since nature resists good, even though the spirit may be willing, I resolve to enter upon a continual warfare against self. The arms with which I shall do battle are prayer, the presence of God, silence; yet I am aware how little I am able to use these weapons. Nevertheless I shall arm myself with complete confidence in you, patience, humility and conformity with your divine will ... but who shall help me to fight a continual battle against enemies such as those which make war on me? You, my God, have declared yourself my captain; you have raised the standard of the Cross, saying: 'Take up the cross and follow in my footsteps.' To correspond with this invitation, I promise to resist your love no longer; rather, I will follow you to Calvary without hesitation."

Deus caritas est! The leitmotiv of her whole spiritual itinerary. She no longer sought to tie herself down to a program of penitential practices, acts of virtue, even of particular methods of prayer. She was now ready to hand over not merely pieces of herself, but her whole being.

During the days of this retreat, Teresa Margaret wrote several observations which she gave to Father Ildefonse, asking him to read the resolutions and give them his approval. Nothing seemed any longer to preoccupy her, she said, save the things of God, and now she appeared to gather all her strength into a movement of love and desire, which culminated in a fervent outpouring of her soul in an act of oblation:

"My God, I desire nothing save to become your perfect image, and since yours was a hidden life of humiliation, love, and sacrifice, so also I wish mine to be. I desire to enclose myself henceforth within your most loving Heart as in a desert, so that I may live in you, and with you, and for you, this hidden life of love and sacrifice."

"O my Lord, you know my great desire to become a victim of your Sacred Heart, wholly consumed by the fire of your holy love. May your Heart be the altar upon which my holocaust shall be made, and you be the priest who will consume this victim by the flames of your burning Love."

Then, suddenly, in the midst of this impassioned flight, the paralyzing awareness of her own insufficiency seemed to over-whelm her, and she broke off abruptly in a plea for assistance, which, however, was full of firm and loving confidence. "But how confused I am, my God, when I see what a worthless victim I am, and how unfitting is this sacrifice I ask you to accept. Yet I am confident that all will be accomplished by the fire of divine love." As she had expressed it on another occasion: "From myself, nothing; from God everything." And in the words of St. Thérèse when faced with the same conflict: "When one casts oneself headlong into the furnace of divine love, how can one fail to be consumed? ... always love knows how to make the best of everything; whatever offends our Lord is burnt up in its fire, and nothing is left but a humble, absorbing peace, deep down in the heart."

This act of oblation contains the clearest and most decisive formulation Teresa Margaret ever made of her desire to be a victim, or her intense love and sense of identification with the Sacred Heart. To be hidden with Christ in God had always been her ambition, and here she has given the hidden life completely new horizons and dimensions. Rather than the theme of self-effacement which had hitherto played so dominant a note in her life, the principle now becomes one of imitation. Hidden with Christ in God she will, like the seed buried in the earth, grow and develop with a marvelous rapidity and fecundity. This she seemed to sense also: that only by hiding herself mystically as well as physically would she attain her full stature. But she could have no intimation of the double effect of the germination, as that of all seeds: undeviating growth, ever struggling upwards, but in the most intense and enveloping darkness.

Her resolutions close with the words: "My God, how well you know my great need of your help. I trust in your infinite mercy, and I shall always do so, regardless of the spiritual state in which I might find myself. Always and everywhere I shall endeavor to recognize your will in all things, even though my eyes see only contradiction and uncertainty. I know that I cannot depend upon myself, and so I shall trust completely in you. 'Nothing shall separate me from the love of Christ,' for 'in you, O Lord, I have hoped; I shall never be confounded.'"

"... In all things I shall be content, knowing that the route I travel leads to Calvary. The thornier the path, the heavier the cross, the more consoled I shall be, because I desire to love you with a suffering love, a selfless love, an active love, with a firm, undivided, persevering love ... I have promised you many things, but in no wise do I depend upon my own indolent spirit. You have enlightened me as to what I must do; now help me to execute it. All this I hope of your infinite mercy."

Teresa Margaret found - as do so many of us - that the simplest form of spirituality was intimacy with Jesus, losing herself in His Sacred Heart. Always she had endeavored to please Him in her renunciations and penances, her prayers and acts of charity. Now, with the grace of transforming love, she appears to have been raised to the mystical state of spiritual betrothal. There are no visions, no external graces to denote this state, such as occurred in the life of St. Teresa of Avila. Even St. Thérèse stepped momentarily out of her ordinariness here with her experience of "the wound of love," confirming God's acceptance of her offering. True to her vocation of hiddenness, Teresa Margaret received no extraordinary mystical graces, even in these high regions. There is, however, the carefully phrased testimony of Father Ildefonse, which makes it possible to delineate the stages of progress with a reasonable degree of certainty, although of their nature they do not fit into any hard and fast categories.

Teresa Margaret was now entering the last phase of her ascent, her soul nearing its final degree of maturity. Her aim in making the oblation of herself, as expressed in her act, was to conform herself more closely to the Sacred Heart, becoming as nearly as possible His "duplicate," hiding herself within that Heart whose flames would consume as rust all those imperfections which had hitherto hindered her complete union with God; so that thus purified and made one with Love, she might become a channel through which His love and graces would be passed on to others.

Of the soul transformed by love, St. John of the Cross writes: "...when it is so far transformed and perfected interiorly in the fire of love, (the soul) is not only united with this fire, but it has now become one living flame within it. Such the soul feels itself to be." St. Teresa, describing this state of the Sixth Mansion, uses words which well describe Teresa Margaret's interior state: "The soul has been wounded with love for the Spouse, and seeks more opportunity of being alone, trying so far as is possible to one in its state, to renounce everything which can disturb it in this its solitude."

The impulse which sought to "hide herself in the Sacred Heart as in a desert" henceforward became the dominant theme of her "hiddenness," a new movement as it were, transposing her ascetical practice of self-effacement into an interior disposition, which had almost the nature of a particular and special vocation, adding a new instrument to her orchestration. Later during the same year, Teresa Margaret sought Father Ildefonse's permission to imitate the hidden life of Christ. In granting it, he thought she referred to the externals of the life of Nazareth, to which she had always been so powerfully attracted. But when she later approached him again on the same subject, she told him that exterior human concerns and material things no longer had the power to absorb her, and that she had no interest but the glory of God and the salvation of souls. After speaking with her for a little while, the priest realized that, as he expressed it, "she was called to imitate a certain aspect of the Savior's life through faith, insofar as it is permitted to a creature to do so: namely, the interior life and hidden operations of the intellect and will of the God-Man."

Teresa Margaret's act of oblation, then, can be regarded as having been made under the influence of the transforming love associated with Spiritual Betrothal, of which St. John of the Cross says: "... in that which God is wont to communicate in such excess the soul feels and knows the truth of that saying which St.

Francis uttered, namely: God is mine and all things."

However, the delights of betrothal do not have the same stability as those of the eventual marriage, of which they are a prelude, and St. John of the Cross warns: "That which is here communicated is the most that is possible in the estate of betrothal; for in the spiritual marriage its profit is much greater. In the betrothal, although in the visits of the Spouse the Bride-soul enjoys these great blessings which we have described, she nevertheless suffers from His absences, and from perturbation and disturbances coming from her lower part and from the devil, all of which things cease in the state of the marriage."

During the subsequent period of intense purgation, the soul is indeed "hidden in the Sacred Heart as in a desert," imprisoned and held by His love, yet like St. Paul on the road to Damascus, blind and dumb, and still having to learn how much she has to suffer for God's sake. It was in this final stage of purification that Teresa Margaret's last two years on earth were to be spent before, at the last, she entered the state of ultimate perfection, spiritual marriage of transforming union. After that nothing remains but "to be dissolved and to be with Christ" in the complete consummation of the beatific vision.

"At the foot of the Cross," wrote Father Gabriel of St. Mary Magdalene, O.C.D., "suffering becomes more a proof of love than a punishment. Teresa Margaret became a saint not through multiplying penitential exercise, but by having effected an uninterrupted adhesion of her will to the crucified Redeemer."

From the commencement of her religious life, as has been seen, she had set herself the ideal of resembling, insofar as possible, through obedience and mortification, her crucified Savior, to become holy, and through submission of will and denial of self, united with prayer, to prepare for her eventual oblation to the Heart of Jesus as a victim of expiation and love. Her ideal was to serve God alone by a life hidden with Christ in God; to love Him in the silence and stillness of her heart; as the grain of wheat must die before it can germinate, as we must die to self before we can expand and grow in the spiritual life.

Suffering in some form or other is inescapable in this life; it is not to be sought as a desirable element in itself, nor is faith designed as a device to ease the process by eliminating the pain. There is a fundamental connection between suffering, joy, and love: hope, that is breathed into our souls by the Holy Spirit, drawing one from the other and leading progressively through the night of suffering to the glorious sunlight of God's love, where "your sorrow shall be turned into joy, and your joy no man shall take from you." It cannot be regarded merely as a just and appropriate punishment meted out to correct the balance of sin in the scales of strict justice, for it is obvious that degrees of suffering are not measured by personal guilt. Our Lord rebuked the apostles for suggesting that the affliction of the man born blind was a divine retribution for some sin committed by himself or his parents. It was, He said, "so that God's action might declare itself in him." Suffering is first and foremost an outstanding proof of love and the means of deepening that love by a more complete and generous giving of oneself, which shrinks before neither sacrifice nor pain. Looked at under the rays of love, suffering assumes vastly different outlines from the aspect it takes beneath the harsher, colder light of retributive justice. The two simply do not mean the same thing but are on entirely different planes.

The divine life cannot be achieved without suffering, however, for suffering and love are inseparable, but the real fruitfulness of suffering lies in the destruction of self-love and transformation of self-centeredness that it effects. "To suffer in peace," St. Thérèse declared, "it is enough to will what Jesus wills." Loving acceptance of suffering and self-love are incompatible; one must go. The lesson St. Teresa Margaret teaches is that suffering and love purchase for the soul that inestimable gift: interior freedom, "the truth that will set us free." From the time charity took possession of her heart, self-love departed, and she was always happy, always content, ready to prove her love by bearing in silence and with joy the trials, great or small, of daily life and finally the desolation and spiritual anguish of the purifying actions of God in the Night of the Spirit. Her own trust and abandonment to God were all-embracing, as indeed they must be if one is to live a life of pure love, patient love, love that sustains, believes, hopes, endures to the last. It was not without struggle or suffering that she won her halo of sanctity. "My Jesus," she affirmed on several occasions, and once wrote the words in her blood, "I will be yours *no matter what the cost; I* am determined to belong to you *despite all repugnance.*"[2]

Lest the fact that sympathy might provide some consolation - for it is well-known that a trial shared loses much of its cutting edge - she endeavored to conceal from those around her any pain or sorrow she endured, or the discomfort of fatigue, the weather, minor indispositions, or the small misunderstandings and inevitable frictions of community life. She continued to practice the incessant mortification of consistently presenting a smiling and serene exterior no matter how harassed she might be by interior sufferings or trials. Detailed like this the bare recital sounds elementary enough, and no more than is demanded by normal self-control; however, many of us might find ourselves in a state of some exhaustion after a day of consistently putting these "little practices" into effect.

"We must so mortify the memory, the intelligence, and each of our senses that all become spiritualized in some way," she said. "Then they, along with the soul, will be contented with God alone, and we shall be able to say: 'My heart and my flesh have exulted in the living God.'" She was truly content with Jesus alone, seeking no consolations in His absences, asking only to be permitted to kneel beside Him in spirit in Gethsemane during His agony and abandonment. To be allowed to share His sufferings was recompense enough for her, and her only comfort was to remain uncomforted. "All my consolation I expect from God, not on earth but in heaven. It matters little

---

[2] I.e., repugnance of nature, or as St. Paul calls it "the sinful principle" that dwells in us all, so that "it is not the good my will prefers, but the evil my will disapproves that I find myself doing."

whether my life is happy or not, provided I correspond with my vocation. With joy I abandon my heart as a prey to afflictions, to sadness, to trials. I enjoy *not* to enjoy, for a fast must precede a feast, and to fast from earthly pleasures will render more joyous the great Banquet of Eternity. I do not take away joy from my heart - I merely postpone it until that happy time when, the fear of losing it being removed, I will be doubly joyous ... I desire nothing but the grace to continue desiring nothing. The door to my heart must remain barred against earthly consolations if I would taste those of heaven."

Following as closely as possible in the footsteps of Jesus through silent and often unsuspected sufferings, she won the fruit of joy. Her happiness, it is true, consisted largely in suffering unnoticed, of having something to offer to God at her own cost, of being humiliated, remaining concealed from the eyes of all in the Heart of Christ; for she had very early discovered that it is only in the obscure and hidden life that one finds Him. He does not frequent the busy and bustling thoroughfares but invites us still as He did the apostles to "come apart with me and rest a while."

A life completely absorbed with the interests of God, conformed to His will, demands incessant abandonment and great confidence, a militant spirit of sacrifice and true humility. The obscurity of Bethlehem and Nazareth, leading to the immolation of Calvary and the silence of the Sepulcher, the unfathomable mystery of God's love; all this must precede the glory of the Resurrection. Such is the ideal of one whose life is a reproduction of the hidden life of Jesus and Mary, and it was perfectly epitomized in St. Teresa Margaret. Her own words completely and concisely sum up her earthly life: To suffer and be silent for Jesus.

More and more insistently Teresa Margaret returned to the theme of "imitation of Jesus" in her conversations with Father Ildefonse, who encouraged her by emphasizing the externals of the hidden life of Christ on earth.

"Certainly," he told her, "it is the shortest and most secure means of arriving at the pure and disinterested love which you seek. Let the words of St. Paul 'You are dead and your life is hidden away now, with Christ in God' become your principal theme for meditation, joining to it the exercise of the presence of God in all external activities." This letter, written on 27th March, 1769, dwells at length on the various aspects of the hidden life of Christ: His election of a lowly trade and humble state of life; unquestioning obedience to His earthly parents; the revelation of Himself finally to the poor, ignorant, and simple; a preference for the "little ones" of this world as His intimate companions; and finally the deliberate choice of a death that was agonizing and degrading. "I think that an exercise such as this, in the secrecy of your heart, can be extremely beneficial to you, perhaps more than determined acts or aspirations ... Accompany your external activity with interior sentiments like these, and you will then seek and esteem humiliations and self-effacement. Cultivate the company of those you find uncongenial or annoying, much as you would prefer to be with the more pious and refined types of persons. Do not try to win the approval of others, whether it be in private or public."

From these directives, it is clear that Father Ildefonse is referring to the external activities of the hidden life of Christ, rather than the "hidden operations of the Sacred Humanity of Jesus Christ, hypostatically united to the Word" which attracted Teresa Margaret like an unobtrusive, but nevertheless supernatural and even mystical grace. However, she returned to the attack with an insistence on which he later commented:

"Repeatedly, during the last two years of her life, she requested permission to imitate the hidden life of Christ. In granting her the permission in the first place, I took great pains to impress upon her the ideal of the exterior life of Christ, completely removed from all that bears even a shadow of esteem and reputation among men."

Teresa Margaret had now reached the age which society and the law recognize as adult and when one is expected to have attained sufficient maturity to make responsible choices and decisions on one's own initiative. She was twenty-one years of age - that is to say she had seen the leaves fall from the trees in autumn, the sap rise again to thrust new life and growth into the bare branches, some twenty times. But there is another way of calculating age, which is an interior and essentially hidden process, unclassifiable by the statistics and computations of the material world. It depends on the awakening of the intelligence, the movement of the will, the response to grace; and in it consists the progress and rate of development made by each individual soul, quite apart from purely physiological developments or precocity of learning in human and profane arts and sciences. As the Psalmist says: "Being young, he fulfilled many years." Our real age depends on the growth that has taken place in our souls, and this varies from person to person. Even identical twins, reared in the same environment, will not duplicate their interior development.

"I find in myself tendencies that I cannot control," she confided on another occasion.

"That is a lack of harmony, of order, partly due to human nature, partly due to weakness of our will," Father Ildefonse told her.

"I assure you it is a source of great suffering and much conflict, for I would like to achieve absolute submission to order."

"What you aspire to is not entirely possible in this life. You must abandon yourself to God, and accept the suffering which is not due to culpable fault or omission. Such acceptance is the only way of arriving at the harmony you seek, until such time as you are able to attain it in the full co-ordination of the faculties of your soul. Abandonment is the crowning of confidence, and it is in this virtue that you will find the secret of entire submission, of refusing nothing to God who is Love, of fearing nothing and accepting all things from His hands as part of His plan for you."

"It is this entire submission I have sought all my life; from the time I was capable of desiring anything, I have always sought God."

"Yes, for it is only in taking the good pleasure of God as one's sole rule in all thoughts and feelings, in accepting whatever is His will without stopping to consider what is painful or difficult in it for sensitive nature, that one can achieve such a degree of abandonment."

"And yet," she sighed, "I seem to be further from, not closer to it."

"One of its fruits is the peace that is enjoyed even in trial and suffering, which surpasses all natural enjoyment, or rather is of an entirely different order. When one is firmly established in this state, nothing can disturb the depths of the soul, although the surface may be ruffled from time to time; not the faults and failings we fall into through forgetfulness and frailty, so long as we are humbly sorry for them and renew again immediately the disposition of entire conformity to the divine will. Above all, you must remember that the repugnance of sensitive nature which you experience does not detract from the perfection of the disposition, although it does add considerably to the suffering and seeming conflict."

Father Ildefonse was exceptionally cautious in handling Teresa Margaret's requests, and he always deliberately guided her with a tight rein. He had no wish to foster any illusions about special graces or mystical states, or even to allow her to think that her spiritual life was in any way different from that of her companions. He said later: "I always gave the impression of understanding what she was explaining of her desires and interior lights in a manner less lofty than I actually knew she meant. I acted thus through considered judgment, in order to prevent any risk of her becoming exposed to subtle temptations or the least trace of vanity or self-complacency, so fatal to the soul in the higher regions of the spiritual life."

Again he recalled: "I well remember explaining to her the words of St. Paul: 'You are dead and your life is hidden with Christ in God.' She had already penetrated deeply into the mysterious, ascetical implications of this profound text, and I realized that *she was called* to emulate by faith the *interior life* of the God-Man."

He pointed out to her that by "dying" in this sense was meant the destruction not of the "self" but of all that is opposed to God and separates us from Him. "Self" must indeed abdicate from its position of sovereignty in favor of God, but should it be destroyed or cease to exist, there would be nothing for Jesus to possess!

Everything that is human (in that it is not animated and directed by the divine life) must wither away, because until all that separates us from Him disappears, there can be no union, which exists only where there is perfect conformity. Therefore true detachment does not consist of "emptying" or "annihilating" so much as desiring nothing apart from the will of God. "This does not mean the annihilation of soul or body, or any of the faculties or activities, but their purification and transformation by the destruction of those ties which fasten one to created things, and a certain degree of self-will and independence, which keeps God at a distance. When the ties which bind us to earth are broken, the soul, far from being annihilated, is set free like the butterfly breaking from its chrysalis. As St. John the Baptist said: 'I must decrease so that He may increase.' There you see the goal of all your asceticism: that Christ may increase in you. He can only live in us as self-seeking decreases and dies. Thus what is merely human satisfaction gradually becomes submerged, dying to rise again in God's glory, undergoing that transformation which is very strikingly illustrated by St. Paul in the comparison with bodily death: 'Sown in corruption it shall rise in incorruption; sown in weakness, it shall rise in power ... and when this mortal body has clothed itself in immortality, shall come to pass those words: Death is swallowed up in victory.' It is in this sense you must understand the term 'dying to self.'"

Thus, while carefully guiding and instructing her, Father Ildefonse gradually came to understand more fully the implication of this repeated request his young penitent made to him during the year. Despite the knowledge he had of her and the way of fidelity and humility she had always trodden, it was only by degrees that he became fully persuaded of the genuineness of this strong impulse. It was not merely her own attraction, he realized, but a definite call from God to enter into a very particular phase of the imitation of Christ.

Teresa Margaret on her part continued to put his counsels into practice; however in 1769 (the last year of her life) she again repeated her request, explaining that "created external things and human concerns no longer caused her even the slightest uneasiness or disturbance. It was as though they no longer existed, and her entire attention was now absorbed in the sole problem of God and her own soul."

This statement needs a little qualification, lest it give the impression that the state of detachment Teresa Margaret had attained be confused with indifference for the welfare of others or the apostolate. Actually, in the degrees that have led to this stage, her main preoccupation had been to maintain the correct balance between God's glory and her own natural satisfaction, and in preventing the latter from trespassing on the honor of God, which must be given the first place in all things. Now that this equilibrium had been established, Teresa Margaret found herself secure in an interior peace and harmony, which was characterized by this exclusive concern for the greater glory of God and a complete forgetfulness of self. Now indeed it could be said of her that she was always about her Father's business, doing always the things that please Him; occupying herself only with His interests, and taking as the criterion of all created things that which has most value for God and His glory.

With God as the center of her life, dominating and absorbing all else, she no longer felt concern for created external matters. Her own human satisfaction and the enjoyment that comes from creature pleasures were forgotten, nor could they cause her "even the slightest uneasiness or disturbance". All that tended to stop short of or turn aside from God's glory was "as though it no longer existed". She now had only one concern, the greater glory of God, and her "entire attention was now absorbed in this sole problem, which was between God and her own soul". One standard alone could now evaluate creatures and created pleasures: the greater glory of God. Where this is to be found matters very little, so that external affairs cause no anxiety. But this state of holy "indifference" or disinterestedness is actually a high degree of perfection in which, without worrying about details, she can obtain more grace for others and is more completely integrated with her fellow men in the Mystical Body than in the lower stages where her spiritual exercises were marked by intense activity and particular acts and intentions. Now, as St. John of the Cross says, "No other task I share, and only in loving is my duty."

"Behold I come to do thy will ... my meat is to do the will of Him who sent me ..." Such was now the disposition of her soul, with no action or thought but for the will and glory of God. But this is very far from saying that she felt no concern for the demands of charity, that her practical interest in her sisters or her affection for her family and friends was any the less. There is only one way of desiring and effectively willing the good of God, and that is by fulfilling His will in things great and small, since His will orders all things for His greater glory. Thus by surrendering herself completely to God's good pleasure, Teresa Margaret gave herself no less to others but was in the condition of willing only what God willed. This she achieved by constant fidelity to the small details and duties of life, all of which are the outward manifestations of His will for us. Self-forgetfulness and consistent self-denial lead to this state of harmony, because pride is annihilated. The love of God should be sufficiently strong to root out all self-love.

Faithfully putting into practice the advice: "Never follow one's own will in anything," Teresa Margaret attained a detachment which was able to declare: "I have completely forgotten myself and have schooled myself never to give way to my inclinations."

Father Ildefonse spoke with her at some length, pointing out that while "hiddenness" and "nothingness" were only negative characteristics, divine grace is always positive, and he was not only impressed by her grasp of what he thought might prove too abstract a consideration for her simple conceptions, but was by now quite convinced that she had indeed achieved the "death to the world" which he had often discussed with her; and that she could now truly say: "My life is hidden away with Christ in God."

He explained further these words of St. Paul to her, no longer as a method of external conformity to the humility and self-effacement of Christ, but in terms of a life mystically hidden in Christ, and he was amazed to find how deeply she had penetrated into the implications of this text.

"I soon realized," he testified, "that she was called to emulate, by faith, insofar as it is possible for a creature, the hidden, interior life and actions of the *intellect and will* of the God-Man." And Teresa

Margaret herself confirmed his conviction by revealing unconsciously that her understanding of this mystic "burial" had indeed progressed into new and deeper abysses or broader horizons. When he had finished his exposition of the Pauline text "hidden with Christ in God," she began to speak of this mystical death, comparing and expounding it in the light of Christ's words: "No one comes to the Father but through Me," joining this to another text of the Apostle: "My just one lives by faith," together with the words from St. John's Gospel: "He who sees me sees the Father," and "None knows the Son truly except the Father, and none knows the Father truly except the Son, and those to whom it is the Son's good pleasure to reveal Him." (Matt. 11:27) Being "buried away with Christ," concealed from all eyes, performing lowly tasks unnoticed and unthanked, had been the ascetical beginnings of her hidden life which, through fidelity and humility, had progressed gradually into a deepening intimacy. Now the full realization of this vocation had flowered, and "hidden with Christ - in God," she had progressed to the depths of a genuine Trinitarian spirituality.

Personal love of the Sacred Humanity of Jesus had formed a simple and attractive spirituality for her tentative footsteps; however, once having become entirely surrendered to Him, she had been led by Him to the Father in the Spirit. "For you are Christ's, and Christ is God's." To live in God one must pass through Christ, who alone is the way, and none comes to the Father except through Him; there is no short-cut that by-passes our Lord. Unless we are conducted by Christ, we cannot come to the Trinity, for He is our guarantee, our letter of introduction as it were, without which we will not be acknowledged. The entire spiritual odyssey of St. Teresa Margaret can be summed up in the words: From the Sacred Heart to the Blessed Trinity.

"Divine charity," said Pope Pius XII, "has its first beginnings in the Holy Spirit who is the personal Love equally of the Father and of the Son in the bosom of the august Trinity ...There is according to Holy Scripture the closest connection between divine charity which must burst into flames in the hearts of Christians, and the Holy Spirit, whose very *property* it is in God to be Love. And this connection

makes clear to us all the real meaning and nature of that cult which is
to be offered to the Heart of Jesus Christ ... the Heart of the Word
made flesh is rightly looked upon as the principal token and sign of
that threefold love wherewith the divine Redeemer ceaselessly loves
both His Eternal Father and all mankind ... and as a mystical Jacob's
ladder by which we climb up to the embrace of God our Savior."

The love of the Sacred Heart - devotion to "the good Jesus,"
rises indeed in a human and sensible symbol of love, but if it is genuine and not merely sentiment, it infallibly terminates in the bosom of
the most Holy Trinity. This is what Teresa Margaret now understood
by the imitation of the hidden life of the Sacred Humanity of Christ,
becoming a "perfect image of Jesus" not merely in the externals and
virtues of the hidden life, but by truly, and in the deepest sense of the
words, hiding with Christ in God.

Father Ildefonse's notes on his penitent's progress become very
much more detailed during these last months, for he followed the
movements of her soul closely, corroborating their ascent and genuineness.

"How do you succeed in maintaining interior recollection with
God during the various duties and distracting occupations you must
do?" he asked her once, thinking no doubt of the constant interrup-
tions and absence of privacy her heavy responsibilities as infirmarian
entailed.

"Oh, that is quite simple," she replied. "External occupations merely
serve as a further means of raising the mind to God. They furnish constantly new motives for loving Him and ever more desiring Him and
seeking Him in others."

"But you tell me that often you are obliged to forego the regular
hours of prayer, and your leisure time is almost negligible."

"Father, I am continually overwhelmed and filled with praise
and wonder at the infinite wisdom and goodness of our God. When I
see how He permits Himself to dwell in souls which are so often
distraught and engrossed in material occupations, I marvel. And yet I
often become more aware of His presence in the midst of such duties
than during the time of prayer itself."

"Yes, when one has acquired the true spirit of prayer, it is certain that work is a prayer so long as one remains united to God. Still it is not always easy when the work is absorbing, requiring all one's attention and concentration."

"It seems to me that it is here the text 'Inasmuch as you did it to one of my least brethren you did it to me' applies. For I have always regarded the service of the sick in that way, and I am always conscious of His presence when I am working among them."

Father Ildefonse pressed her further.

"God is not tied by time or space. We are doing His will as perfectly when obedience keeps us at tasks which we find irksome."

"For me," she replied, "it suffices to work in silence as our Rule commands, because then all things will help to unite us to God. It is enough to keep the outer doors closed, for then the heart and soul have no other place to go than into their center, where God is to be found. As He is the beginning of all our work, so He is its end; and with His aid we accomplish it quickly and well, so that He is also the way."

"Then you do not regret that you no longer have the leisure to spend much time in visits to the Blessed Sacrament, or at other devotions such as the Rosary or the Stations of the Cross?" he asked, for he was well aware of her earlier attraction and fidelity in performing them all.

"Oh, Father," she reminded him, "you just said that God is not tied. How great are the gifts which we continually receive from Him. We swim like little fish in the ocean of His mercy. We can make Him no suitable return, for we have nothing that we have not already received from Him. That being so, we are perpetually in debt, and that knowledge leads us back to the pure, generous beneficence of our God."

"So it is just as easy - or even easier - for you to remain recollected in the presence of God than be distracted and concentrated on mundane things?"

"If you put it like that," she said simply, "I suppose so. But I think of it rather as two people, let us say two sisters, who love each other very dearly. Although they are constantly thrown into the closest companionship, they will never find such ubiquity distasteful, but rather in their mutual affection they will draw help and strength for their external occupations. It seems to me that living in the presence of God is as simple as that. Just as someone who loves a person often recalls that person to mind, so too we must constantly recall to mind that God is present and always working for our greater good. All that we have to do is to return love of Love. Our whole exercise and obligation is in loving alone."

18

The Night of the Spirit

I missed Him when the sun began to bend;
I found Him not when I had lost his rim;
With many tears I went in search for Him ...
I found Him nearest when I missed Him most;
I found Him in my heart, a life of frost.
(George MacDonald)

Both St. Teresa of Avila and St. John of the Cross state that could the soul know in advance the intensity of the sufferings caused by the purgations of God before union with Him can be achieved, few, if any, would have the courage even to pray for it; for in truth, says St. John, they go down alive into purgatory, being cleansed here on earth in the same manner as there.

"O my God," cries St. Teresa, "how great are the trials which the soul will suffer, both within and without, before it enters the seventh mansion! ... If we realized their intensity beforehand, it would be most difficult for us, naturally weak as we are, to muster determination enough to enable us to suffer them."

Teresa Margaret was now to be led through the desert of spiritual aridity. All the consolation and fervor of her devotions had disappeared, and she found herself, as it were, abandoned, in the grip of one of the most searching trials by which God perfects the soul, detaching it from every human support, so that its only alternatives lie in either turning back to the sunshine of sensible consolations, or casting itself unreservedly

235

on His merciful love with an abandonment and confidence that requires near heroism.

Apart from occasional fleeting glimpses of light and rare moments of a return of spiritual joy, Teresa Margaret walked this path during the last year of her life. She prayed without emotion or fervor, but she continued to pray, faithfully performing all her religious duties, despite the dryness and actual repugnance with which they were often carried out.

It is a strange and seemingly conflicting situation in which one finds oneself when plunged into the Night of the Spirit. The soul is starving in dryness, distaste, weariness; yet it rests in a gentle tranquility that has nothing to do with the emotions. It is, rather, the peace of knowing that behind all the clouds, despite her own inability to see or even approach Him, God is there, loving her as He did in the days of light and fervor. And through all the doubts and anxieties, the soul perseveres in loving, although in the dark, and in a manner that requires heroic faith, hope, and love.

To love, and yet to enjoy no feeling or consolation of that love, was the spiritual martyrdom of these final months.

It is the fashion nowadays to thumb through the popular handbooks on applied psychology in an attempt to equate the effects of the purifications of the soul in this crucible - termed by St. John of the Cross "the dark night of the spirit" - with the symptoms of mental illness. Certainly some of the exterior manifestations of one undergoing these intensive passive purifications might appear similar to the visible effects of a nervous condition. But one of the surest guarantees that they are the purifying and unifying actions of God on the soul is the growth and enrichment of the personality, the flowering of a genuine spirituality, the ever-deepening humility that ensures the absence of delusions. These cannot possibly be effected by mental imbalance or hysteria. In St. Teresa Margaret's case, the question should not even arise, since we have the very detailed testimony of Father Ildefonse, who observed her closely all during this trial, and do not rely merely on the impression of credulous nuns, wise after the event.[1]

Father Ildefonse was not the kind of person to enroll himself as a disciple of his penitent, or sit at the feet of a child prodigy of spurious sanctity; nor would he be deceived by pious sentiment parading as holiness. He had, in fact, shown extreme caution from the outset in admitting the reality of the attractions and spiritual horizons that were opening out so rapidly now that Teresa Margaret was nearing the final goal. He had deliberately restrained her ardor in the matter of ascetical exercises, and later in giving herself up to these impulses of the spirit; and had observed her complete obedience to his instructions, as well as the detachment with which she relinquished her own natural desires in order to submit to his judgment.

Teresa Margaret's trial by fire actually began with the reception of the grace of 1767: *Deus caritas est.* But the infusion at first seemed all light, and the pain and conflict at that stage consisted in the awareness of her nothingness and human misery, and the limitations imposed on a soul burning with the longing "to be dissolved and to be with Christ," who is still detained in a body that insists on claiming its own rights. The fact is that the increasing dissatisfaction with oneself, and the growing awareness of the abyss that separates her sinfulness from God's purity, is in itself a sign of growth in the knowledge and love of God; however, being hidden from the soul, it is a cause of further pain and conflict.

Again there is Father Ildefonse's testimony: "This sharp, mortal pain, caused by the belief that she did not love God, as He loved her,

---

[1] As a matter of fact, the sisters were so far from hero-worshipping Teresa Margaret with naive, uncritical enthusiasm, or of losing themselves in admiration for her gifts of prayer and recollection, that they expressed concern about her constant and apparent abstraction. They had the unfortunate Sister Louise ever present to remind them of the result of neglecting symptoms of what in those days went under the general title of "melancholy." Was Sister Teresa Margaret suffering from a similar depression? The Prioress mentioned her concern to the Provincial, who decided to interview the young nun and form his own opinion. At the end of the consultation, he delivered his verdict: "I would indeed very happily see every sister in this community afflicted with such 'melancholy' as that of Sister Teresa Margaret!" It was only later that they came to attribute her "faraway look" to her habitual awareness of the presence of God and His continual operations in her.

became insufferable from the year 1767 when she experienced the
intense joy which accompanied the graces she received upon hearing
the words: God is Love."

But the light had gone out. The transports, the overwhelming
ardor of her loving intimacy suddenly ceased, leaving her alone and
seemingly lost in the mists and darkness. In her anguish it seemed
that the light of faith was eclipsed, hope had vanished, and the love of
God that had filled her from earliest years was only a remembrance of
some experience in a faraway existence, even the memory of which
added torture to this pain of desolation and seeming abandonment.

"Whither art thou gone, leaving me full of woe?" The opening
lines of St. John of the Cross' *Spiritual Canticle* could very well have
been on her lips at this time. "Thou didst flee, having wounded me; I
went calling after thee, and thou wert gone."

In her fear of being cast off by God, she asked Father Ildefonse
in anguish: "Father, shall I lose my soul?"

The love of God had been so certain and concrete a reality to her
before, that she could not understand how anyone could fail to love
Him wholeheartedly or dare to offend Him. But now she asked did
she herself love Him any longer? Without waiting for a reply, she
asserted confidently: "Yes, of course. And I hope and believe I shall
be saved through the love and infinite goodness of my heavenly Father and through the merits of Jesus Christ His Son, who is also mine."
And then, apparently in defiance of the lack of "feeling" which seemed
to her to be a temptation against faith, she echoed the cry of Tertullian
'I believe because it seems to unbelievers impossible'; saying with
great vehemence to Father Ildefonse: "Like our Holy Mother, St.
Teresa, I am more prompted to believe revealed truths which seem
impossible to the intellect, because in them shines all the more brightly
the power and wisdom of our God."

Externally nothing had changed. Although the spiritual exercises
that had hitherto afforded her such joy and consolation now became a
source of acute pain and conflict, to her sisters she appeared the same,
eagerly making her way to choir at the appointed hour when not detained by her duties in the infirmary; always prompt, and first in her

place when the bell rang for morning prayer; going about her duties, cheerful, affable, kindly; undertaking additional irksome tasks unasked; always ready with a word of sympathy for anyone looking distressed or in pain, without ever seeking it herself. None guessed the anguish of her own soul, the martyrdom of love that was being accomplished there in the purifying flames of the night of the spirit. Father Ildefonse alone realized the full violence of the trial and the agony and desolation of soul as his spiritual daughter was led towards her final goal of transforming union, through the barren desert of interior sufferings. He remarks on the inexpressible purity of her conscience, and her constant fear of the least failure in love or response to grace, her humble resignation in accepting everything from the hand of God, and in suffering willingly all dryness, aridity of soul, and interior desolation, which sufferings she attributed solely to her own demerits and lack of fervor. "But her strength and generosity, her fidelity and courage, far from wavering, grew daily stronger, making her undertake all things however difficult and repugnant, for the love of God," says Father Ildefonse.

"I had recognized in her," he continued, "that supreme state of union through faith, the simplicity and sublimity of which carried her, without any assistance from the senses of imagination, to the abstract and pure consideration of the most hidden and highest perfections of the divinity. The natural facility, as it were, of this deep union with God no longer met any obstacle, nor did it even hinder her in her varied external occupations, especially during the last two years of her life, in duties imposed by obedience, or prompted by charity. It even appeared that such occupations served her rather as a means to fly more easily and more perfectly to God; and this is how she managed to appear externally still more disengaged and active, as the Sisters have told me that she did." Having clearly understood the aspirations and tendencies of her soul and carefully classified its stages of spiritual development, he was able to identify the sudden onslaught of interior sufferings as the passive purifications of God.

During these days of trial and darkness, Teresa Margaret wrote to him: "I find myself in complete interior abandonment, seeing nowhere the least ray of light. The very thought of having to apply myself to the things of God is a torment. Finding myself in utter darkness and fearing in this state to offend our Lord very much I thought it proper to tell you, so as to receive suitable counsel. My former desires scarcely make themselves felt, and if by means of spiritual reading they come once more to mind, the reading seems endless and wearisome, because of the struggle I have to endure within myself. I feel in the depths of my heart that God wishes me for Himself alone, but I am deaf to His voice, particularly in the practice of virtue, for which I experience a keen repugnance."

Sufferings, says St. John of the Cross, when they are spiritual, seem as though they will never come to an end, and that all our days of light and blessing are now over.

Teresa Margaret had never imagined suffering comparable to this. When hitherto she had begged to be allowed no consolation on earth, she had had in mind mainly earthly pleasures and sensible consolations. Now she understood what it meant to be deprived of all spiritual comfort, abandoned in the emptiness of a great void, feeling no attraction in the service of God. And yet her confidence in Him remained steady, and her fidelity and regularity were as constant as in the days when spiritual exercises and devotions had been the source of all her joy and delight.

During this period of interior purgation and seeming abandonment, she continued to practice her customary penances, but in spirit her participation in the Passion had also moved from exterior to interior imitation, becoming like her practice of the hidden life, refined or transformed into a more spiritual and mystical grace. It was not the scourging or crowning with thorns, the cynicism of Pilate or the mockery of Herod, the furious hate of the crowd or the agony of cross, thorns and nails, but the interior anguish of desolation, the intolerable loneliness of one abandoned and afflicted in soul and body that was now her lot. Thus she entered into the corporal Passion of her divine Master, but also and even more particularly into the interior Passion of His soul and into His dispositions, becoming more and more conformed to Jesus crucified, her lifelong goal and ambition, the awful reality of which she had at last plumbed.

In proportion as her faith and hope were purified, her love increased, and with it a deep grief caused by the belief that she neither loved nor served God as she should; that perhaps He was displeased with her and for this reason had cast her out from His presence. No longer the sweet abiding presence dwelt in her, into which she could withdraw herself and find her "paradise on earth"; there was nothing. She sought for another road to lead her back to Jesus, since the old one was blocked. What caused the greatest pain in her soul, says Father Ildefonse, was Divine Love Himself. The more He perfected her, the more closely did He conceal Himself from her sight.

"I could understand something of the mortal anguish she suffered in being no longer able to live without loving God as much as she desired - indeed death would, she felt, be a great consolation. I understood her martyrdom by seeing her quite transformed by that love, which represented to her vividly the excellence and infinite merit of the object of her love; so that her own response appeared feeble and shabby. Yet in reality it was increasing and being perfected in her. The profound disgust she experienced in prayer tormented her more than all else."

She felt that she had been unfaithful to Him who had lavished such great and undeserved graces on her, and given her so many proofs of His love for her. She suffered intensely, and seeing herself in this state of torment and unable to control herself, she cried out one day, "What will become of me?" This painful condition lasted through the latter months of her life.

It is difficult not to write off (or at least discount to some extent) as mere paradoxical exaggerations, the language of affliction, of which Job is the exponent *par excellence*. But it is the only medium by which one in this distressing state can hope to express the interior trials through which she is passing. It is a condition that appears contradictory. To all intents and purposes, God, heaven, all that had given purpose and goal to life are as though they no longer exist; and yet, in this aridity, the genuine saint clings with her whole soul to God as firmly as she has ever done when upheld by the certitude of His love and the fervor of its consolations. But there is, in fact, no antinomy. What has disappeared is the joy in that supernatural love. The whole exercise is now transferred to the will, which remains united to God, and never for a single instant withdraws itself from Him. No matter how high the waves rise, it remains immovable, like a rock-built lighthouse. Eventually the storm dies down, the seas grow calm, and it remains intact. So with the will, for our feelings, while they are sometimes as turbulent and seemingly uncontrollable as the angry waters, are destined in the end, like the mountainous waves, to subside.

St. John of the Cross explains the state very closely: "The nearer the soul approaches God, the blacker is the darkness which it feels and the deeper is the obscurity which comes through its weakness; just as the nearer a man approaches the sun, the greater are the darkness and the affliction caused him through the great splendor of the sun and through the weakness and impurity of his eyes." The reason for our "blindness" is not through any fault in the sun, but because of the feebleness of our eyes and our inability to endure its blinding light, which forces us to close them in order that it should not rob us of what sight we have.

He further states, however, that in spite of this blindness and affliction, "the soul immediately perceives in itself a true determination and an effectual desire to do naught which it understands to be an offence to God, and to omit to do naught that seems to be for His service. For that dark love cleaves to the soul, causing it a most watchful care and an inward solicitude concerning that which it must not do, for His sake, in order to please Him." No sharper vignette, one feels, could possibly be given of the condition of soul of Teresa Margaret during this period.

Clinging to the bare wood of the cross, she accepted this interior martyrdom with resignation, while tasting its bitterness to the full. No longer was there any sense of pleasure in the love of God. "I would no longer know HOW to love God!" she exclaimed. Yet at the same time she lived only for Him, setting about her work with energy, volunteering for additional tasks to relieve the burden of others, while her sufferings, far from depressing her, only stirred in her the desire to suffer more. This was something still possible to her. She could no longer love God - or rather feel she loved Him - but she could and would continue to suffer for Him, as long as there was breath left in her body. God, she insisted, was punishing her for her sins and imperfections, particularly for her ingratitude and slothfulness in His service, and she accepted the chastisement humbly and patiently. Fear of not responding sufficiently to God's love and graces is one of the infallible signs of a faithful soul.

God does not abandon us, however unworthy we have proved ourselves to be, and despite the darkness that engulfed her soul, Teresa Margaret remained confident that, although she could neither see nor feel Him, He was there as He had always been - guiding, protecting, correcting - like a loving Father. Abandonment in this degree requires great courage and trust. It sounds easy enough in theory to surrender oneself unreservedly to the operations of God, which can only be for our greatest good and ultimate happiness. We may even feel in advance that, with St. Paul, we reckon the sufferings of this present time not worthy to be compared with the joys of which they are the price. But when the time of testing comes, nothing is so difficult as to summon up the necessary confidence to step forward blindly into the darkness, trusting only in the support of God's unseen and unfelt hand.

St. John of the Cross teaches that the duration and intensity of the suffering will vary in each individual soul, but he says that "those who have the disposition and greater strength to suffer, He purges with greater intensity and more quickly."

On March 31st, 1767, Father John Colombino had written a long letter to Teresa Margaret, reassuring her about the aridity and "indolence" which was causing her such perplexity.

"Although you feel yourself deprived of all feeling and 'in the dark,' I repeat what I have told you before: that the painful trial which afflicts you, rising as it does from the vehemence of your desires, actually IS love. It will profit you much in securing you a purer, stronger charity through the exercise of naked, arid faith which must now guide you in the accomplishment of your tasks and the various functions of your spiritual life (and how costly this latter will be to you!), in fighting distractions and temptation, in overcoming the coldness you feel towards everything. You must be concerned about this point and be vigilant, and courageous ... Try to stay close to the Lord, and that will surely help you to be faithful to Him regardless of the contrary insinuations of the world and the adverse opinion of others."

Now she grew increasingly anxious about faults and imperfections, considering them culpable, and fearing that she might have gravely offended God. She confided these doubts and scruples to Father Ildefonse and to Father Colombino, as well as another of the Carmelite Friars who replaced Father Colombino for a time as ordinary confessor to the convent, Father John of the Cross. This trial increased during 1768, when a temporary confessor was appointed to whom Teresa Margaret was not able to confide her troubles. It is probable that she had been instructed by her director not to do so, that being normally the advice given in dealing with scruples. The only hope of combating them is to discuss them with only one confessor and obey his instructions implicitly. Thus she began to add an extra worry as to whether she was now making her confessions badly, and her troubles multiplied. "I accuse myself to the best of my ability," she told Father Ildefonse, "but since he is unaware of my interior struggles, I can scarcely explain myself to him."

Teresa Margaret had always been thorough in her self-examination, mentioning the slightest involuntary failings in thought, word, or deed, or any lack of response to the promptings of grace, resistance to some interior inspiration, etc. She was almost inconsolable over the least defect or involuntary fault, and this inability to speak openly to the confessor was a form of torture in her present hypersensitive condition, which made her confess absurd "faults" such as "an inordinate love for her parents." Here, as St. Teresa says, "the soul sees clearly how extremely unworthy it is - for in a room bathed in sunlight not a cobweb can remain hidden. It sees its own wretchedness ... and every little speck of dust, however small, however hard a soul may have labored to perfect itself, once this Sun really strikes it, it sees that it is wholly unclean."

It would be difficult to decide whether scruples are a greater source of embarrassment to the one afflicted or the confessor who has to deal with them. Certainly it is painful to read all these agonizing doubts and torturous worries, which would no sooner be allayed than they would return in another form. Actually it is impossible adequately to describe scrupulous fears and spiritual distress, which are all the more humiliating because of their obvious unreasonableness. Formerly, Teresa Margaret had been established in a peace and confidence that was tranquil and seemingly unshakable. A word should have sufficed to relieve her anxieties, for she was frank and candid with her director, going to unnecessary pains to make known, simply and clearly, her states of mind and soul, which were now in such marked contrast to her former life of prayer and spiritual experience. She was intelligent, and most of her confessors found that very little explanation was needed to make her understand and implement their directions, and usually no counsel ever had to be repeated. It seems certain that her inability to find peace in the reassurance of her directors was because the scruples themselves were part of God's purifying actions, and in no way a psychological condition.

Her faith made her accept whatever counsel she was given, and this obedience enabled her to attain some degree of peace, for she knew she could not be deceived if she frankly opened her soul and then accepted the advice given in God's name. Still, the struggle was a long and bitter one, for the old scruples, or a fresh crop, would reappear as soon as she had been reassured and set at ease; and so the whole process would be put in motion once more. On one occasion she wrote several notes during the day to her confessor after having spoken to him on that same morning, later becoming disturbed lest she had omitted to make some doubt quite clear.

Even the things which had hitherto constituted all her joy no longer brought tranquility, but rather they became the cause of further suffering, as she was unable to find any attraction in those prayers and devotions from which formerly she had been almost unable to drag herself away. Everything was a source of pain and difficulty as she forced herself to persevere in the various exercises and practices.

She felt that she was not corresponding with the continual graces God bestowed upon her, and of this she also accused herself in confession. She commenced to keep in a notebook a balance-sheet of her accounts of conscience, to which she gave the revealing and formidable title: "Render an account!"

However, it would appear that common sense prevailed, from the following letter written to Teresa Margaret by Father John of the Cross: "From your letter I understand the reason of your fear regarding your confession this morning. You did well to receive Communion in spite of this, because there is no sufficient matter to impede you. Go again tomorrow morning ..."

All during 1768 the priest was writing such reassuring notes to his young penitent on this theme. "It may be that after you receive this letter you will begin worrying: 'I have not explained it properly', or 'He did not understand fully'; but stand firm and ignore these doubts, even though you may be convinced you have deliberately deceived me. Insist to yourself 'I wish to obey'... I imagine you obeyed me this morning by dispelling your fears and receiving Holy Communion. I want you to do the same thing tomorrow morning ... Hold firmly to holy obedience; do exactly as I have told you and you will be victorious ... dispose of all these fears by going to Holy Communion tomorrow without a previous confession." He kept reiterating that imperfections and involuntary faults are found in the most spiritual people, and are mostly accepted as part of our human frailty, with which we will have to live all our lives. They are not sinful because they do not constitute a formal offence against God, or the culpable transgression of a precept.

These letters from Father John ceased in November, 1768, and the following month began a regular correspondence with Father Ildefonse which lasted until Teresa Margaret's death sixteen months later. Father Ildefonse was to guide her soul through this ultimate phase of testing and see her placed firmly in the way of union. Whereas Father John of the Cross had been content with simply dispelling her scruples and reassuring her that obedience was her surest guide in the labyrinth; that she could not be deceived, for even were he mistaken, God would ratify his decisions; and that only in the Blessed Sacrament would she find the strength she needed to overcome her temptations, Father Ildefonse's direction was more fundamental. He went to the very root of the trial, showing her how she must draw profit from it for the greater glory of God, the progress of her own soul, and the salvation of others.

On December 29th, 1768, Teresa Margaret wrote to him: "In all confidence, I tell you that I find myself in torment because I do nothing to respond to the demands of love. I feel that I have fallen from the grace of the Supreme Good ... Everything seems to hinder and impede me from a single-minded flight toward God; frequently I do not even know how to occupy myself; what ought to move me to love causes me anxiety lest I become disgusted with it. I have thus far found no remedy except to work by faith; even this becomes a suffering to me because of my insensitivity which makes it painful. Although I am constantly vigilant over nature, I feel that I shall emerge from this trial very much less than perfect. One must experience it to realize how painful a thing it is to live without any love when one is at the same time burning with an ardent longing to possess it."

On another occasion, when speaking with Father Ildefonse, she tried to explain this conflict.

"I truly do not want to offend God, nor can I find that I have done so. And yet I must try to make a complete manifestation of conscience, or else I have no peace, for I cannot rely on my own judgment in these matters. Then again, no sooner have I done this, than I become troubled lest I have deceived you. I fear that I color my trials so as to represent them as those agonies suffered by the great saints, whereas in fact I am certain that they are the result of my lack of virtue and recollection - not even punishments for great faults and sins, but merely the outcome of my own negligence and failures."

"Yet despite the repugnance you tell me you feel in applying yourself to prayer and the spiritual life, you persevere in all these practices. If they give you no pleasure, you must be doing them solely for God."

"I try to, but all is dark everywhere, and I feel so afraid when I move in any direction. Everything requires an effort of the will, whether it is spiritual exercises or my duties and ordinary work. And sometimes this effort is almost beyond me."

"You must abandon yourself completely to God," the priest told her. "You should not be thinking of yourself at all, but of saving souls for Him. If God gives you no feeling of love and fervor, offer Him that deprivation, despite the feeling of frustration and emptiness. But most of all I think you should be careful not to indulge too much in writing letters. It gives you temporary relief to pour out all your anguish, but it is better to forget self than to be over-solicitous in probing and dissecting the least motive and movement. Just keep the general direction of doing all things for God, and leave the particulars to Him."

Teresa Margaret left, comforted and firmly resolved not to write again unless absolutely necessary, and this brought some return of calm. But before the afternoon had passed, she was distraught and anxious, and, feeling that he could console and reassure her, she took up her pen to write to Father Ildefonse. However, remembering her promise, she refrained from writing for another week, when she felt unable to resolve her conflict. Father Ildefonse did not reply to her appeal, but came in person.

"Your words always encourage me greatly," she told him, "and I am much in need of encouragement at the moment."

But he would not allow her to discuss her scruples in detail.

"My dear Sister," he reminded her, "you have not, I think, forgotten the promise which you made to the Sacred Heart a few months ago, and which you submitted to me for approval? - to offer no resistance to His love. Nor have you, I take it, withdrawn that promise. Well, it is not for you to lay down what direction that love shall take, what form it will assume. If it is all sweetness and light, then there is no suffering, for consciousness of His nearness always upholds one and takes all the bitterness from any burden. But when one follows Him to Calvary, it is a different matter altogether. Of course, at the time you could not have foreseen or understood the reality, but I am certain that would not have made any difference. However, the essence of a holocaust - and you yourself used that term - is that it must be entirely consumed by fire. That is not a pleasant operation."

"No," she replied without hesitation, "it is true that I do not withdraw what I promised then, nor do I regret it. I desire to be a victim of love - of His Sacred Heart. I do not fear suffering, but I cannot under-

stand the contradictions within me, the very violence of these oppos-
ing desires which tear me apart. I long to give myself entirely to Him,
and yet there is this timorousness which makes me so fainthearted."

"Do not expect to see the handiwork of God, whether it is in
your own soul or anywhere else. Love means union, and He will draw
you into the union you desire in His own fashion and time, provided
you do nothing to oppose His action. But love not only transforms, it
consumes ... burns away not only the rust and dross of our imperfections, but consumes us utterly. Remember the words of Scripture:
'The Lord thy God is a consuming fire.' Well, let the fire attack you,
consume you utterly. To yourself all that appears is the smoke, the
acrid fumes, the charred and blackened wood, and not the single, glowing coal that burns within."

"I fear that ignoring all these imperfections might be a form of
complacency."

"That is nothing but a scruple. Ignore it."

"Yes, I do that. I seek God's pardon and tell Him of my longing to
be entirely His, and renew my resolution to suffer in silence. But I fall so
often that I fear I have sinned gravely, and if only I could be certain that
this is not so, I think I would not grow so fearful and disturbed."

"Ah," he told her, "Certainty is something you must not expect
while God holds you in this painful state. Close your eyes like a child
and throw yourself upon His mercy with boundless faith and hope in
His goodness and willingness to aid you, of which you have had so
much experience in the past. Always remember that He is infinitely
more loving and merciful than you are weak and sinful. Try to preserve peace of mind whatever the turmoil in your emotions or the
rebellions of sensitive nature, and He will give you the victory, I promise that. Indeed, I would go so far as to say that never has your adherence to God been as complete or perfect as now when you feel no
fervor or delight, because you are obliged to cling to Him with your
will, and not because of any joy in His consolations."

This purifying trial, placed by Father Ildefonse at a time when,
in his opinion, Teresa Margaret was approaching the state of transforming union, has been clearly described by St. John of the Cross

in *The Living Flame of Love:* "Before this divine force of love is introduced into the substance of the soul and is united with it by means of a purity and purgation which is perfect and complete, this flame which is the Holy Spirit is wounding the soul and destroying and consuming in it the imperfections of its evil habits, and this is the operation of the Holy Spirit, wherein He prepares it for divine union and the transformation of love in God."

Again: "And in its substance the soul suffers from abandonment and the greatest poverty. Dry and cold, and at times hot, it finds relief in naught, nor is there any thought that can console it, nor can it even raise its heart to God." A purification of such intensity comes to pass in few souls, he says, only in those whom God intends to raise to a higher degree of union, "for He prepares each one with a purgation of greater or less severity, according to the degree to which He desires to raise it."

This dark night is an inflowing of God into the soul, for by purging and illuminating it, He prepares it for the union of love with Himself. The suffering and the fruitfulness of the night of the spirit have often been compared with the agony of Jesus in Gethsemane; the victory He won there initiated the redemption of mankind, and from it issued the birth and development of His Mystical Body, the Church. The dark night is the individual soul's participation in that suffering and triumph, for its purpose is not merely the purification of one particular soul; it has that object, of course, but much more also: a segment of the total work of human redemption. In this, as in all else, we are united in one single body, and the degree of perfection of each soul is a matter of vital importance to the whole Mystical Body. In this sense, all suffering is redemptive suffering, and it embraces our love of God and of our fellow-men. Far from causing us to ignore our neighbor, a God-centered outlook permits us to grasp the full implications of the intimate links which bind us to all humanity in a solidarity which allows none to remain outside the orbit of our own pursuit of God. All mankind is involved - we cannot advance without drawing them all along with us; and the weight of the burden would crush us were it not for the union of our suffering and travail with that of Christ, from whom it obtains its fruitfulness and we our strength.

Father Ildefonse, by explaining her trial in this light, seems to have finally settled most of the fantastic scruples that had tormented Teresa Margaret for the past year. The aridity remained, and in April, 1769, she wrote to him, acknowledging the letter quoted earlier, in which he set out practical suggestions for imitation of the hidden life of Jesus:

"Your letter was a great consolation to me," she said, "and it gave me exactly what I was searching for: a method enabling me to attain the object of my desires. As soon as I received it I set about implementing your suggestions, but it is always with dryness, sometimes more, sometimes less. I seem to be fighting against the current on account of my great repugnance and lack of sensitivity ... Father, I am so confused! I do not seem to offend God and I do want to belong wholly to Him, but I find myself adrift on a sea so buffeted by storm and tempest that I do not know what to do to avoid shipwreck and arrive safely in port."

The metaphors "tempest" and "shipwreck" are strong ones for Teresa Margaret, usually so reserved in her manner and restrained in her language. Her interior sufferings continued to increase in intensity. Shortly afterwards she again told Father Ildefonse:

"I feel so abandoned that I do not seem able to find the faintest glimmer of light anywhere. The prospect of applying myself to the things of God torments me; sometimes I wonder how long I will be able to hold out. I do not seem even to want God's help, so cold is my heart."

He continued to reassure her.

"Prayer is not only our privilege, but it is also our first duty, as you know," he said. "Every soul, even our Blessed Lady, owes a duty to God of worship, reaching if necessary to annihilation. When we consciously turn to God and focus our highest faculties of mind and will upon Him, we are putting them to the noblest use possible. The physical order is ruled by necessity; but obedience rules in the moral sphere. It alone puts order into the domain of the free will, and spiritual beauty as well as harmony depend upon it."

"Father, the mode of life you prescribed before comforted me very much at the time, but now I seem to have settled once more 'into a rut' … I cannot even explain adequately the paradoxes which seem to exist in me, so that I feel torn apart by the pull of strong impulses in the opposite directions. I have no 'feeling.' Prayer appears utterly futile, because of my state of mind and my indifference; it is just a fatiguing task performed in complete darkness which presents an almost insuperable difficulty for my already lazy will."

"Feelings or emotions can be a cause of great pain as well as a considerable nuisance, for flesh and blood ever struggle against the spirit," he reminded her. "Yet it is not with them, but with the will that one prays. We sometimes enjoy the exercise, when God so permits; however often it is painful and difficult, and we have no right to expect that it should be a source of pleasure. Prayer is a duty - our first and foremost. Always keep that thought before you. And as with every duty, it must be performed whether or not we like or enjoy it."

But she could not overcome her distress.

"Time is very short", she said significantly, "and yet I must do myself great violence lest I waste it. I try to aim for the stars in my resolutions, especially in the matters for which I feel least attraction. And then as soon as an occasion for practicing them presents itself, I fall flat on my face in the dust…"

"My child, I know that in reality you do understand this matter quite well, and that it is only the violence of the struggle in your emotions that causes such conflict. Basically, in prayer we make an act of utter and unreserved surrender to God, of all we are - we who are His creatures, His slaves. This abandonment is united with Christ's surrender to His Father's will in Gethsemane and on Calvary, since it is as members of His Body that we pray. It is, therefore, no cause for surprise, and certainly none for distress, if it sometimes costs us tears and sweat and blood also. But is this too great a price to pay for the attainment of life that is more perfect?"

"I truly cannot understand these contradictions within myself. Even the least act of virtue repels me, and yet I am on fire with the longing to be conformed to the Heart of Jesus - to die to myself that He may live in me."

"That can only be achieved by allowing Him to do it in His own way and at His own time. You will suffer, for this conformity you speak of can be attained by no other means, but it must always be in peace and abandonment to His will. Read again and ponder carefully what our Holy Mother Teresa said in *The Way of Perfection:* 'It seems very easy to say that we will surrender our will to someone, until we try it and realize that it is the hardest thing we can do if we carry it out as we should ... I want you to realize with whom you are dealing, and what the good Jesus offers on your behalf to the Father, and what you are giving Him when you pray that His will may be done in you ... Would you like to see how He treats those who make this prayer from their hearts? Ask His glorious Son who made it thus in the Garden. Think with what resolution and fullness of desire He prayed; and consider if the will of God was not perfectly fulfilled in Him through the trials, sufferings, insults, and persecutions which He gave Him, until at last His life ended with death on a Cross.' It is with our Lord in Gethsemane that you too must perfect the conformity of your will; and that, as you know, is not the place where one looks for spiritual consolations."

Teresa Margaret could never have struggled out of this imprisoning chrysalis without damaging her new and excessively fragile wings, had she not had the help of an experienced director; rather, she would have gone round in circles, failing to extract the full value from her trial, or else inevitably falling back somewhat and missing the full goal of complete union. For while spiritual direction can be dispensed with in many cases without great loss by those in the "ordinary ways" of prayer, it is highly improbable that one will, through trial and error, successfully direct himself in the confusing ways of mystical prayer, and certainly not to the height of transforming union.

Father Ildefonse continued to encourage and explain her to herself, but the trial was now reaching a peak of crisis. "Suffer and be silent for Jesus, return love for Love." It had been her shield and buckler in the early days of her religious life; now she again sought protection in this resolution.

"I try to cling to my determination of suffering and being silent, internally as well as externally, in preserving serenity whatever the outcome," she told Father Ildefonse, and it must be remembered that her self-control was so great that none of this anguish showed itself in her manner or in the mode in which she performed her work. She was still the loving, sympathetic, hard-working infirmarian, whose time and charity were completely at the disposal of her suffering sisters, none of whom had any inking of the aridity and desolation in which she lived her own spiritual life, "burning in ice and freezing in fire."

Three months before her death, on the 6th of December, 1769, she wrote: "Once more I find myself beaten to the ground as before. I feel myself abandoned and indifferent ..."

"The whole point of surrender," Father Ildefonse replied, "is that we *blindly* throw ourselves upon God; but there is no guarantee that we shall feel ourselves upheld by Him. We may seem to have thrown our selves upon nothing and be falling through space. You have to believe you are supported without any feeling of it."

And a month later, on 6th January, 1770, she again confided "The tempest seems to be increasing in its fury, and I simply cannot see how to make any progress. Everything seems dark and dangerous all around me. Even the things that once helped me so much only add to my sufferings. I must do violence to myself to perform my ordinary tasks, be they temporal or spiritual. Holy Communion and all other spiritual exercises are performed with the same coldness and apathy..."

Speaking of these last months of her life, Father Ildefonse said: "Her keenest suffering was divine Love itself, which, as it increased, simultaneously hid itself from the eyes of her soul. She loved without thinking that she did so. And as her love increased in its hidden existence, so did her desire for greater love, coupled with a sense of utter frustration and the conviction that she was completely failing God."

Even in these last stages of spiritual growth, Teresa Margaret did not depart from her characteristic path of silent suffering. In the final analysis, perfect conformity with the will of God is the real criterion of sanctity, and as Father Ildefonse has pointed out repeatedly, despite the tempest that raged in her emotions and senses, her will was firmly and undeviatingly fixed in God. To be holy, to be a saint, one has to be what God wills one to be - neither more nor less. Mystical states are not essential; in fact, they often carry the risk of attributing virtue to what appeals to the senses, while ignoring the hidden and obscure, forgetting the lesson of Jesus and Mary and the thirty years at Nazareth. Perfect union cannot exist without perfect purity of soul and heart and conscience, but this is not necessarily accomplished through any exterior graces which signal their presence or manifest their perfection.

Others might be privileged to witness the operations of divine grace within them, to assess and classify their various stages. For Teresa Margaret, right up until the end, her union with God was expressed as had been her union by charity with her sisters - in self-effacement and hiddenness. Now, her face still concealed by the veil she had worn for so long, she continued on her way of solitary suffering, feeling herself devoid of merit, of fervor, of any virtue.

"I desire nothing save to become a perfect copy of yourself," she had told our Lord in her act of oblation. "And since yours was a hidden life of humiliation, love, and sacrifice, such shall mine be also." This was no fanciful metaphor; she understood what she was offering, and she knew it had been accepted by the awful reality of its accomplishment.

19

A Victim of the Fire of Divine Love

When weight of all the garner'd years
Bows me, and praise must find relief
In harvest-song, and smiles and tears,
Twist in the band that binds my sheaf.
(Edward Dowden)

As has been demonstrated by both St. Teresa Margaret and St. Thérèse, the life of love and the attainment of a high degree of union with God, can be lived without the manifestation of mystical phenomena or extraordinary favors; similarly they both show us that the death of love is no less simple and may be effected without the transports and ecstasies so often associated with it. As in life she had sought to remain hidden from the eyes of all, so in death Teresa Margaret aspired to nothing spectacular, desiring to be forgotten or neglected rather than cause trouble and inconvenience to others.

Her life is full of paradoxes. She had truly passed unnoticed in her community, yet all were aware of her extraordinary holiness. Her seeming dryness and dissipation were combined with fidelity and an unshakeable confidence in God's mercy, even when she feared most that she had offended Him and was cast off by Him. She had been introduced into the lofty regions of the unitive way, yet to all intents and purposes, God blinded her so completely with the dazzling light of His infused graces that she felt herself lost and abandoned. The raptures and flights of the spirit, the visions and revelations that characterized the Sixth Mansion for St. Teresa of Avila, make no appearance in the life of her daughter.

But St. Teresa herself affirms that these graces are not a necessary part of sanctity, whereas the fullness of charity and union of conformity are essential to moral perfection. "This is the union I have longed for all my life, and which I never cease to beg of God; for it is the surest and safest," she said. "His Majesty can bestow no greater favor upon us than to grant us a life conformable to that of His beloved Son, so I hold it for certain that these graces are sent to strengthen our weakness, so that we may imitate Him by suffering much."

Could anything be clearer? To imitate Christ in His suffering is the proof of our love, and God can give no greater token of His choice of us than to permit us to share in the redemptive work of His Son.

Teresa Margaret had learned gradually to live in a state of constant warfare, as a soldier who cannot even lay aside his armor while he sleeps, yet with a trusting surrender that was almost relaxed, resting peacefully on His loving Heart. In one sense her ascent was exceedingly complex, and yet it is no exaggeration to say that there have been few simpler forms of spirituality. To her last breath, she adhered faithfully to the first and strongest motivation of her whole life, but by now the hiddenness, originally conceived of as an ascetical practice, had become transformed into a truly mystical grace. Rightly had Father Ildefonse termed it "imitation of the interior operations of the will of the God-Man."

Perfection does not mean that goodness has reached its maximum peak and that the soul is capable of no further increase. Perfection in such a sense of fullness belongs only to God. But we say that one has achieved perfection when there no longer remains in the soul any of the disorder which is caused by the dominance of creature pleasures over the glory of God; when the soul loves God and seeks His will, putting it always in the first place and her own desires being completely subordinated thereto.

Perfection, then, is the full realization of the commandment: *Thou shalt love the Lord thy God with thy whole heart and thy whole soul, and with all thy strength and with all thy mind.* In this state we see, love, seek God first in every place and in all things, however trivial. In other words, one's whole life is subordinated to the honor and glory of God, not only does one avoid all sin, but one never trespasses or usurps God's rights in the least thing. God is truly in His rightful place, and the soul in hers: He holds the first place in her life, and anything or anybody that would infringe thereon is excluded. A single act is perfect when this subordination is effected; when the whole of one's life reflects and produces it, one is in the state of perfection.

This had been the state of Teresa Margaret's soul, despite her conviction of her lack of virtue, for the past two years. The influence of the singular mystical grace *Deus caritas est* never lost anything of its first fragrance. Its influence remained in her soul, not as a static impression, reduced to the ranks of happy memories of the past, but as a dynamic force, ever deepening, as the Holy Spirit little by little assumed the initiative in her soul, gradually developing and fostering the impulse He had planted there until finally God absorbed her faculties more or less completely. All her resolutions from this time onwards were an outcome of that sublime touch of the Spirit, breathing into her soul an awareness of His nature, Love, and her need to respond to Love with love. Her increasing consciousness of her own powerlessness and indigence never bred discouragement, but rather a loving admission of her dependence on divine assistance, and an experience of it that is both sustaining and delightful. The more complete her self-surrender, the more intense grew her determination to yield nothing to nature, to give herself completely to God in all things and in all places, keeping back nothing of self. But such total surrender does not imply passivity. In no way are the human faculties impaired or "negatived" by abandonment of them to the divine will. Rather they draw from Him fresh spiritual energy. God does not interfere with our wills, does not force us to accept His gift of love or our own happiness.

Teresa Margaret seems to have had a premonition that her life would be short. On several occasions she referred to the fact that "the time is very brief ..." and Father Ildefonse speaks of her "vivid desire" for an early death, not as an escape from the trials and sufferings of life, but that she might the sooner come to love God without hindrance or interruption. She often repeated the words of the Psalmist: "When shall I come and stand before thy face?"

To be able to love God without fear of placing obstacles between Him and the soul, with no danger of ever again offending Him, to see Him face to face and to love Him directly, no longer through the mists and veils of earthly experience, but in the full contemplation of His glory, and that for all eternity: this was what death represented for her, rather than a relief from pain and stress.

"May I request this favor of God?" Teresa Margaret asked one day, when she had spoken with Father Ildefonse on the subject of an early death. "I am not trying to evade suffering in asking not to be left long on earth, because in this life it has become my only consolation."

Father Ildefonse told her that she might follow the movement of her heart in this matter, so long as she remained perfectly submissive to the divine will. Having received this permission, she promptly entered into the "compact" previously mentioned with her old patient, Sister Adelaide, who apparently fulfilled her part of the agreement promptly. Within a few months of the old nun's death, Teresa Margaret too had departed this life.

On learning of the sudden death of his spiritual daughter - which seems to have occurred during a short absence - Father Ildefonse showed no surprise. "I marveled greatly when I heard of her happy death," he remarked later. "And I have no doubt that its cause was the intensity and fervor of her petitions to that effect. She was indeed a very responsive soul, a victim of the fire of divine Love which consumed her so rapidly because she offered no resistance to His action."

In mid-February, 1770, Teresa Margaret wrote her last letter to her father, in which she enclosed the symbol of the human and divine love which linked their own hearts and souls: a heart cut from a piece of red paper, affixed to a blank sheet of white notepaper. She asked him to keep this carefully, and begged that he begin a novena to the Sacred Heart at once for a most pressing intention of hers.

It is not easy to decide that at this stage she had a definite premonition of the imminence of her death, but a strange incident is recorded at about the same time. A former acquaintance, Teresa Rinuccini, who was about to enter the Benedictine Monastery of St. Apollonia, had been doing the rounds of the convents in Florence, making the customary conventional farewell visits. On leaving the Carmel parlor where she had been talking to Teresa Margaret, Teresa said: "Before taking the habit, I will come and see you once more."

"If you can see me," was the enigmatic reply.

"Why, what do you mean?" asked the visitor, surprised. "Will Mother Prioress be displeased if I visit you again?"

But Teresa Margaret changed the subject, and would not explain her cryptic remark. Yet her unexpected prediction was fulfilled. Before Teresa could make a second call, Teresa Margaret was dead.

During these last weeks, it really seemed as though she were making conscientious preparations for her final journey. Her charity, which had always been poured out prodigally on her sisters, appeared to acquire a new quality of tenderness, especially in her contacts with the sick, whom she was still tending. She had, on one occasion, expressed a wish that she should die "in harness" as infirmarian, able to console and assist the suffering up to the last. But a new tranquility now became apparent, an interior peace and stability that flowed over into her external actions, and which seems to place her final achievement of full union in these last weeks. No longer tortured by fears and doubts, she recovered her old serenity, and if she was not aware of her impending death, she was at least secure in the consciousness of the one thing that had made death welcome - the possession of God, the transformation in love. All that now remained was for her to break free of the bonds that held her prisoner in the flesh, "to be dissolved and to be with Christ."

On Sunday, the 4th of March, she asked Father Ildefonse to allow her to make a general confession, as though it were to be the last of her life, and to receive Communion the following morning in the same dispositions. Whether or not she had any presentiment that this was indeed to be her Viaticum one cannot know, but in the event it proved to be so.

The general confession was a very long and detailed affair, occupying much time. Teresa Margaret accused herself of her least imperfections, and with such deep contrition that even Father Ildefonse, accustomed as he was to her minute self-examinations and manifestations of conscience, was surprised. This was not merely a crop of scruples; she was not anxious or confused as to the gravity of these things as sins, but saw them as so many infidelities, for which she was sincerely and deeply repentant. Before he had finished she was in tears; nevertheless, she left the confessional with a radiantly happy face and appeared more contented and serene than she had been for many months.

This was the last time Father Ildefonse saw Teresa Margaret. Perhaps he had been called away from Florence, or was giving a retreat elsewhere; for it seems likely that otherwise he would have been called to assist her, or at least received notification of her illness. But the first intimation of anything untoward was the news of her death.

Teresa Margaret was twenty-two years and eight months of age, in excellent health, never having had any serious illness or even the threat of one. She was tall, well-built, robust, with a clear, fresh complexion and vivacious manner. The overwork and lack of sleep during the past few years had left no trace of physical exhaustion; she was bright, alert, and active. In fact, many marveled at her resilience and stamina, and Mother Anna Maria once remarked that she seemed to thrive on hard work, which had the effect of strengthening rather than fatiguing her.

Yet in the full bloom of healthy, young womanhood, she suddenly and inexplicably made these elaborate preparations for an imminent and precipitate death.

On Tuesday, the 6th of March, at about 6 p.m., Teresa Margaret made her customary rounds of the infirmary, visiting each patient. She stayed a little longer than usual in the cell of Sister Teresa Mary of the Immaculate Conception, chatting with her, and explaining a devotional practice which she had discovered in a book by a Jesuit and pleased her very much. It was a method of drawing spiritual profit from one's illnesses and indispositions, and she did not waste the opportunity of passing on such good advice.

The Lenten fast had not ended, and the evening meal was quickly disposed of. When Teresa Margaret reached the refectory, the community had finished their collation and departed, dispersing to perform their various chores before assembling for evening recreation. There was a piece of fruit and some bread under her folded napkin. She went to the serving hatch and fetched her bowl of soup from the kitchen where it had been left to keep hot and took her seat in the otherwise deserted room. Immediately as she began to eat the simple meal, an acute abdominal pain almost doubled her up. She rose to leave the refectory, but realized that she could not manage to climb the stairs to her cell. Entering a room nearby, she waited until the first violence of the attack had passed, then made her way upstairs. As she closed the door of her cell another spasm overwhelmed her, and she fell on to the floor, unable to reach the bed on the opposite side of the room.

Sister Mary Victoria, who was assistant infirmarian, happened to pass through the corridor just in time to hear Teresa Margaret's call for help. Entering, she found her lying on the floor, writhing in pain. Within a matter of minutes she had summoned help, and, assisted by many hands, the sufferer was undressed and put into bed and the doctor summoned. He was not alarmed, but merely diagnosed a bout of colic - extremely painful, he agreed, but in no way serious. He prescribed a mild sedative, and advised that she should drink plenty of liquid. Then he left, with the assurance that if she followed these directions the colic would pass and there would be no complications.

The sisters breathed a sigh of relief at this sanguine prognostication. However, as Teresa Margaret was still in acute pain, they decided she should not be left alone during the night, and arranged to take relays watching with her; but she refused their offers.

"No, you must not put yourselves to any trouble for me. You need sleep more than I need attention. I will be quite all right."

They insisted, but finally, seeing they were causing her more distress than relief by their well-meaning ministrations, they decided that Virginia Martelli, a young and rather simple girl whom Teresa Margaret had prepared for her first Communion should stay with her.[1]

Teresa Margaret did not sleep at all during the night, and she tried to lie still so as not to disturb those in the adjoining cells, for in the emergency, she had not been removed to the infirmary. Several times she whispered to Virginia, cautioning her to be more careful in her movements, lest she should make any noise or waken the others. With her usual exactitude she followed the doctor's direction quite literally, and consumed an amazing quantity of liquid. Earlier in the evening she had been given broth and barley-water, and during the night two flasks, one of well water and another of mineral water, had been left with her; she drank the entire contents of both. It is hardly surprising that this course of hydro-therapy increased rather than lessened her sufferings. Her face and body were bathed in perspiration, but when Mother Anna Maria came first thing in the morning to see her, she seemed to have taken a slight turn for the better. She was less oppressed by pain, and seemed even inclined to talk a little.

"You must go and take some rest now, Virginia," she said, and when the girl had departed, asked Mother Anna Maria about her patients, requesting a detailed report on the condition of each one.

"Do not forget the herbs for our Mother," she reminded her.

"What about yourself. Do you need anything?"

"No, thank you. I have everything."

Later in the morning Doctor Pellegrini returned, but as soon as he saw the patient his optimism evaporated. By this time her internal organs had become paralyzed, and after an examination he announced gravely that he would have to call in the services of a surgeon.

None of the saint's biographers seem to have made any attempt at diagnosing her illness, apart from the rather vague "inflammation of the intestines," but it appears possible that the various symptoms recorded could spell "strangulated hernia." This

---

[1] According to the custom of that time, children were permitted to enter an enclosure, and while no hard-and-fast definition of the term "children" seems to have been made, it was generally taken to mean "up to the use of reason," or those who had not yet made their first Communion, so that it was often the practice to admit them into the community for instruction by one of the nuns. This process must have been very retarded in Virginia's case, for she was about fourteen.

usually makes itself manifest first by violent stomach pains (which even today are often wrongly diagnosed as colic, so we need not be too hard on Doctor Pellegrini), followed by a continuous vomiting, which also appears to have afflicted Teresa Margaret. Sometimes there is a brief respite, and then the acute pains recur. These symptoms could also describe gallstones, but with strangulated hernia, the intestines become twisted, so that nothing can pass either way, and unless an immediate operation is performed, death is almost inevitable within forty-eight hours; whereas from ordinary hernia, a good recovery can be expected. In strangulated hernia, however, the intestines could very well become paralyzed, as the internal functions are impeded and finally halted.

However, nothing of this was known in 1770, when the remedy for all ills seemed to be, when in doubt, draw some blood. Leeches were applied as relief for the most astonishingly varied ailments from asthma to sunstroke. So now the medicos proceeded to bleed Teresa Margaret's left foot. A vein was opened, and there was a sluggish flow of congealed blood. And then for the first time it dawned upon Doctor Romiti the surgeon, how grave her condition was. Taking Sister Magdalene aside, he advised that the sister should receive the Last Sacraments without delay. She, however, felt that this was not necessary, and was reluctant to send for a priest because of the patient's continued vomiting. Also Sister Teresa Margaret's pain appeared to have lessened, and she suggested that instead of preparing for her death, he should endeavor to cure her. The seeming asperity of this reply was probably due to anxiety, but she passed on his message to the Prioress, who seemed to share the infirmarian's opinion, for, strangely, none of them made any attempt to have a priest summoned.

The apparent improvement in her condition was, in fact, due to an internal hemorrhage which gave temporary relief to the congested organs, but nobody suspected this. The spasms of pain lessened, but only because she herself was growing rapidly weaker, and her general condition deteriorating alarmingly.

The patient offered no comment, nor did she ask for the Last Sacraments. She seemed to have had a premonition of this when making her last Communion "as Viaticum" the previous Sunday. She held her crucifix in her hands, from time to time pressing her lips to the five wounds, and invoking the names of Jesus and Mary, but she continued to pray and suffer, as always, in silence.

By 3 p.m. her strength was almost exhausted, and her face had assumed an alarmingly livid hue. Thoroughly frightened now, the Prioress sent hastily for Father Covari, a Dominican, who was then extraordinary confessor to the convent. He arrived in time to anoint the young nun, pronouncing in the name of the Church those portentous words of release which down the centuries have echoed for the departing soul the cry of the dying Christ: "Into thy hands I commend my spirit." "Go forth, Christian soul, from this sinful world, in the name of God the Father Almighty who created you; in the name of Jesus Christ, Son of the living God, who suffered and died for you; in the name of the Holy Ghost, who sanctified you."

Silent and uncomplaining to the end, with her crucifix pressed to her lips and her head slightly turned towards the Blessed Sacrament, Teresa Margaret took her flight to God.

All the nuns, kneeling huddled against each other in the confined space of the little cell, seemed stunned with the suddenness and unexpectedness of it all. A passing fit of colic ... in a few hours they had expected to see her moving once more through the corridors, serene and kindly as ever. The Prioress' hands trembled as she closed the door after the departing community.

"Mother Anna Maria," she said quietly, laying a detaining hand on the other's arm, and drawing her aside. The two stood gazing down on the familiar face, quiet and still now, but almost unrecognizable under that ghastly discoloration. They turned the bedclothes back. The hands and feet were almost black. Her body seemed to be decomposing almost under their eyes.

"You must arrange for the funeral without delay, Mother," said Mother Anna Maria quietly. "It would be most unwise to leave her body for any length of time."

"Yes, but the obsequies ...?"

"There's nothing to be done but hurry them forward."

Deftly, and as quickly as possible, they clothed the already rigid body in the serge habit and enfolded it in the white choir mantle, now to be her shroud. Her billet of profession and crucifix were placed in the still hands folded on her breast, and a wreath of white flowers laid on her head over the black veil.

Suddenly the complete silence that hung heavily over the monastery was shattered by the sound of the house bell. At the summons for which all had been waiting, the community assembled quickly, wearing their choir mantles and holding lighted candles to form a procession in the cell, where the cross-bearer stood at the head of the sister who, twenty-four hours before, had been walking down this corridor. It was not easy to concentrate on the prayers with their reiterated reminders that it is death which, opening onto infinite horizons, gives life its ultimate meaning and purpose.

With a startling suddenness the voices of the chantresses rang out: *Libera me, Domine.* Four sisters bent to raise the black pallet on which the body lay, the community continuing the responsory as they made their way to the choir.

"Deliver me, Lord, from everlasting death in that dread day when heaven and earth will rock and thou wilt come to judge the world by fire. I tremble and am full of fear as I await the day of reckoning, that day of wrath, calamity, and sorrow... ."

Reverently they laid the pallet on the simple bier - two trestles covered with a black cloth - at each corner of which stood a large candlestick in which mournful brown candles flickered sullenly. The bare feet were near the open grille, and two of the nuns took their places, kneeling beside the almost unrecognizable head of their deceased sister, to begin the perpetual vigil which would end only when they laid her body in the tomb.

Requiem aeternam, dona ei Domine, et lux perpetua luceat ei.

As the Prioress sprinkled the still form with holy water, she uttered a silent, unrubrical prayer that the rapidly approaching corruption of that once lovely body would be arrested until tomorrow, so that no unseemly accident should mar the grave solemnity of the ceremonies.

Thou wilt not permit the holy one to see corruption (Ps. 15:10).

There are few ceremonies more trying than the singing of a Requiem Mass for a deceased member of one's community. Her body lies in the middle of the choir, and the beautiful words of the liturgy, as well as the hauntingly simple melody take on a new poignancy when applied to one with whom all have lived so intimately.

"What shall wretched I be crying
To what friend for succor flying
When the just in fear are sighing?"

The holy apostles and doctors, the virgins and martyrs, our own saintly foundresses, and those who have worn this habit and won the halo of sanctity - none of them can lend it to us. It is their own, and cannot be borrowed. When the soul stands before her maker, she cannot hide behind the holiness of the saints; rather it will accuse her by a damning comparison. But

"Remember that my lost condition
Caused, dear Lord, thy mortal mission;
Thou with weary steps hast sought me,
Crucified hast dearly bought me ..."

Should the weary Christ have labored in vain? For one soul - even for such as mine - the divine exile would have renounced His godhead and taken the form of a slave, even had the salvation of all the rest of the world been guaranteed.

"Lord of mercy, Jesus blest,
Grant her everlasting rest."

Mass ended, all waited with veils lowered, as the celebrant Father Gregory, accompanied by Father Valerian, entered the choir to give the three absolutions.

"Lord, do not call thy servant to account, for no one can stand guiltless in thy presence unless thou grant her forgiveness ..."

In Paradisum, deducant to Angeli ... in civitate sanctam Jerusalem. The solemn chant began, as the angels were called upon to bear another redeemed soul to Paradise.

The bier was raised, and slowly the procession wended its way to the crypt for the burial. And now, after a lifetime of silent self-effacement, God lifted the veil beneath which His humble, unassuming spouse had so long concealed herself from all eyes. She was His, and He had a mission and message to pass on to us through her. This He now proclaimed, in the words of Pope Pius XI, "with that powerful voice of miracles, which is indeed His voice."

Surely, of all the wonders worked by Almighty God through this most unassuming instrument, none has been more outstanding than the preservation of her own body, after the apparent symptoms of early decomposition that everyone had observed with such alarm. Yet now, as they entered the vault, all noticed that there was another change taking place in the face; the alarming blue-black discoloration was much less pronounced, and, temporarily, the burial was postponed. Within a few hours another examination revealed that face, hands, and feet had regained their natural coloring, and the nuns felt immensely consoled to see that lovely, childlike face looking once more as they had always known it in life.

They begged the Provincial's permission to leave her unburied until the next day, a request which he, dumbfounded at this astonishing reversal of natural processes, readily granted. The final burial of the body was arranged for the evening of the 9th of March, fifty-two hours after her death. By that time her skin tint was as natural as when in life and full health, and the limbs, which had been so rigid that dressing her in the habit had been a difficult task, were flexible and could now be moved with ease.

This was all so unprecedented that the coffin was permitted to remain open. The nuns, the Provincial, several priests and doctors all saw and testified to the fact that the body was as lifelike as if she were sleeping, and there was not the least visible evidence of corruption or decay. Her face regained its healthy appearance, there was color in her cheeks. Suddenly the real depth and wealth of the hidden, silent, self-effacing life that had been lived in their midst, in charity, humility and never-failing kindness which each had experienced at some time, dawned in full force on the nuns, when they understood the import of what was happening. Mother Victoria, who had been Prioress in 1766 and received the profession of this young nun, and had later been the recipient of her loving ministrations in the infirmary, suggested that a portrait should be painted before the eventual burial. This was unanimously agreed to, and Anna Piattoli, a portrait painter of Florence, was taken down to the crypt to capture forever the features that looked so serenely life-like in death.

The Carmel burial vault was a scene of much coming and going during these days, and had assumed anything but a mournful atmosphere. By the time the painting was completed, a hitherto unnoticed fragrance was detected about the crypt. The flowers that still remained near the bier had withered, and fell to dust when touched. But the fragrance persisted, and grew in strength, pervading the whole chamber. And then, miles away in Arezzo, Camilla Redi also became aware of the elusive perfume of narcissi, so beloved by her Anna Maria, which noticeably clung to certain parts of the house - the room formerly occupied by Anna, the clothes she had worn, the golden hair cut from her head on the day of her investiture ... "The odor of sanctity," Sister Teresa Margaret had once laughingly called this perfume, and indeed it now proved to be so.

Several times her body was visited by the surgeon, Doctor Romiti. On the fourth occasion, which was about a week after her death, he testified that the complete absence of any sign of decomposition was not a natural event, and he advised that the proper ecclesiastical authority should be informed of the prodigy, which must have a supernatural cause.

Mgr. Francis Icontri, Archbishop of Florence, was accordingly approached by a priest attached to the Carmel, Father Augustine Losi. His Grace did not seem particularly impressed, thinking no doubt that the nuns' imagination had been at work. However, he decided to investigate the matter in person, and either confirm the marvel or squash the rumor. But he allowed another week to pass before taking any action.

On March 21st, a fortnight after Teresa Margaret's death, he made an official visit, accompanied by a Canon, the Chancellor, and three priests from the Cathedral. There had been ample time for the natural processes of decay and dissolution to complete their work upon the body, and if, as claimed, there was no sign of corruption, it would indeed seem that a supernatural power held them in check.

His Grace descended into the crypt at about 4 p.m., accompanied by his own priests, the Carmelite Provincial and another friar, two doctors and the surgeon. Three nuns were present, including Mother Anna Maria and Sister Magdalene, the infirmarian. The doctors again examined the body, which had the appearance of a child who had just fallen into a relaxed sleep. The incision on her left foot, which had been made for the "blood-letting" was quite fresh, and her skin clear and rosy. The doctors conferred together, and finally informed the Archbishop that the condition of the body could only be regarded as miraculous. Then Mother Anna Maria records an incident which impressed her deeply:

"All were speaking of the prodigy, when the Archbishop arose, and himself uncovered the face of our dead sister. He stood there, looking at it very fixedly, startled to see the blue eyes slightly open and the whole face seemingly relaxed as one in a light but peaceful slumber."

Did he, one wonders, recall this young girl who had knelt before him only thirteen years previously, when as a student at St. Apollonia's, he had sealed her with the sacrament of Confirmation?

The surgeon noticed a little moisture that had gathered on her upper lip below the nostril, and wiped it off with a piece of cloth. He then smelled it, with the thought that here indeed would be a definite proof. It emitted so sweet an odor that he immediately offered it to His Grace, who stated that he also perceived "a heavenly fragrance."

The coffin was then closed and sealed by the Archbishop, who left the crypt to visit the Prioress, at that time indisposed and confined to bed, and give her the consolation of his blessing.

"They are all elated by the great treasure you possess," he told her, "and I too am very happy that we have so wonderful a thing in our midst. I believe it is indeed a miracle, and yet I do not think that we have yet witnessed the greatest miracle of all. In years to come she will be seen again, and those who will still be alive then shall have a great consolation."

"Did your Grace perceive anything extraordinary?" the Prioress enquired.

"Extraordinary! Indeed, it is a miracle to see a body completely flexible after death, the eyes those of a living person, the complexion that of one in the best of health. Why, even the soles of her feet appear so lifelike that she might have been walking about a few minutes ago. She appears to be asleep. There is no odor of decay, but on the contrary a most delightful fragrance. Indeed, it is the odor of sanctity."

That day the coffin was finally closed with twelve nails, and secured by eight episcopal seals in red wax upon black and white linen tapes. It was then placed inside a large cypress coffin, with a parchment giving the name of the deceased. The coffin was firmly placed in a niche over the door of the crypt, and a small metal plate, according to the simple Carmelite custom, recorded:

"Sister Teresa Margaret of the Most Sacred Heart of Jesus, died on the 7th of March, 1770, in the twenty-third year of her age, and the fourth year of her religious profession."[2]

In the busy world outside the quiet cloister, rumors were traveling. The word "miracle" was at first whispered, and then shouted. Several people reported having "cured" themselves or others of various ailments by applying flowers taken from the bier before the young nun was buried or articles that had touched her body. But the continued reports that the body remained incorrupt were the cause of the greatest speculation. Father Ildefonse has recorded some sixty miraculous answers to prayer through Teresa Margaret's intercession within three years of her death.[3]

---

[2] She was only five days short of completing her fourth year of profession. Thirteen year later in 1783 another examination of the body was made in the presence of the Archbishop, at which her father, Sir Ignatius Redi, was a witness. Twenty-two years later the body was transferred to the nuns' choir on the 21st of June, 1805, the day on which, in that year, was celebrated the Feast of the Sacred Heart.

It seemed that popular acclaim would carry the day and that, swayed by such obvious proof of divine intervention, the customary delay in introducing a cause for beatification would be waived and steps taken to raise her to the altar.

Teresa Margaret was not, however, destined for the people of her own century, but for ours. Each generation, G. K. Chesterton once said, seeks its saints by an instinct; and they are not so much what the people want, as what they need. God has the antidote for the ills of every age, and canonization is the halo which He places on the brow of certain of His children for His own glory, and to achieve this work. Everything depends on the work which God desires to achieve through saints in the world. It is to meet our need; we can never be said to deserve any saint which the Church gives us, in the same way that at the Incarnation:

"Christ took our nature on Him, not that He

'Bove all things lov'd it, for the puritie:

No, but He drest Him with our human Trim,

Because our flesh stood most in need of Him." (Robert Herrick)

The workings of Divine Providence are never haphazard. If God has preserved St. Teresa Margaret's body until this present day, and delayed her canonization for our generation, it must be because He wishes to teach us some lesson through her example, to offer her to us as a model for imitation. The fact that He has so palpably intervened is surely a proof that she has a special message and doctrine for us of this century deafened with noise and numbed by speed. We need to be taught anew the lesson that "the kingdom of God is within you," and until we learn how to enter within ourselves and find Him, our age of space, speed and hyper-activity will never know peace. The late Holy Father, Pope John XXIII, writing in August 1962 to com-

---

[3] There is a charming anedote related in one of the miraculous cures accepted for her canonization. A nun, suffering from galloping consumption, had been given only a few more days to live by the doctor. The community made a novena to Teresa Margaret for her cure, and on the night of its conclusion, the sufferer felt a sudden great weight oppressing her chest. "I am dying!" she cried. Then the comforting voice of the former infirmarian whispered words that seemed to the sister to be quite audible: "Why, silly one! You are cured!" And she was.

memorate the fourth centenary of the Discalced Carmelite Reform stressed the need for silence and recollection, "and that precisely in these days of accentuated activity." The silent, self-effacing saint, exemplar of the hidden life, comes to our troubled, restless, rootless generation, saying to us: "Peace, be still."

In the collect of the Mass for her feast, the Church prays: "O God, who didst grant to blessed Teresa Margaret to draw from the founts of the Savior, priceless treasures of purity and love, grant that through her intercession, we may abound in these same heavenly gifts."

The treasures drawn by St. Teresa Margaret from this "fount which freely flows" (namely purity and charity) are the two virtues so sorely lacking in the world today, as Pope Pius lamented. In face of the evils of modern society, which in the encyclical *Haurietis Aquas* he named as "unrestrained sensuality and charity grown cold" he offered the Sacred Heart as a remedy. *"Thou shalt drink water in joy from the founts of the Savior ..."* "Anyone attempting to follow St. Teresa Margaret in her characteristic devotion will necessarily reproduce her characteristic virtues: purity of body and soul which have won for her the title "the spotless lily of Florence," and charity. Penetration into the depths of the Savior's life, "imitation of the interior operations of the God-Man," necessarily requires spotlessness in one's own life, purity of body and heart and conscience. Through the loftiness of her own spiritual aim, St. Teresa Margaret gives us a practical demonstration of the love of God and love of neighbor, rising in the Heart of Christ, fed by the "water from the founts of the Savior," and leading to the eternal embrace of the Blessed Trinity.

Pope Pius XI who beatified and canonized St. Teresa Margaret, sev times expressed his desire that modern society, obsessed and distracted by material things, should look to the young and humble Carmelite's example to find a remedy for those ills that afflict souls when they lose the sense of the supernatural in their absorbed and distracted pursuit of riches, pleasures, and comfort. Desire feeds on the quest of the unattainable, fading when its object is grasped. But love rests tranquilly in the possession of its object, seeking not more and better things to pursue, but to possess more totally, to identify itself more completely with the object of its love. The desire is for the possession of some material good, and such things can never satisfy, but only create further desire for more possessions, a higher standard of well-being, a greater degree of comfort. But love is spirit, and the fruits of the Spirit are joy and peace.

The political upheavals of the French Revolution which broke out shortly after her death and later spilled over the Alps into Italy, resulted in a series of vicissitudes for the Carmel of Florence, including eviction from their Monastery,[4] which put an end for the time being to all thoughts of beatification. The cause was resumed in this century, and finally on the 19th of March, 1934, Pope Pius XI placed the halo of canonization on the head of St. Teresa Margaret of the Sacred Heart, with the words: "Truly, it is such souls as these, so pure and noble, who, by their suffering, their love, and their prayers, carry on silently in the Church the most far-reaching and fruitful apostolate."

Time and time again the Popes have returned to this theme: the apostolic value of prayer, penance, and the hidden life. Recently Pope John XXIII, quoting the above words of his predecessor (taken from the homily given at the Mass of Canonization of St. Teresa Margaret) said: "The real apostolate consists very precisely in participating in the work of the salvation of Christ, a participation that is impossible without an intense spirit of prayer and sacrifice, for the fundamental requirements of the spiritual life are prayer, contemplation, silent labor, sacrifice."

These words of the Holy Father sum up admirably the life and apostolate of St. Teresa Margaret, whose body, still perfectly incorrupt after almost two hundred years, lies in the chapel of the Carmel of St. Teresa on the Via dei Bruni in Florence. But she herself stands, with outstretched hands, to lead us - if we will but accept her guidance - to the kingdom of God which is reserved for the meek, the

---

[4] The former monastery on the Porta alla Croce was (like most requisitioned monastic buildings) turned into a prison, but the community was never dispersed and managed to stay together throughout this troubled period. Eventually they took the building on Via dei Bruni, which still bears the title of their original dedication, St. Teresa's Carmel, where today the incorrupt body of St. Teresa Margaret lies.

patient, the humble, the charitable. For we must all enter that kingdom as little children, poor in spirit, loving, confident. Our Lord has told us so Himself. It is not merely a highly recommended way; it is the only one. There is no other entrance.

* * * * *

The Institute of Carmelite Studies promotes research and publication in the field of Carmelite spirituality. Its members are Discalced Carmelites, part of a Roman Catholic community—friars, nuns, and laity—who are heirs to the teaching and way of life of Teresa of Jesus and John of the Cross, men and women dedicated to contemplation and to ministry in the Church and the world. Information concerning their way of life is available through local diocesan Vocation Offices or from the Vocation Directors' Offices:

5345 South University Avenue, Chicago, IL 60615

2131 Lincoln Road, NE, Washington, DC 20002

P.O. Box 3420, San Jose, CA 95156-3420

4600 West Davis St., Dallas, TX 75211